WEBSTER'S
Español/Inglés English/Spanish

Spanish Pronunciation Guide

Letter	Spanish	English	Description Guide
a	papá	father	
b	blusa	blouse	At the beginning of a word
	cabo	·	Between vowels, closer to v
c	cacto	cactus	Before a, o, u like k
	cedro	cedar	Before e, i like s; frequently
ch	cheque	check	
d	distante	distant	At the beginning of a word
	cada		Between vowels, like th of rather
e	eche	cafe	
f	fantasia	fancy	
g	gente		Before e, i, like h of ha!
	guerra	*guide*	With u before e, i a hard g
	ganar	gain	Before a, o, u, a hard g
h	honor		Always silent
i	machina	machine	
j	juego		Like h in ha!
k	kilo	kilogram	
l	lista	list	
ll	llama		IIn Spain, like lli of million, elswhere llike Spanish consonant y (as below)
m	mamá	mama	
n	norte	north	
ñ	niño		Like ny of canyon
o	solo	alone	
p	papá	papa	
q	que	raquet	
r	cara		
rr	carroza		Strong trilled r
s	sal	salt	
t	té	tea	
u	refugio	refuge	
ue	bueno		Like k
v	vino		Same as initial Spanish b
	lava		Same as intervocalic Spanish b
w	wat	watt	Prounounced either like English v or w
x	existir	exit	Exception: in Mexico x is like the Spanish j
y	y		Like i of machine
		yes	Like s of vision
z	zona		Like s in salt: in much of Spain,

Tex
Cover Co
Character Illus
Dist

D0951501

a *prep.* at; to
abacería *f.* grocery
abacero *m.* grocer
ábaco *m.* abacus
abad *m.* abbot
abadesa *f.* abbess
abadía *f.* abbey
abajo *adv.* beneath; down; below; *interj.* down with
abalanzar *v.* to hurl
abanderamiento *m.* registration (nautical)
abanderar *v.* to register
abandonado, da *adj.* derelict; careless
abandonar *v.* to desert; forsake; abandon; give up
abanicar *v.* to fan
abanico *m.* fan
abarajar *v.* to catch
abaratar *v.* to lower; become cheaper
abarcar *v.* to embrace; coprise; encompass
abatimiento *m.* dejection
abatir(se) *v.* to depress; to discourage
abdicar *v.* to abdicate
abdómen *m.* abdomen
abdominal *adj.* abdominal
abedul *m.* birch
abejón *m.* hornet
aberración *f.* aberration
abertura *f.* aperture; gap
abeto *m.* fir
abierto, ta *adj.* open; clear
abismal *adj.* abysmal
abismo *m.* abyss
abjurar *v.* to abjure
ablandar(se) *v.* to soften; mollify
ablativo *m.* ablative
ablución *f.* ablution
abnegación *f.* abnegation
abnegar *v.* to renounce
abocar *v.* to decant
abocardar *v.* to ream
abochornar *v.* to blush; suffocate
abofetear *v.* to slap
abogacía *f.* bar; law
abogado *n., adj. m. f.* attorney; counsel; lawyer
abolengo *m.* ancestry
abolición *f.* abolition
abolir *v.* to abolish
abolladura *f.* dent
abollar *v.* to emboss; dent
abominar *v.* to abominate; to loathe
abono *m.* manure; fertilizer
aborrecer *v.* to hate; abhor
aborrecimiento *m.* hate; hatred; abhorrence; loathing
abortar *v.* to abort
abotonar *v.* to button up
abozalar *v.* to muzzle
abra *f.* cove; small boy
abrasión *f.* abrasion
abrasivo, va *adj.* abrasive
abrazar(se) *v.* to hug; cuddle
abrazo *m.* hug; embrace
abrecartas *m.* letter opener
abrevar *v.* to soak; water
abreviación *f.* abbreviation
abrigar(se) *v.* to shelter; harbor; protect
abril *m.* April
abrillantar *v.* to cut into parts; polish; brighten
abrir(se) *v.* to open up; spread out; open
abrochar *v.* to button up; fasten; buckle
abrogación *f.* abrogation
abrogar *v.* abrogate; repeal
abrumar *v.* to overwhelm
abrupto, ta *adj.* abrupt; steep
abrutado, da *adj.* bestial
absceso *m.* abscess
absolución *f.* absolution
absoluto, ta *adj.* complete; absolute
absolvente *adj.* absolving
absolver *v.* to acquit; clear
absorbencia *f.* absorbance
absorbente *m.* absorbent
absorber *v.* to soak up; engross
absorción *f.* absorption
abstención *f.* abstention
abstenerse *v.* to abstain; refrain
abstinencia *f.* abstinence
abstracto, ta *adj.* abstract
abstraer *v.* to abstract

abstruso, sa *adj.* abstruse

absurdidad *f.* absurdity

absurdo, da *adj.* silly; preposterous; absurd

abundancia *f.* abundance; amplitude

abundante *adj.* plentiful; abundant; ample

abundar *v.* to abound

abundoso, sa *adj.* abundant

aburrimiento *m.* boredom

aburrir *v.* to bore

abusar *v.* to misuse; maltreat

abusivo, va *adj.* abusive

abyección *f.* abjectness

abyecto, ta *adj.* abject

acá *adv.* here

acabado, da *adj.* end; conclusion

academia *f.* academy

académico, ca *adj.* academic

acampar *v.* to camp

acariciar *v.* to pet; pat; caress

acarrear *v.* to cart

acarreo *m.* cartage

acceder *v.* to accede

accesible *adj.* accessible

acceso *m.* approach; access

accesorio, ria *m. f.* accessory

accidentado, da *adj.* uneven

accidente *m.* casualty; accident

acción *f.* movement; action

aceite *m.* oil

aceituna *f.* olive

acelerar(se) *v.* to speed; accelerate

acentuar(se) *v.* to emphasize; accent; stress

aceptar *v.* to adopt; accept

acercar(se) *v.* to bring near

acero *m.* steel

acertijo *m.* riddle

acético, ca *adj.* acetic

acetona *f.* acetone

ácido, da *adj.* acid; sour

ácido cítrico *m.* citric acid

aclamación *f.* acclamation

aclaración *f.* clarification

aclarar *v.* to clear; clarify; rinse

aclimatar *v.* to acclimate

acné *m.* acne

acogida *f.* welcome; reception

acolchar *v.* to pad

acometer *v.* to attempt; undertake; overcome; attack

acomodar *v.* to suit; accommodate; put up

acompañante *m., f.* escort; music accompanist

acompañar *v.* to escort; attend; go with; accompany

aconsejar(se) *v.* to take advice

acontecer *v.* to chance; happen

acontecimiento *m.* occasion; event; occurrence.

acordar(se) *v.* to agree on

acordeón *m.* accordion

acorralar *v.* to round up; corral; intimidate; pen

acortar(se) *v.* to clip; shorten; lessen; obstruct

acosar *v.* to harass; pursue

acostar(se) *v.* to lie down

acostumbrar(se) *v.* to be accustomed to; be used to

acre *adj.* acrid; sour

acrecentar *v.* to augment

acreedor *m.* creditor

acrimonia *f.* bitterness

acróbata *m., f.* acrobat

activar *v.* to activate

activo, va *adj.* active; brisk; quick; alive

acto *m.* event; act; function

actor *m.* actor

actriz *f.* actress

actual *adj.* present; actual

actualmente *adv.* at present

actuar *v.* to perform; act

acuario *m.* aquarium

acuátil *adj.* aquatic

acueducto *m.* aqueduct

ácueo, a *adj.* watery

acumular *v.* to stockpile; accumulate; congest

acuñación *f.* coinage

acuñar *v.* to coin; mint

acusar *v.* to impeach; charge; indict; accuse

acústica *f.* acoustics

achispado, da *adj.* tipsy

adagio *m.* adage

adalid *m.* commander

adaptable *adj.* adaptable; versatile

adaptación *f.* adaptation

adaptar(se) *v.* to fit; adapt; adapt oneself to; adjust

adecuado, da *adj.* fit; suitable

adefesio *m.* something gaudy; extravagant; ridiculous

adehala *f.* tip; bonus

adelantado, da *adj.* fast; advanced

adelantar(se) *v.* to advance; gain; accelerate

adelgazar(se) *v.* to lose weight; taper; make thin; attenuate

ademán *m.* attitude; gesture

además *adv.* besides; moreover

adentro *adv.* inside; within

adepto, ta *adj.* adept

aderezo *m.* finery; adornment; dressing

adestrar *v.* to train

adeudar *v.* to debit; owe

adherente *adj.* adherent

adherir(se) *v.* to cling; stick

adhesión *f.* adherence

adición *f.* addition

adicional *adj.* more; extra; additional

adicto, ta *adj.* addicted

adiestrar(se) *v.* to exercise; train; practice

adiós *m., interj.* farewell; goodbye

adiposo, sa *adj.* fat; adipose

aditamento *m.* attachment; addtion

aditivo *m.* additive

adivinar *v.* to foretell; to guess

adjetivo *m.* adjective

adjuntar *v.* to annex

administración *f.* administration; management

administrar *v.* to manage; dispense; administer

admirable *adj.* fine; excellent; admirable

admiración *f.* admiration

admirar(se) *v.* to wonder; admire; amaze

admisible *adj.* acceptable; admissible

admitir *v.* to acknowledge; permit; admit

adobe *m.* adobe

adoptar *v.* to adopt

adoptivo, va *adj.* adoptive

adorable *adj.* adorable

adoración *f.* adoration

adorar *v.* to worship; adore

adormecer(se) *v.* to fall asleep; drowse

adormidera *f.* poppy

adornar *v.* to adorn; deck; decorate; grace

adorno *m.* adornment; ornament; array

adquirir *v.* to obtain; secure; acquire

adrenalina *f.* adrenaline

aduana *f.* customs

aduanero, ra *adj.* customs

aducir *v.* to cite; adduce

adujado, da *adj.* coiled

adulador, ra *m.* flatterer

adular *v.* to flatter; adulate

adulto, ta *adj.* adult

adulzar *v.* to make sweet

adverbial *adj.* adverbial

adverbio *m.* adverb

adversario, ria, *m., f.* opponent; adversary

adversidad *f.* adversity

adverso, sa *adj.* averse; unfavorable; adverse

advertido, da *adj.* skillful; informed; intelligent; capable; sagacious

advertir *v.* to notify; advise; caution

adyacente *adj.* adjacent

aeración *f.* aeration

aéreo, a *adj.* aerial

aeroplano *m.* airplane; aeroplane

aeropuerto *m.* airport

afabilidad *f.* affability

afán *m.* anxiety; solicitude

afanar *v.* to urge; toil; strive

adyfanoso, sa *adj.* anxious

afectación *f.* pretense; affectation

afectado, da *adj.* affected

afectar *v.* to affect

afecto *m.* affection

afeitar v. to shave
afeite m. shave; cosmetic
aferrar(se) v. to grasp; furl
afianzar v. to bail; clinch
afición f. liking; affection; inclination
aficionado, da m. fan; amateur
afijo, ja adj. affixal
afilar(se) v. to sharpen
afiliar(se) v. to join; affiliate; adopt
afín adj. related; contiguous
afinación f. refining; tuning
afinar v. to refine; polish; tune
afirmar(se) v. to secure; assert; contend; affirm
aflicción f. anxiety; bereavement
afligido, da adj. stricken
afligir(se) v. to afflict
aflojar(se) v. to loosen; slacken; weaken
aflorar v. to emerge; sift
afluencia f. affluence; crowd; jam; fluency; abundance
afluente adj. affluent
aforar v. to appraise; gauge
afortunado, da adj. prosperous; lucky; fortunate
afrenta m. f. insult; affront
afrentar(se) v. insult; affront
afuera adv. outside; outskirts; suburbs
agalla f. gill
agarrar(se) v. to grasp; seize; clutch; clinch
agarre m. influence; pull
agarro m. grip; lutch; grab
agarrotar v. to compress; bind tightly
agasajar v. to entertain
agencia f. bureau; agency
agenciar v. to obtain; promote
agenda f. diary; notebook
agente m., f. officer; agent
ágil adj. nimble; agile; lithe
agilidad f. agility
agitación f. flurry; flutter; stir; excitement; agitation
agitar(se) v. to stir up; churn
aglutinante adj. adhesive
aglutinar v. to agglutinate
agonía f. pain; agony

agonioso, sa adj. persistent
agorar v. to foretell
agostar v. to consume
agosto m. August; harvest
agotamiento m. exhaustion; depletion
agotar(se) v. to drain; give out; tire; exhaust
agraciar v. to award; grace
agradable adj. gracious; nice; pleasant; agreeable
agradar v. to please
agradecer(se) v. to appreciate; acknowledge; thank
agrado m. liking; taste
agravación f. aggravation
agravante adj. aggravating
agraviar v. to harm; wrong
agravio m. offense; injury; grievance; harm
agredir v. to assault
agresión f. aggression
agresivo, va adj. aggressive
agresor, ra m. aggressor
agriar v. to annoy; sour
agricultura f. farming
agrietar v. to split
agrimensura f. surveying
agrio, gria adj. acid; sour
agro m. farming
agrupación f. group
agrupar(se) v. to cluster; bunch; group
agua f. water
aguacate m. avocado
aguado, da adj. diluted; watery
aguantar(se) v. to support; endure; hold
aguante m. endurance
aguardar v. to await
agudeza f. acumen; keenness; sharpness; brightness
agudizar v. to sharpen
agudo, da adj. sharp
agüero m. omen
águila f. eagle
aguja f. needle
agujero m. hole
aguoso, sa adj. watery
aguzar v. to sharpen
ahí adv. there
ahijar v. to adopt

ahilado, da *adj.* faint; soft
ahilar *v.* to faint from hunger; line up
ahíto, ta *adj.* stuffed
ahora *adv.* now
ahorcajar(se) *v.* to straddle
ahormar *v.* to fit; mold
ahorrar *v.* to save
ahorro *m.* savings
ahumado, da *adj.* smoky; cured; smoked
ahumar *v.* to cure; smoke
airar *v.* to annoy; anger
aire *m.* aspect; air
aireado,da *adj.* aired out
airear(se) *v.* to air
aireo *m.* ventilation
aislado, da *adj.* alone
aislar *v.* to seclude; isolate
ajado, da *adj.* withered
ajar *v.* to mar; spoil
ajedrez *m.* chess
ajenjo *m.* bitterness
ajeno, na *adj.* alien; strange; foreign
ajetreo *m.* agitation; bustle
ajo *m.* garlic
ajobo *m.* burden; load
ajustar *v.* to settle; adapt; adjust; fix; tighten
ajuste *m.* fitting; accommodation
ala *f.* wing
alabanza *f.* praise
alabar *v.* to praise
alacrán *m.* scorpion
alacridad *f.* eagerness
alambre *m.* wire
álamo *m.* poplar
alardeo *m.* bragging
alargar(se) *v.* to lengthen
alarma *f.* alarm
alarmar *v.* to alarm
alba *f.* daybreak; dawn
albaricoque *m.* apricot
alberca *f.* tank; pool; swimming pool
albergar *v.* to shelter; lodge
albino, na *adj.* albino
alborotar *v.* to excite; incite
alborozo *m.* joy
alcalde *m.* mayor

alcaloide *m.* alkaloid
alcanzar *v.* to attain; reach; grasp
alce *m.* moose
alcoba *f.* bedroom
alcohol *m.* alcohol
alegoría *f.* allegory
alegrar(se) *v.* to be happy; cheer; rejoice
alegre *adj.* joyous; gay; glad
alegremente *adv.* gaily
alegría *f.* gladness; gaiety
alegrón *m.* joy
alejamiento *m.* distance; with drawal; estrangement
alelado, da *adj.* bewildered; dull; stupid
alentador, ra *adj.* encouraging
alentar *v.* to animate
alergia *f.* allergy
alérgico, ca *adj.* allergic
alertar *v.* to alert; warn
aleteo *m.* flapping
alfabeto *m.* alphabet
alfarería *f.* pottery
alfilerar *v.* to pin
alfombra *f.* carpet
alfombrar *v.* to carpet
alforza *f.* pleat; tuck
álgebra *f.* algebra
algo *pron.* anything; something
algodón *m.* cotton
alguien *pron.* someone; anyone
algún *adj.* some
alguno, na *pron.* someone
alhaja *f.* gem
aliado, da *m.* ally
alianza *f.* alliance
alienar *v.* to alienate
aliento *m.* courage; breath
aligerar(se) *v.* to relieve; lighten
alimentar *v.* to feed
alimento *m.* food
alineación *f.* alignment
alisar *v.* to smooth
alistar *v.* to enlist
aliviar *v.* to alleviate; allay
alivio *m.* easing; relief
alma *f.* spirit
almeja *f.* clam
almidón *m.* starch
almidonar *v.* to starch
almohada *f.* pillow

almorzar *v.* to lunch
almuerzo *m.* lunch
alocado, da *adj.* crazy
alocución *f.* allocution
alojar(se) *v.* to house
alongar *v.* to stretch; make longer
alquilar *v.* to hire; rent
alquimista *m. f.* alchemist
alrededor *m., adv.* around; *prep.* round
altamente *adv.* extremely
altar *m.* altar
alteración *f.* alteration
altercación *f.* altercation
alternado, da *adj.* alternate
alternar *v.* to rotate; alternate
alternativa *f.* alternative
altimetría *f.* altimetry
altitud *f.* altitude
alto, ta *adj.* upper; high
altruista *adj.* altruistic
altura *f.* elevation; height
aludir *v.* to allude
alumbrado *m.* lightening
aluminio *m.* aluminum
alumno, na *m., f.* student
alusión *f.* allusion
alzado, da *adj.* heightened
alzar *v.* to hoist; lift up; raise
allá *adv.* there
allegado, da *adj.* related; close; near
allí *adv.* there
amabilidad *f.* kindness
amable *adj.* lovable; amiable
amado, da *adj.* beloved
amaestrar *v.* to train
amanecer *v.* to dawn
amanecida *f.* daybreak
amansar *v.* to soothe; tame
amaño *m.* skill
amar *v.* to love
amargar *v.* to make bitter
amargor *m.* bitterness
amarillo, a *adj.* yellow
amarrar *v.* to fasten; tie
amateur *adj.* amateur
ámbar *m.* amber
ambición *f.* ambition
ambigüedad *f.* ambiguity
ambiguo *adj.* uncertain

ambulancia *f.* ambulance
ambulante *adj.* ambulatory
ambular *v.* to amble
ameba *f.* amoeba
amenaza *f.* threat
amenazar *v.* to menace
amenidad *f.* amenity
americano, na *adj.* American
amiga *f.* girl friend
amigar *v.* to reconcile
amigo *m.* friend
amilanar *v.* to discourage; intimidate; scare; frighten
amistoso, sa *adj.* friendly
amo *m.* master; boss
amolar *v.* to sharpen
amoldar *v.* to adjust; mold
amontonar(se) *v.* to amass; hoard;
amor *m.* love; lover
amoralidad *f.* morality
amparar *v.* to defend; protect
ampliar *v.* to expand; increase
amplificar *v.* to amplify
amputar *v.* to amputate
ánade *m.* duck
anagrama *f.* anagram
análisis *m.* analysis
analista *m.,f.* analyst
anaquel *m.* shelf
anatomía *f.* anatomy
anatómico, ca *adj.* anatomic
anciano, na *adj.* aged
ancla *f.* anchor
ancho, cha *adj.* broad, wide
andar *v.* to go; ambulate
andrajoso, sa *adj.* ragged
anécdota *f.* anecdote
anegar *v.* to flood
anémico, ca *adj.* anemic
anestesiar *v.* to anesthetize
ángel *m.* angel
angélico, ca *adj.* angelical
angora *f.* angora wool
anguila *f.* eel
ángulo *m.* angle
anguloso, sa *adj.* angular
angurria *f.* greed
angustiar *v.* to anguish
anillo *m.* ring

animación *f.* animation
animal *m.* animal
animar *v.* to become animated
aniquilar *v.* to destroy; annihilate
anoche *adv.* last night
anormal *adj.* abnormal
anotación *f.* note
anotar *v.* to note
ánsar *m.* goose
ansia *f.* yearning
ansiar *v.* to long for
ansiedad *f.* anxiety
ante *prep.* before
antebrazo *m.* forearm
antedecir *v.* to predict
antepasado *m.* ancestor
anterior *adj.* prior; anterior
antes de *adv.* before
antiácido *adj.* antacid
antibiótico *m.* antibiotic
antídoto *m.* antidote
antílope *m.* antelope
antinatural *adj.* unnatural
antiséptico *m.* antiseptic
antonimia *f.* antonym
anual *adj.* annual
anuario *m.* yearbook
anublar *v.* to cloud
anular *v.* to cancel
anunciación *f.* announcement; annunciation
anunciante *m., f.* advertiser
anunciar *v.* to announce
anzuelo *m.* fishhook
añadido *m.* addition
añadir *v.* to add
añejo, ja *adj.* old; mature
añil *adj., m.* indigo
año *m.* year
apabullar *v.* to squash
apacible *adj.* gentle
apaciguar(se) *v.* to appease
apadrinar *v.* to support
apaleo *m.* thrashing
apañar *v.* to mend; seize; grasp
aparcar *v.* to park
aparente *adj.* seeming
aparición *f.* appearance
apartado, da *adj.* isolated
apartamento *m.* apartment
apartar(se) *v.* to divide; remove

aparte *adv.* aside; apart
apasionar *v.* to captivate
apatía *f.* apathy
apático, ca *adj.* apathetic
apear *v.* to chock; fell
apelable *adj.* appealable
apelar *v.* to appeal
apellidar *v.* to name; be called
apellido *m.* family name
apenar *v.* to sadden; grieve
apero *m.* farm gear, tools
apestar *v.* to infect with the plague; nauseate
apetencia *f.* appetite
apetito *m.* appetite
apetitoso, sa *adj.* delicious
apio *m.* celery
aplacar *v.* to placate
aplanar *v.* to flatten; stun
aplastar(se) *v.* to flatten
aplaudir *v.* to clap; applaud
aplicable *adj.* applicable
aplicación *f.* application; diligence
aplicar *v.* to apply
apocado, da *adj.* timid
apodo *m.* nickname
apolítico, ca *adj.* apolitical
aporrear(se) *v.* to beat
aportar *v.* to bring; arrive
aposición *f.* apposition
apóstol *m.* apostle
apóstrofe *m.* apostrophe
apoteosis *f.* apotheosis
apoyar(se) *v.* to rest on; support
apoyo *m.* support
apreciación *f.* appreciation
apreciar *v.* to value; appreciate
aprehender *v.* to seize
aprehensión *f.* apprehension; comprehension
aprender *v.* to learn
aprensión *f.* fear
apresar *v.* to seize
apresurar *v.* to hurry
apretar *v.* to tighten; press
aprobar *v.* to pass; approve
aproximar(se) *v.* to approximate
aptitud *f.* talent; aptitude
apuesto *f.* wager
apuntar(se) *v.* to aim; point
apunte *m.* notation; note

apurar(se) v. to worry
aquejar v. to distress
aquel adj. that
aqué pron. that one
aquí adv. now; here
aquietar v. to quiet; calm down
ara f. altar
araña f. spider
arbitrar v. umpire; arbitrate
árbitro m. arbitrator
árbol m. tree
arboreto m. arboretum
arbusto m. shrub
arco m. arch
archivar v. to file
archivo m. archives
arder(se) v. to burn
ardilla f. squirrel
ardor m. heat
árduo, dua adj. arduous
área f. area
arenoso, sa adj. sandy
arenque m. herring
argolla f. ring
argüir v. to prove; argue
argumentar v. to argue
árido, da adj. dry; arid
arisco, ca adj. wild; unfriendly; surly; churlish
aristocracia f. aristocracy
aristócrata f., m. aristocrat
aritmético, ca adj. arithmetic
armario m. closet; cabinet; cupboard
armiño m. ermine
armisticio m. armistice
armonía f. harmony
aro m. hoop; ring
aroma m. f. fragrance
aromar v. to scent; perfume
aromatizar v. to perfume; to scent
aromoso, sa adj. aromatic
arpista m., f. harpist
arqueología f. archaeology
arquitecto, ta m., f. architect
arrancar v. to seize; pull up; obtain; stem
arrasar v. to clear; level
arrastrar(se) v. to pull; crawl; drag
arrear v. to harness; herd

arrebato m. rage
arrecife m. reef
arreglado, da adj. neat
arreglar(se) v. to order; settle; dress (up)
arreglo m. understanding; arrangement
arremedar v. to copy; mimic
arremeter v. to attack
arrendar v. to rent
arreo m. drove; herd; appendages
arrepentirse v. to regret
arrestado, da adj. arrested
arresto m. arrest
arriba adv. above
arribar v. to arrive
arribo m. arrival
arriendo m. renting
arriesgado, da adj. hazardous; daring
arriesgar(se) v. to venture; jeopardize; risk
arrimar v. to draw or bring near
arrimo m. approach; help; crutch
arrinconado, da adj. distant
arrinconar v. to corner; to place in a corner
arrítmia f. lack of rhythm
arrobamiento m. rapture; ecstasy
arrobar v. to enrapture
arrodillar(se) v. to kneel
arrogante adj. proud; arrogant
arrojar(se) v. to fling; emit; throw
arrojo, ja m. boldness
arrollador, ra adj. overwhelming
arrollar v. to carry or sweep away
arropar v. to tuck in; wrap with clothing
arrorró m. lullaby
arroyo m. brook; stream
arroz m. rice
arruga f. crease; fold; wrinkle line
arruinar v. to destroy; ruin
arrullar v. to lull to sleep; to coo
arrumaco m. caress
arrumbar v. to neglect; to put or cast aside
arsenal m. storehouse; shipyard
arte m., f. craft; art
artefacto m. appliance
arteria f. artery

artero, ra *adj.* sly; cunning
artesanía *f.* craftsmanship
articulación *f.* joint
articular *v.* to articulate
artista *f., m.* artist
artificio, *m.* item; article; thing; cunning; trick
artificial *adj.* artificial
artístico, ca *adj.* artistic
artritis *f.* arthritis
as *m.* ace
asado *m.* roasted; roast meat; barbecue
asador *m.* grill; roasting spit
asalariar *v.* to set a salary for someone
asaltador, ra *m. f.* assailant
asamblea *f.* conference; meeting; legislature
ascendencia *f.* ancestry
ascendente *adj.* ascending
ascender *v.* to promote; ascend
ascensión *f.* rise; ascension
ascensor *m.* lift; elevator
ascensorista *m., f.* one who operates an elevator
asco *m.* disgust
asear *v.* to clean; wash
asechar *v.* to set a trap
asediar *v.* to bother; to pester
asedio *m.* siege
asegurar(se) *v.* to fasten; assure; secure
asentar *v.* to record; settle
asentimiento *m.* consent
asentir *v.* to agree
aseo *m.* tidiness; neatness
asequible *adj.* attainable; accessible
aserción *f.* affirmation
aserrar *v.* to saw
asesinato *m.* murder; assassination
asesor, ra *adj.* advisory; advising
asesorar *v.* to advise
asestar *v.* to aim
aseverar *v.* to assert
aseverativo, va *adj.* affirmative; assertive
asfaltar *v.* to asphalt
asfixia *f.* suffocation
asfixiar *v.* to asphyxiate

así *adv.* so
asiento *m.* seat
asignar *v.* allot; assign
asignar *v.* to appoint; to assign
asilar *v.* to give shelter
asilo *m.* asylum; home for the aged or poor
asimilar(se) *v.* to assimilate
asimismo *adj.* in a like manner; likewise
asir(se) *v.* to grip; hold on to
asistencia *f.* attendance; assistance; aid
asistir *v.* to accompany; aid; attend
asma *f.* asthma
asociación *f.* association
asociar(se) *v.* to associate with
asolador, ra *adj.* ravaging
asolar *v.* to scorch
asomar *v.* to begin to show; appear
asombrar(se) *v.* to amaze; astonish
aspirar *v.* to breathe; inhale
aspirina *f.* aspirin
astrología *f.* astrology
astronomía *f.* astronomy
astuto, ta *adj.* artful; sly; canny; cunning
asunto *m.* matter; subject; concern
atacar *v.* to assault; charge
ataque *m.* attack
atar(se) *v.* to rope; tie; brace
atención *f.* attention
atender *v.* to heed; attend
atestiguar *v.* to testify
atiesar(se) *v.* to tighten; stiffen
atleta *f., m.* athlete
atlético, a *adj.* athletic
atómico, *adj.* atomic
átomo *m.* atom
atracción *f.* attraction
atractivo, ca *adj.* engaging
atraer *v.* to attract; lure
atrás *adv.* aback; back
atrasado, da *adj.* backward
atribuir *v.* to ascribe
atrocidad *f.* atrocity
aturdir(se) *v.* to daze; muddle; bewilder

audición *f.* audition
augusto, ta *adj.* august
aumento *m.* raise; increase, expand
aún *adv.* still
aunque *conj.* although
ausente *adj.* missing
autobús *m.* bus
autógrafo *m.* autograph
automóvil *m.* car
autorización *f.* authorization
avanzar(se) *v.* to advance
ave *f.* bird
avenida *f.* avenue
aventura *f.* adventure
aversión *f.* aversion
aviación *f.* aviation
avión *m.* plane; airplane
ayuda *f.* aid; help
ayudar *v.* to assist; help
azorar *v.* to alarm
azorrado, da *adj.* foxy
azotar *v.* to beat upon
azote *m.* spanking; whip
azúcar *m., f.* sugar
azucarado, da *adj.* sweet
azul *m.* blue
azulado, da *adj.* bluish
azular *v.* to color or dye blue
azulejo *m.* glazed tile; cornflower; blue jay

B

baba *f.* spittle
babarse *tr.* to dribble
babaza *f.* slime
babear *v.* to drool
babel *m.* confusion
babero *m.* bib
babieca *adj. m. f.* simple person; silly
babor *m.* port side of ship
babosear *v.* to slobber
bacalao *m.* codfish
bacanal *a.* bacchanalian
bacilo *m.* bacillus
bacteria *f.* bacterium
bacteriología *f.* bacteriology
bacteriólogo, ga *m., f.* bacteriologist
bache *m.* pothole

badajo *m.* bell clapper
badulaque *adj. & m.* foolish person
bagaje *m.* luggage; a person's knowledge
bagatela *f.* trinket; trifle
bagre *m.* catfish
bahía *f.* bay
bailador, ra *m., f.* dancer
bailar *v.* to dance
bailarina *f.* ballerina
baile *m.* ball; dance
baja *f.* drop; fall
bajar(se) *v.* to fall; lower
bajeza *f.* lowliness
bajo, ja *adj.* short; small; lower; *adv.* low
bajón *m.* decline bassoonist
bala *f.* bale; bullet
balada *f.* ballad
baladí *adj.* trivial
baladro *m.* shout
baladrón *m.* braggart; bully
baladronada *f.* boast
baladronear *v.* to brag; boast
balancear(se) *v.* to teeter
balanceo *m.* rocking
balanza *f.* scale
balar *v.* to bleat
balbucear *v.* to stammer; babble
balcón *m.* balcony
balido *m.* bleat
balística *f.* ballistics
balístico, ca *adj.* ballistic
baloncesto *m.* basketball
balonmano *m.* handball
balonvolea *m.* volleyball
balota *f.* ballot
balsa *f.* balsa
bálsamo *m.* balsam
baluarte *m.* bastion
ballena *f.* whale
ballenato *m.* whale calf
ballenero, ra *adj.* whaling
ballesta *f.* crossbow
ballestear *v.* to shoot with a crossbow
ballestería *f.* archery
bambolear *v.* to sway
bamboleo *m.* swaying; swinging
ballet *m.* ballet

bambú *m.* bamboo
banana *f.* banana
banca *f.* banking
bancarrota *f.* bankruptcy
banco *m.* bank; slope; pew; bench
bandada *f.* flock; group
bandera *f.* banner; flag
bandeja *f.* tray
banderola *f.* pennant
bandido *m.* bandit
bandolero *m.* bandit
banqueta *f.* stool; sidewalk
banquete *m.* feast; banquet
banquetear *v.* to feast
bañar(se) *v.* to bathe
baño *m.* bathtub
barajar *v.* to shuffle
barato, ta *adj.* cheap; inexpensive; *adv.* cheaply
barba *f.* beard
barbacoa *f.* barbecue
barbado, da *adj.* bearded
barbaridad *f.* outrage
bárbaro, ra *adj.* savage; wild
barbear *v.* to shave
barbero *m.* barber
barbilla *f.* chin
barbotar *v.* to mutter; mumble
barboteo *m.* murmuring
barbulla *f.* chatter; jabbering
barca *f.* small boat
barcaza *f.* launch; barge
barco *m.* ship; boat
barítono *m.* baritone
barniz *m.* glaze; varnish; lacquer
barnizar *v.* to varnish; lacquer
barómetro *m.* barometer
barón *m.* baron
baronesa *f.* baroness
barra *f.* bar; ingot
barraca *f.* booth; hut
barrer *v.* to sweep
barrera *f.* barricade; barrier
barriga *f.* belly
barril *m.* barrel
barrio *m.* neighborhood
basalto *m.* basalt
basar *v.* to base
base *f.* foundation; basis; base
básico *adj.* basal; basic
basílica *f.* basilica

básquetbol *m.* basketball
bastante *adj.* sufficient
bastar *v.* to suffice
bastardear *v.* to debase
basto, ta *adj.* rude; coarse
bastón *m.* baton; walking stick
basura *f.* rubbish; garbage
bata *f.* negligee; dressing gown; bathrobe
batalla *f.* battle
batallar *v.* to battle
batallón *m.* battalion
batería *f.* battery
batido *m.* batter; a fruit and milk drink
batir(se) *v.* to churn; beat; whip; whirl
batuta *f.* baton
baúl *m.* luggage; trunk
bautismo *m.* christening
bautizar *v.* to baptize
baya *f.* berry
bayo, ya *adj.* bay
bazar *m.* bazaar
beatificar *v.* to beautify
beatífico *adj.* beatific
beatitud *f.* beatitude
bebé *m.* baby
beber *v.* to drink
bebida *f.* beverage
beca *f.* scholarship
becerro *m.* calf
befar *v.* to taunt
beige *m.* beige
béisbol *m.* baseball
belicoso, sa *adj.* warlike
beligerante *adj.* belligerent
belleza *f.* beauty
bello, lla *adj.* beautiful
bemol *m.* flat
bendecir *v.* to bless
bendición *f.* blessing
bendito, ta *adj.* holy
beneficiar(se) *v.* to benefit
beneficioso, sa *adj.* beneficial
benéfico, ca *adj.* charitable
benévolo, la *adj.* benevolent
bengala *f.* flare
benignidad *f.* kindness
benigno, na *adj.* kind; mild
berrinche *m.* tantrum
besar(se) *v.* to smooch; kiss

beso m. kiss
bestia f. animal; beast
bestial adj. bestial
Biblia f. Bible
bíblico, ca adj. Biblical
bibliografía f. bibliography
bibliógrafo, fa m. bibliographer
biblioteca f. library
bíceps m. biceps
bicicleta f. bicycle
biciclista m., f. bicyclist
bicho m. insect
bien m. good; adv. well
bienvenida f. welcome
bifurcarse v. to fork
bigote m. mustache
bilateral adj. bilateral
bilioso, sa adj. bilious
bilis f. bile
billar m. billiards
billete m. bill
billón m. billion; one thousand, million
binario, ria adj. binary
biografía f. biography
biográfico, ca adj. biographic
biógrafo m. biographer
biología f. biology
biológico, ca adj. biological
biólogo m. biologist
biopsia f. biopsy
bisabuela f. lo m. greatgrand-mother; -father
bisecar v. to bisect
bisección f. bisection
bisonte m. bison
bizguear v. to squint
blanco, ca adj. blank; white
blandir v. to flourish
blando, da adj. bland; soft
blanquear v. to whiten
blasfemar v. to swear; curse
blasfemia f. blasphemy; insult
blindado, da adj. armored
bloque m. block
bloquear v. to block
blusa f. blouse
bobo m. fool; ninny
boca f. mouth
bocadillo m. sandwich; morsel; appetizer
bocado m. bite; mouthful

boda f. marriage; wedding
bodega f. wine cellar; warehouse; small grocery store
boicoteo m. boycott
bola f. fib; ball
boletín m. bulletin
boliche m. bowling
bolita f. pellet; a type of armadillo
bolsa f. bag; pouch
bolsillo m. pocket
bolsista m. stockbroker
bolso m. handbag
bollo m. bump
bomba f. pump; bomb
bombardero m. bomber
bombear v. to pad; pump
bombilla f. light bulb
bombón m. candy
bondad f. kindness
bondadoso, sa adj. good
bonito, ta adj. pretty
boqueada f. gasp
boquilla f. nozzle
borde m. edge
bordillo m. curb of sidewalk
borracho m. drunkard
borrador m. eraser
bosque m. woods
bosquejar v. to outline
bota f. wine bag; boot
botánica f. botany; herbs and religious articles store
bote m. pot; tin can; small boat
botella f. bottle
boticario, a m., f. druggist
botín m. loot
botón m. stud; button
botones m. bellhop
bóveda f. vault
bovino, na adj. bovine
boxeador m. boxer
boxear v. to box
boya f. buoy
boyante adj. buoyant
bozal m. muzzle
bramante m. thin twine; adj. bellowing; roaring
bramar v. to bluster; roar
bramido m. bellow
bravo, va adj. brave; ferocious; angry

brazado *m.* armful
brazo *m.* arm
breve *adj.* short
brevedad *f.* conciseness
bribón, na *adj.* rascally
brillante *adj.* bright; shiny
brillar *v.* to glow; beam
brillo *m.* glow; shine
brincar *v.* to jump; gambol
brío *m.* jauntiness
brisa *f.* breeze
brocado *m.* brocade
broche *m.* brooch; fastener; hook and eye
bromear(se) *v.* to joke
bromista *f.* joker
bronce *m.* bronze
bronceado *m.* suntan; bronze
broncear *v.* to tan; to bronze
bronco, ca *adj.* coarse; rough
bronquio *m.* bronchial tube
bronquitis *f.* bronchitis
broquél *m.* small shield
brotadura *f.* budding
brotar *v.* to bud
brujería *f.* witchcraft
brujo, ja *m.* wizard *f.* witch
brújula *f.* compass
brumoso, sa *adj.* foggy; misty
bruñidura *f.* polishing; burnishing
bruñir *v.* to burnish; polish
brusco, ca *adj.* sudden
bruto *m.* beast; brute *adj. m., f.* stupid; unpolished
bubón *m.* swelling or very large morbid tumor
bucear *v.* to swim under water; dive
bucle *m.* curl; ringlet
budín *m.* pudding
buenaventura *f.* good luck; good fortune
bueno, na *adj.* fit; good
buey *m.* ox
búfalo *m.* buffalo
bufanda *f.* muffler; scarf
bufón *m.* clown; buffoon
buhonero *m.* hawker; peddler
buitre *m.* vulture
bujía *f.* candle

bulbo *m.* bulb (plant)
bulevar *m.* boulevard
bulto *m.* bulk; bundle
bulla *f.* uproar; brawl; noise
bullicio *m.* riot; racket
bullir *v.* to boil; budge
buñuelo *m.* a type of doughnut or cruller
buque *m.* vessel; ship
buqué *m.* bouquet
burbuja *f.* bubble
burdeos *adj.* deep red in color
burdo, da *adj.* rough; coarse
burguesía *f.* middle class
burilar *v.* to engrave
burla *f.* taunt; joke
burlar(se) *v.* to gibe; joke
burlesco, ca *adj.* burlesque
burócrata *m., f.* bureaucrat
burra *f.* stupid woman
burro, rra *m., f.* donkey; stupid
bursa *f.* rubbish
bursátil *adj.* pertaining to stock market
busca *f.* search
buscaplé *m.* feeler word
buscar *v.* to look or search for
buscavidas *m., f.* busybody; hustler
búsqueda *f.* search
busto *m.* bust; chest
butaca *f.* armchair
butano *m.* butane
buzo *m.* deep-sea diver
buzón *m.* mailbox

C

cabal *adj.* fair; precise
cábala *f. relig.* cabala
cabalgar *v.* to ride on horseback
cabalgata *f.* cavalcade
caballería *f.* cavalry
caballeriza *f.* stable
caballero *m.* gentleman
caballete *m.* easel; sawhorse
caballito *m.* pony; small horse
caballo *m.* horse
caballón *f.* ridge between furrows
cabaña *f.* cabin
cabaret *m.* cabaret; night club
cabecilla *m.* ringleader

cabellera f. head of hair
cabello m. hair
caber v. to fit
cabestrillo m. sling for injured arm
cabestro m. halter for horses
cabeza f. skull; chief
cabezón, na adj. bigheaded; obstinate
cabezota m., f. very big head
cabildear v. to lobby
cabildo m. town council
cable m. cable; cablegram
cablegrafiar v. to cable
cablegrama m. cablegram
cablevisión f. cable television
cabo m. corporal; cape;
cabra f. goat
cabrío m. rafter
cabrito m. young goat; kid
cabronada f. coll. dirty trick; indignity
cacahuate m. peanut
cacao m. cocoa
cacarear v. to crow; cackle
cacatúa f. cockatoo
cacerola f. casserole
cacique m. Indian chief
caciquear v. to order people around
caco m. burglar
cacto m. cactus
cachalote m. sperm whale
cachar v. to split; chip
cachaza f. sluggish
cachear v. to frisk, to search
cachemira f. cashmere
cachetear v. to slap; hit
cachetina f. fist fight
cachetudo, da adj. plump or chubby cheeks
cachorro m. puppy
cada adj. every; each
cadalso m. platform; scaffold for capital punishment
cadáver m. body; corpse
cadavérico, ca adj. cadaverous
cadena f. chain
cadencia f. rhythm; cadence
cadera f. hip, hip joint
cadete m. cadet
caduco, ca adj. lapse; senile

caer(se) v. to fall
café m. coffee; cafe
cafeína f. caffeine
cafetal m. coffee plantation
cafetería f. cafeteria; cafe
caída f. downfall; tumble
caimán m. alligator; cayman
caja f. cabinet; chest; box
cajero m. cashier; teller
cajista m., f. typesetter; compositor
cal f. lime; limestone
cala f. cove; small bay
calabaza f. pumpkin; gourd; squash
calabozo m. jail; underground prison cell
calador m. driller
calafatear v. to calk; caulk
calamar m. squid
calambre m. cramp
calamidad f. calamity; misfortune
calamitoso, sa adj. calamitous
calaña f. character; nature
calar(se) v. to swoop; penetrate
calcetería f. hosiery
calcetín m. sock
calificación f. assessment; qualification; grade; mark
calcificar(se) v. to calcify
calcio m. calcium
calco m. tracing
calcomanía f. decal
calculador, ra m., f. calculator; adj. calculating
calcular v. to estimate; calculate
cálculo m. calculation; calculus
caldera f. boiler
caldo m. soup; broth; stock
calefacción f. heating; heat
calefactor m. heater
calendario m. calendar; schedule
calentador, ra adj. warming; heating m. heater
calentar(se) v. to heat; warm
caliente adj. warm; hot
calina f. haze
calipso m. calypso
calma f. calm
calmante adj. sedative; m. tranquilizer
calmar(se) v. to soothe; calm;

settle

calofrío *m.* chill; fever

calor *m.* warmth; heat

caloría *f.* calorie

calórico, ca *adj.* caloric

calumnia *f.* slander; calumny

calumniador, ra *adj.* slanderous

caluroso, sa *adj.* warm; hot

calvario *m.* Calvary

calvicie *f.* baldness

calvo, va *adj.* bald

calzada *f.* causeway; drive; highway; road

calzones *m., pl.* trousers

callado, da *adj.* silent; quiet

callar (se) *v.* to keep quiet; hush

calle *f.* street

callejuela *f.* alley

callo *m.* callus; corn

cama *f.* bed

camada *f.* litter; brood

camafeo *m.* cameo

cámara *f.* room; chamber; camera

camarada *m., f.* comrade

camarera *f.* waitress

camarero *m.* waiter

camarote *m.* cabin

cambiar(se) *v.* to change; alter

cambiavía *m.* rail switch

cambio *m.* shift; change

cambista *m., f.* broker; money-changer

camelear *v.* deceive

camella *f.* camellia

camello *m.* camel

camero, ra *adj.* pertaining to double; bed; bedmaker

camilla *f.* stretcher

caminar *v.* to walk; travel

caminata *f.* hike; walk

camino *m.* route; road

camión *m.* truck; bus

camionero, ra *m., f.* truck driver

camioneta *f.* van; station wagon

camisa *f.* shirt

camiseta *f.* tee-shirt; undershirt

camisola *f.* camisole

camisón *m.* nightgown

camorra *f.* squabble; quarrel

camorrear *v.* to quarrel;squabble

campamento *m.* camp

campana *f.* bell

campaña *f.* campaign

campesino, na *adj.* country; peasant

campestre *adj.* rural

campista *m., f.* camper

campo *m.* country; field

camposanto *m.* graveyard; cemetery

camuflaje *m.* camouflage

camuflar *v.* to camouflage

canal *m.* canal; channel

canalete *m.* paddle; small oar

canasta *f.* hamper; basket; a card game

cancelación *f.* cancellation

cancelar *v.* to cancel; void; annul; negate

cáncer *m.* cancer

canciller *m.* chancellor

cancillería *f.* chancery

canción *f.* song

cancionero *m.* songbook

cancro *m.* cancer; canker

candado *m.* padlock

candela *f.* candle; taper

candelero *m.* candlestick

candidato *m.* candidate

candidatura *f.* candidacy

canela *f.* cinnamon

canesú *m.* bodice; yoke

cangrejo *m.* crab

canica *f.* marble

canícula *f.* midsummer heat; dog days of summer

canilla *f.* shinbone

canillita *m.* newspaper boy

canino, na *adj., m.* canine

canje *m.* trade; exchange

canjeable *adj.* exchangeable

canjear *v.* to trade; exchange

cano, na *adj.* gray-haired

canoa *f.* canoe; rowboat

cansado, da *adj.* weary; tired; rundown

cansancio *m.* tiredness

cansar(se) *v.* to weary; tire

cantante *m., f.* singer

cantar *v.* to sing; chant; *m.* song

cantera *f.* quarry

cantidad *f.* quantity; amount

cantimplora *f.* canteen

canto m. singing; song; croak
canturrear v. to croon; hum
caña f. cane; reed
caño m. pipe; spout
cañón m. cannon; barrel
caos m. chaos
capa f. cape; coating; layer
capataz m. foreman
capaz adj. roomy; capable
capcioso, sa adj. deceitful
capellán m. chaplain
caperuza f. hood
capilar adj., m. capillary
capilaridad f. capillarity
capilla f. chapel
capillo m. baby bonnet; cap
capital m. capital
capitán m. captain
capitolio m. capitol
capítulo m. chapter
capó m. car hood
capón adj. castrated
capricho m. whim; fancy; caprice
caprichoso, sa adj. temperamental; whimsical
cápsula f. capsule
captura f. capture; catch
capucha f. hood; cowl
capullo m. cocoon; flower bud; corn husk
caqui m. khaki
cara f. face
caracol m. snail
carácter m. nature; character
carámbano m. icicle
caramelizar v. to cover with caramel
caramelo m. caramel
caravana f. caravan
carbohidrato m. carbohydrate
carbón m. coal; charcoal
carbonato m. carbonate
carbono m. carbon
carburador m. carburetor
carburante m. fuel
cárcel f. prison; jail
cardenal m. cardinal
cardíaco, ca adj. cardiac
carecer v. to lack
carencia f. need; lack of
carey m. sea turtle
carga f. burden; load

cargadero m. loading platform
cargamento m. cargo
cargar(se) v. to burden; load
cargo m. responsibility; charge; burden; load
cariarse v. to decay teeth
caridad f. charity
cariño m. affection; love
caritativo, va adj. charitable
carnal adj. carnal
carnaval m. carnival
carne f. pulp; flesh; meat
carnear v. to slaughter
carnicero m. butcher
carpeta f. folder; table covering
carpintería f. carpentry
carpintero m. carpenter
carrera f. career; race
carrero m. carrier; cart driver
carretaje m. cartage
carrete m. reel; spool; coil; bobbin
carretera f. road; highway
carroza f. coach; chariot
carruaje m. carriage
carrusel m. merry-go-round
carta f. card; letter
cartapacio m. notebook; portfolio
cartel m. poster
cartelera f. billboard
cartera f. billfold; wallet
cartero m. postman
cartílago m. gristle; cartilage
cartografía f. mapmaking; cartography
cartógrafo, fa m., f. map maker, cartographer
cartón m. cardboard
cartucho m. cartridge; brown paper bag
casa f. home; house
casaca f. dress coat
casado, da adj. married
casar(se) v. to wed; marry
cascabel m. small bell
cascabelear v. to jingle
cascado, da adj. cracked; decrepit
cascada f. cascade
cascajo m. gravel
cáscara f. hull; shell; skin

caseta f. cottage; sentry box
casete m., f. tape cartridge; cassette
cascote m. rubble
casi adv. almost
casimir m. cashmere
casino m. casino
caso m. happening; case
caspa f. dandruff
casta f. breed; caste
castañetear v. to chatter teeth; play the castanets
castidad f. chastity
castigar v. to punish
castillo m. castle
castor m. beaver
casual adj. accidental; coincidental
casualidad f. coincidence; chance
catalejo m. small telescope; spyglass
catalogar v. to catalog; catalogue
catar v. to taste; sample
catástrofe f. catastrophe
catedral f. cathedral
caterva f. gang; crowd
catéter m. catheter
catinga f. body odor
catorce adj. fourteen
catre m. cot made of canvas
cauce m. channel; riverbed; ditch
caución f. bail; caution
caucho m. rubber; rubber tree or plant
caudillo m. leader
causa f. cause
cautela f. cautiously
cautela f. caution
cauteloso, sa adj. cautions
cauterizar v. to cauterize
cautiverio m. captivity
cautivo, va adj., m., f. captive
cauto, ta adj. cautious
cavar v. to dig
caverna f. cave, cavern
caviar m. caviar
cavidad f. cavity
caza f. hunt game
cazador, ra adj. hunting
cazar v. to hunt
cazo m. ladle

cazuela f. casserole
cebar v. to fatten
cebolla f. onion
cebra f. zebra
ceceo m. lisp
cedro m. cedar
cédula f. ID document
céfiro m. zephyr
cegar v. to blind
ceguera f. blindness
ceja f. eyebrow
cejar v. to go back
celada f. ambush
celador, ra adj. vigilant; watchful
celar v. to comply with something
celda f. cell; prison or beehive
celebración f. celebration
celebrar v. to celebrate
célebre adj. famous; celebrated
celebridad f. celebrity
celeridad f. speed
celestial adj. heavenly
celibato m. celibacy
célibe adj.; m., f. celibate
celofán m. cellophane
celoso, sa adj. zealous; jealous
célula f. cell
celuloide m. celluloid
celuloso, sa adj. cellulose
cellisca f. sleet storm
cementerio m. cemetery
cemento m. cement
cena f. supper; dinner
cenar v. to have dinner
cencerro m. cowbell
cenicero m. ashtray
cenit m. zenith
censor m. censor
censurar v. to censor
centella f. flash
centenar m. one hundred
centeno m. rye
centésimo, ma adj. hundredth
centígrado, da adj. centigrade
centímetro m. centimeter
centinela m., f. sentry
centolla f. spider crab
centrado, da adj. centered
central adj. central; f. head office
centralizar v. to centralize
caseta v. to center

céntrico, ca *adj.* central

centro *m.* core; middle; center

ceñir *v.* to encircle; bind; be tight on

ceño *m.* frown; scowl

cepa *f.* stump; stock; origin of family

cepillo *m.* brush

cera *f.* wax

cerámica *f.* ceramics

cerca *adv.* near; close

cerca *f.* fence

cercanía *f.* nearness; *pl.* outskirts

cercano, na *adj.* near; close

cercar *v.* to surround; to fence something in

cercenar *v.* to cut off

cerciorar *v.* to assure

cerco *m.* hoop; siege

cerda *f.* sow; horsehair; bristle

cerdo *m.* pig

cerdoso, sa *adj.* bristly

cereal *m.* cereal

cerebral *adj.* cerebral

cerebro *m.* brain; mind

ceremonia *f.* ceremony

ceremonial *m.* ceremonial

cereza *f.* cherry

cerillo *f.* match

cero *m.* zero

cerrado, da *adj.* shut

cerradura *f.* lock

cerrar(se) *v.* to close; seal

cerrojo *m.* bolt

certificado *m.* certificate

certificar *v.* to certify

cervato *m.* fawn

cerveza *f.* ale; beer

cesar *v.* to cease

cesión *f.* grant; cession

césped *m.* grass; sod; lawn

cesta *f.* basket

cetrino, na *adj.* sallow

cíclico, ca *adj.* cyclic

ciclista *m., f.* cyclist

ciclo *m.* cycle

ciclón *m.* cyclone

cicuta *f.* hemlock

ciego, ga *adj.* sightless; blind

cielo *m.* heaven; sky

cien *adj.* hundred

ciénaga *f.* swamp

ciencia *f.* science

científico *m.* scientist

ciento *adj.; m.* hundred

cierre *m.* snap; fastener

ciertamente *adv.* certainly

cierto, ta *adj.* certain; sure

ciervo *m.* hart; stag

cifra *f.* figure; cipher

cifrar *v.* to cipher

cigarrillo *m.* cigarette

cilindro *m.* cylinder

cima *f.* crest; summit; top

cinco *adj.* five; fifth (of month); *m.* five

cincuenta *adj.* fifty

cine *m.* movies

cinta *f.* reel; tape; ribbon

cinto *m.* girdle

cinturón *m.* belt

ciprés *m.* cypress

circo *m.* circus

circulación *f.* circulation

circular *adj.* circular

círculo *m.* circle

cirio *m.* candle; taper

cirro *m.* cirrus

ciruela *f.* plum

cirugía *f.* surgery

cirujano *m.* surgeon

cita *f.* meeting; date; appointment

citación *f.* citation; subpena

citar(se) *v.* to quote; summon

ciudadano, na *m. f.* citizen

cívico,ca *f. adj.* civic

civil *adj.* civilian; civil

civilización *f.* civilization

clamor *m.* outcry; clamor

clamoroso, sa *adj.* clamorous

clan *m.* clan

claramente *adv.* clearly

claridad *f.* clearness; clarity

clarificación *f.* clarification

clarificar *v.* to clarify

clarín *m.* bugle

clarinete *m.* clarinet

claro, ra *adj.* clear; light; lucid

clase *f.* grade; class; sort

clásico *adj.* classic; classical

clasificar(se) *v.* to classify; class

clavar(se) *v.* to nail; to thrust

clave *adj.* key; clef

clavel *m.* carnation
clavija *f.* peg
clavo *m.* spike; nail
clemencia *f.* mercy; clemency
clemente *adj.* clement
clerical *adj.* clerical
clérigo *m.* priest; parson
clero *m.* ministry; clergy
cliente *m., f.* client; customer; patron
clima *m.* climate
clímax *m.* climax
clínica *f.* clinic
cloquear *v.* to cluck
cloro *m.* chlorine
coacción *f.* compulsion; constraint
coagulación *f.* coagulation
coagular(se) *v.* to coagulate; clot
coalición *f.* coalition
cobalto *m.* cobalt
cobarde *adj.* cowardly
cobra *f.* cobra
cobrador, ra *m.* bill collector
cobrar(se) *v.* cash; collect
cobre *m.* copper
cobro *m.* recovery
cocer *v.* to bake; cook
cociente *m.* quotient
cocina *f.* kitchen; stove
cocinar *v.* to cook
coco *m.* coconut
coctel *m.* cocktail
coche *m.* automobile
codicia *f.* greed
codiciar *v.* to covet
codicioso, sa *adj.* greedy
codificar *v.* to codify
código *m.* code
codo *m.* elbow
coeducación *f.* coeducation
coetáneo *m.* contemporary
cofradía *f.* gang; sisterhood; brotherhood
cofre *m.* chest
coger *v.* to get; risk; take
cogida *f.* catch
cohechar *v.* to bribe
cohecho *m.* bribery
coherente *adj.* coherent
cohete *m.* rocket; firecracker
coincidente *adj.* coincidental

coincidir *v.* to coincide
coito *m.* intercourse
cojear *v.* to hobble
cojera *f.* limp
cojín *m.* cushion
cojo, ja *adj.* lame
col *f.* cabbage
cola *f.* tail; line; glue
colaborar *v.* to collaborate
colador *m.* strainer
colapso *m.* collapse
colcha *f.* quilt; bedspread
colchón *m.* mattress
colección *f.* collection
coleccionar *v.* to collect
colega *m.* colleague
colegio *m.* academy; college; high school
colgadura *f.* drape
colibrí *m.* hummingbird
cólico *f.* colic
coliflor *f.* cauliflower
colina *f.* hill; knoll
colmenar *f.* hive; beehive
colmillo *m.* fang; tusk; canine tooth
colmo *m.* height; overflow
colocar(se) *v.* to place; locate; put
colon *m.* colon
colonia *f.* colony
colonial *adj.* colonial
colono *m.* settler
color *m.* color
colorete *m.* rouge
columna *f.* pillar; column
columnista *m., f.* columnist
columpiar(se) *v.* to swing
colusión *f.* collusion
coma *f.* comma; coma
comadre *f.* midwife; godmother of a woman's child
comandante *f.* commander
comandar *v.* to command
comatoso, sa *adj.* comatose
comba *f.* bend; rope-skipping
combar(se) *v.* to bend; sag
combate *m.* fight
combatir(se) *v.* to combat
combinación *f.* combination
combinar(se) *v.* to blend; combine

combustible *adj.* combustible

compeler *v.* to compel

compensación *f.* compensation

competir *v.* to compete

compilar *v.* to compile

compinche *m.* chum

complacer(se) *v.* to please; humor

complemento *n.* complement

completar *v.* to complete

completo, ta *adj.* full; absolute; thorough; complete

complicar(se) *v.* to involve

cómplice *m.* accessory

componer(se) *v.* to make; compose

comportar(se) *v.* to behave

composición *f.* composition

comprar *v.* to purchase; trade

comprender *v.* to understand

comprensivo, va *adj.* comprehensive

compresión *f.* compression

comprimir *v.* to compress

comprobación *f.* proof

comprobar *v.* to verify

compuesto *m.* compound

compulsión *f.* compulsion

computador, ra *m. f.* computer

computar *v.* to compute

común *adj.* common

con *prep.* towards; with; by

concavidad *f.* hollow

concebir *v.* to conceive

conceder *v.* to concede; accord

concejo *m.* council

concepción *f.* conception

concepto *m.* concept; opinion

concesión *f.* allowance; concession

conciencia *f.* conscience

concierto *m.* concert

concluir(se) *v.* to end; conclude

concordar *v.* to tally; agree

concordia *f.* concord; harmony

concreto, ta *adj.* concrete

concubina *f.* concubine; mistress

concurrir *v.* to meet; concur

concursante *m., f.* participant

concurso *m.* contest

condado *m.* county

conde *m.* count

conde *m.* earl; count

condecorar *v.* to decorate

condena *f.* sentence

condesa *f.* countess

condición *f.* state; condition

condicionar *v.* to condition

condimento *m.* condiment; seasoning

condolencia *f.* condolence

condonar *v.* to condone

conducir(se) *v.* to steer; lead; conduct; drive

conducta *f.* behavior

conducto *m.* duct; conduit

conectar *v.* to connect

conejito *m.* bunny

conejo *m.* rabbit

conexión *f.* connection

confección *f.* confection

confeccionar *v.* to make up; prepare

conferencia *f.* lecture; conference

conferir *v.* to grant; bestow

confesar(se) *v.* to confess; admit

confesor *v.* confessor

confeti *m.* confetti

confiable *adj.* reliable

confianza *f.* dependance; confidence

confiar *v.* to trust; rely; confide

confidencial *adj.* confidential

confín *m.* confines; bound

confirmar *v.* ratify; confirm

confiscar *v.* to confiscate

conflagración *f.* conflagration

conflicto *m.* clash; conflict

conformar(se) *v.* to adjust; conform

conforme *adj.* similar; agreeable

conformidad *f.* conformity

confrontar *v.* to confront

confundir(se) *v.* to confound; perplex; puzzle; baffle

confusión *f.* mess; jumble; confusion

congelación *f.* frostbite

congelar(se) *v.* to freeze; congeal

congénito, ta *adj.* congenital

congestión *f.* congestion

conglomerado *m.* conglomerate

congregar(se) *v.* to flock; assemble

congreso *m.* convention; congress

conjetura *f.* surmise; guess; conjecture

conjeturar *v.* to conjecture

conjugar(se) *v.* to conjugate

conjunción *f.* conjunction

conjunto *m.* whole; ensemble

conjurar *v.* to conjure

conmoción *f.* stir; concussion; commotion

conmovedor, ra *adj.* stirring

conmover(se) *v.* to shake; move; disturb

cono *m.* cone

constructivo, va *adj.* constructive

consuelo *m.* consolation

consultar *v.* to consult

consumar *v.* to carry out

consumidor *m.* consumer

consumir(se) *v.* to waste away; consume

consumo *m.* consumption

consunción *f.* consumption

contacto *m.* contact

contagiar(se) *v.* to catch; infect

contagio *m.* contagion

contagioso, sa *adj.* catching

contaminación *f.* pollution; contamination

contaminar(se) *v.* to contamnate

contar(se) *v.* to number; count; relate; tell

contemplar *v.* to view; look at

contemporáneo *adj.* contemporary

contender *v.* to compete; contend; contest

contendiente *m.* contender; rival

contener(se) *v.* to hold; include; contain

contenido *m.* content

contestación *f.* answer

contestar *v.* reply; answer

contienda *f.* contest; strife; strugle

contiguo, gua *adj.* adjacent

continente *m.* mainland; continent; container

continuar *v.* to continue

continuo, nua *adj.* continous; perpetual

contonear(se) *v.* to strut

contorno *m.* contour; outline

contra *prep.* versus; against

contrabajo *m.* bass; basso

contrabando *m.* smuggling; contraband

contracción *f.* contraction

contradecir *v.* to contradict

contraer(se) *v.* to contract

contralto *m., f.* alto; contralto

contrariedad *f.* snag; vexation

contrario, ria *adj.* adverse; contrary

contrastar *v.* to contrast

contraste *m.* contrast

contraventana *f.* shutter; storm window

contribución *f.* task; contribution

contribuir *v.* to contribute

control *m.* control

controlar *v.* to control

controversia *f.* controversy

contusión *f.* bruise; contusion

convalecer *v.* to convalesce

convaleciente *m., f.* convalescent

convencer *v.* to convince

convención *f.* convention

convencional *adj.* conventional

conveniencia *f.* expediency

conveniente *adj.* proper; fitting; convenient

convenir(se) *v.* to agree; befit

convento *m.* abbey

convergir *v.* to converge

conversación *f.* conversation

conversar *v.* to converse

convertir(se) *v.* to turn into

convexo, sa *adj.* convex

convicción *f.* conviction

convidado, da *m. f.* guest

convidar(se) *v.* to invite

convite *m.* invitation; party

convocar *v.* to summon

convoy *m.* convoy

convulsión *f.* convulsion

coñac *m.* brandy

cooperación *f.* teamwork

cooperar *v.* to cooperate

coordinación *f.* coordination

coordinar *v.* to coordinate

copa f. goblet; drink
copete m. tuft; crest
copia f. imitation; copy
copiar v. to copy
copioso, sa adj. copious
coqueta f. coquette
coquetear v. to flirt
coral adj. choral m. coral
corazón m. heart
corazonada f. hunch
corbata f. neck tie
corcel m. steed
corchete m. clasp; bracket
corcho m. cork
cordero m. lamb
cordón m. cord
corneta f. bugle; m. bugler
cornisa f. cornice
coro m. chorus
corola f. corolla
corona f. crown
coronar v. to crown
coronario, ria adj. coronary
corpiño m. bodice
corporal adj. corporal
corpóreo, a adj. bodily
corral m. corral
correa f. strap; belt
corrección f. correction
correcto, ta adj. right
corredor, ra m. broker
corregir(se) v. to correct; modify
correría f. foray
corriente adj. current
corroer(se) v. to erode
corromper(se) v. to rot
corrosión f. corrosion
corrosivo, va adj. corrosive
corrupción f. corruption
corsé m. corset
cortado, da adj. abrupt, choppy
cortadura f. slit; cut
cortante adj. edged
cortar(se) v. to chop; cut; clip
corte m. court
cortés adj. civil; polite
cortesía f. civility
cortijo m. grange
corto, ta adj. brief; short; scarce
cosa f. affair; thing
cosecha f. crop
coser v. to sew

cosmético, ca adj. m. cosmetic
cosmos m. cosmos
cosquillear v. to tickle
costo f. cost
costar v. to cost
coste m. price, cost
costilla f. rib
costoso, sa adj. expensive
costumbre f. custom
costura f. seam; sewing
cotidiano, na adj. daily
coyote m. coyote
cráneo m. skull
craso, sa adj. thick; gross; fat
cráter m. crater
creación f. creation
creador m. creator
crear v. to make; create
crecer(se) v. to increase; grow
creciente f. swelling (of river)
crecimiento m. growth
crédito m. credit
credo m. credo
crédulo, la adj. credulous
creencia f. faith
creer(se) v. to think
creíble adj. plausible
crema f. cream
cresa f. maggot
crespo, pa adj. curly; kinky hair
cresoón n.m. crépe
creta f. chalky lime
criada f. maid
criar(se) v. to raise; nurse
crimen m. felony; crime
cripta f. crypt
crisis f. breakdown
crisol m. crucible
cristal m. crystal; glass
cristianismo m. Christianity
Cristo m. Christ
criterio m. criterion
crítica f. censure; criticism
criticar v. to criticize
crítico, ca adj. critical
cromático, ca adj. chromatic
cromo m. chrome
crónica f. chronicle
crónico, ca adj. chronic
cronista m. f. reporter
cronometrar v. to tell time
croqueta f. croquet

croqueta f. croquette
cruce m. intersection; crossing
crucial adj. crucial
crucificado da adj. crucified
crucificar v. to crucify
crucifijo m. crucifix
crucifixión f. crucifixion
crucigrama m. crossword puzzle
crudeza f. crudeness
crudo, da adj. crude; raw; unripe
cruel adj. heartless; cruel, harsh
crueldad f. harshness, cruelty
crujido m. creak
crujir v. to crunch; to crackle; to creak
crustáceo adj. & m. shell fish
cruz f. cross
cruzada f. crusade
cruzado, da m. crusader; knight
cruzar(se) tv. to cross
cuaderno m. notebook, exercise-book
cuadra f. stable
cuadrado m. square
cuadrante m. quadrant
cuadrar(se) v. to tally
cuadrilongo m. oblong
cuadro m. square; picture; frame
cuajada f. curd
cual adv. as
cuál pron. which, what, which one
cualidad f. quality; characteristic
cualquier adj. any
cuan adv. how
cuando conj. when; although
cuándo adv. when; since
cuantía f. amount; quantity; importance
cuanto, ta adj. & pron. as much as
cuanto adv. how much
cuánto, ta pron. how much
cuarenta adj. forty
cuarentavo, va adj. fortieth
cuaresma f. Lent
cuartear v. to cut up; quarter; to divide
cuartel m. mil. barracks; section, ward
cuarto m. quarter; fourth; room
cuarzo m. quartz
cuasi adv. almost

cuate adj.; m., f. twin; alike
cuatro m. four; small four-string guitar
cuatrocientos adj. four hundred
cubeta f. bucket; tray
cubierta f. cover
cubil m. den; lair
cubilete m. tumbler; dice box
cubo m. cube; socket; bucket
cubrir(se) tr. to conceal; cover
cucaracha f. cockroach
cuco adj. neat
cuchara f. spoon
cucharada f. spoonful
cucheta f. cabin (ship or train)
cuchicheo m. whispering
cucharilla f. small spoon
cuchilla f. knife, cutting tool
cuello m. collar; neck
cuenta f. count, account; bill
cuentagotas m. dropper
cuentero, ra adj. gossipy
cuentista m. f. storyteller; story writer
cuento m. tale, story
cuerda f. cord; rope, string
cuerdo, da adj. ; m. f. sensible; sane; wise
cuerno m. horn
cuero m. hide; pelt; leather
cuerpear v. to dodge something
cuerpo m. corpus; body
cuervo m. crow; raven
cuesta f. hill; slope
cuestión f. question; matter; affair; dispute
cuestionable adj. debatable; questionable
cuestionar v. to debate; discuss; dispute
cueva f. cave; cellar
cuidado m. care; caution; worry
cuidador, ra m., f. caretaker
cuidadoso, sa adj. careful; watchful
cuidar(se) v. to look after; to care for
cuita f. grief; sorrow; worry; trouble
culantro m. coriander
culebra f. snake
culinario, ria adj. culinary

culminar v. to culminate

culo m. buttocks, behind, seat

culpa f. fault

culpabilidad f. guilt

culpable adj. guilty, culpable

culpar v. to blame; to accuse; to criticize

cultivar v. to farm; cultivate, till

cultivo m. cultivation; tillage; farming

culto, ta adj. cultured, cultivated m. worship, cult

cultura f. culture

cultural adj. cultural

cumbre f. peak; top

cumpleaños m. birthday

cumplido, da adj. perfect; complete

cumplidor, ra adj. reliable; trustworthy

cumplimiento m. fulfillment

cumplir v. to accomplish; to be (years) old

cundir v. to expand; spread

cuñada f. sister-in-law

cuñado m. brother-in-law

cuneta f. ditch, gutter

cuplé m. a type of popular song

cupo m. quota; share

cupón m. coupon

cura f. cure; priest

curable adj. curable; remediable

curación f. treatment, cure

curandero, ra m., f. healer; medicine person

curar(se) v. to heal; to treat; to cure

curia f. court; curia

curiosear v. to pry, snoop

curiosidad f. curiosity; neatness; cleanness

curioso, sa adj. curious; inquisitive

cursar v. to study; to frequent; to haunt; to attend

cursi adj. affected; tasteless

cursivo, va adj. cursive

curso m. course; circulation

curtido tanned; expert

curtir(se) v. to coarsen; tan hides

curva f. bend; curve

curvatura f. curvature

curvado, da adj. bent; curved; angled

curvar v. to curve

curvatura f. curvature

curvo va adj. curve, curved

cúspide f. top, summit, peak

custodia f. keeping; care; guard

custodiar v. to protect; watch over

custodio m. guard, custodian

cutícula f. cuticle

cutis m. complexion; skin

cuyo, ya pron. whose

CH

chabacanear v. to act in a gross, crude or vulgar way

chabacano, na adj. tasteless; crude

chacarero, ra m. f. farmer

chacota f. fun; merriment

chacotear v. to kid; to joke

chacotero, ra m. f. kidder; one who kids

chacra f. farm

cháchara f. chatter

chacharear v. to chatter; to make small talk

chafalonía f. a scrap of gold or silver.

chaira f. knife used by a shoemaker

chal m. shawl; stole

chala f. corn shuck or husk

chalán, na, adj. horse trader or dealer

chalar(se) v. to go crazy or mad

chaleco m. vest; waistcoat

chalet m. chalet

chalina f. neckerchief; small or narrow shawl

chalote m. shallot

chalet m. chalet

chalupa f. lifeboat; small sailing boat; small canoe; a Mexican dish

chambelán m. chamberlain

chambergo m. soft broad brimmed slouch hat

chamizo *m.* half-burnt log or tree; hut; cottage

champán *m.* champagne

champiñón *m.* mushroom

champú *m.* shampoo

champurrar *v.* to mix drinks

chamuscar *v.* to scorch; to singe

chamusquina *f.* scorching; to look fishy or like trouble

chance *m.* chance; a type of lottery ticket

chancear *v.* to joke

chancillería *f.* chancery

chancho, cha *adj.* filthy; dirty

chanchullo *m.* a crooked deal; trick

changar *v.* to work at odd jobs

chango, ga *adj.* playful; *m.* monkey

chantaje *m.* blackmail

chantilli *m.* whipped cream

chanza *f.* joke; jest

chapa *f.* plate; veneer

chapotear *v.* to splash

chapucear *v.* to bungle; to botch

chapucería *f.* botch; mess up; bumble

chapucero *adj.* bungling; crude, rough

chapurreo *m.* jabber; language spoken poorly

chapuzar(se) *v.* to duck, to plunge, to dive

chaqueta *f.* jacket

charada *f.* charade

charca *f.* pond, pool

charco *m.* puddle, pool

charla *f.* talk; gossip; chat; lecture

charlar *v.* to gossip; talk

charlatán, na *m.* quack

charro, rra *adj.* ill-bred; flashy; *m.* Mexican cowboy

chasis *m.* chassis, body

chasquear *v.* to click; snap; crack

chato, ta *adj.* squat; snubnosed

che *inj.* hey!

cheque *m.* check

chica *f.* girl

chicle *m.* chewing gum

chico *m.* boy *adj.* little, small

chiflado, da *adj.* cranky; crazy; madly in love

chile *m.* chili; chile

chillar *v.* to screech; scream

chillido *m.* scream, shriek

chillón, na *adj.* shrill

chimenea *f.* chimney; fireplace

chimpancé *m. f.* chimp; chimpanzee

china *f.* china; porcelain

chinchar *v.* to bother

chinchilla *f.* chinchilla

chipén *m.* activity, excitement

chiquillería *f.* youngsters

chiquitín, na *adj.* tiny

chiripa *f.* fluke

chirona *f.* jail

chirriar *v.* to sizzle; to shriek; to creak

chirrido *m.* squeak; creak

chismear *v.* to gossip

chispa *f.* drop of rain; spark

chiste *m.* joke

chistera *f.* top hat; basket

chocante *adj.* shocking

chocar *v.* to knock; hit; bump to collide; to shock

chocolate *m.* cocoa; chocolate

chofer *m.* chauffeur; driver

choque *m.* crash; collision

chorizo *m.* sausage

chorrear *v.* to spout; gush

choza *f.* shanty; shack

chubasco *m.* shower; storm; squall

chuchería *f.* knickknack

chuleta *f.* cutlet; chop

chupado *adj.* skinny; lean

chupar(se) *v.* to sip; to suck

chupechup *m.* lollypop

chupete *m.* pacifer

churruscar *tr.* to burn

chuscada *f.* joke

chusco *adj.* funny; droll

D

dable *adj.* feasible; possible

dactilografía *f.* typewriting; typing

dactilógrafo, fa *m. f.* typist

dádiva *f.* gift; present

dadivosidad *f.* liberality; generosity

dadivoso, sa *adj.* liberal; generous

dado, da *adj.* given

dama *f.* lady; dame

damisela *f.* damsel; young lady

damnificar *v.* to harm; to damage; to hurt

damnificado, da *adj.* harmed; damaged

danza *f.* dance; dancing

danzar *tr.* to dance

danzarin *adj.* dancing

dañar(se) *v.* to hurt; to damage; to harm

dañino, na *adj.* harmful; damaging; destruction

daño *m.* damage; hurt; harm

dar *v.* to give; to cause

dardo *m.* arrow; dart

dársena *f.* dock; inner harbor; port

data *f.* items; date

datar *v.* to date

dato *m.* fact, detail

de *prep.* of; from; with

deambular *v.* to roam or wander around

debajo *adv.* underneath; below

debate *m.* discussion; debate

debatir *v.* to discuss; to debate

debe *m.* debit

deber *v.* to owe *m.* obligation or duty; homework

debidamente *adv.* duly; properly

debido, da *adj.* fitting; due

débil *adj.* feeble; weak; faint; lame

debilidad *f.* weakness

debilitar *v.* to weaken

debut *m.* opening; debut

debutante *f.* debutant *adj.* beginning

decadencia *f.* decline; decadence

decadente *adj.* , *m. f.* decadent

decaer *v.* to decay; weaken

decaimiento *m.* feebleness, weakness; dejection; decay

decanato *m.* deanship

decano *m.* dean

decantación *f.* pouring off

decantar *v.* to pour off; decant; exaggerate

decapitar *v.* to behead

decencia *f.* decency

decenio *m.* decade

decente *adj.* decent; dignified, clean, honest

decepción *f.* deception; disappointment, delussion

decepcionar *v.* to disappoint

deceso *m.* death; decease

decidido, da *adj.* resolute; determined

decidir *v.* to resolve

decimal *adj.* decimal

decir *v.* to say; to tell

decisión *f.* decision; verdict; ruling; resolution

decisivo, va *adj.* crucial; conclusive; decisive

declamar *v.* to recite

declaración *f.* declaration; statement; evidence

declarar(se) *v.* to propose; to declare; to declare oneself

declinación *f.* decline; declination

declinar *v.* to decline; to refuse

declive *m.* incline; slope

decoloración *f.* discoloration; stage set

decolorante *m.* decolorant

decolorar *v.* to fade; to discolor

decomisar *v.* to seize; confiscate

decorado *m.* scenery or set in a theater

decorador, ra *adj.* ornamental; decorative

decorar *v.* to decorate

decorativo, va *adj.* ornamental; decorative

decoro *m.* honor; respect

decoroso, sa *adj.* decent; honorable

decrecer *v.* to diminish

decrépito, ta *adj.* aged; decrepit

decretar *v.* to decree; order

dedal *m.* thimble

dedicar(se) *v.* to devote

dedo *m.* finger

deducir *v.* to conclude; deduce; subtract

defección f. defection

defecto m. flaw; defect

defectuoso, sa adj. faulty; imperfect; defective

defender v. to defend

defensa f. defense

defensor m. supporter; defender; protector

deferencia f. deference

definición f. definition; determination

definir v. to define

deformar(se) v. to loose shape

defraudación f. cheating; fraud

defraudar v. to cheat; defraud

defunción f. death; demise

degenerar v. to decline; degenerate

degolladero m. windpipe; throat; slaughter house

degollar v. to cut the throat; decapitate

degradar(se) v. to demean; degrade

degustación f. sampling; tasting

deidad f. deity

dejado, da adj. negligent; careless

dejar(se) v. to quit; let

dejo m. abandonment; accent; lilt

del contr. of "de" and "el"

delante adv. ahead; before; in front

delantero, ra adj. forward; front

delatar v. to inform; denounce, expose

delegación f. delegation

delegar v. to delegate

deleitable adj. enjoyable; delightful

deleitar(se) v. to delight

delgado, da adj. thin; slim

delicado, da adj. sensitive; gentile; delicate

delicia f. pleasure; delight

delincuente adj. delinquent

delinear v. to outline; delineate

delirante adj. delirious

delirar v. to rave; be delirious

demanda f. challenge; demand; claim; suit

demandar v. to demand; ask for; file a suit

demasía f. surplus; more than what is needed

demasiado adj & adv. too much

demérito m. demerit

democracia f. democracy

demoler v. to demolish; destroy

demolición f. destruction

demora f. wait; delay

demorar(se) v. to delay

demostrar v. to display; demonstrate

demudar v. to change; alter

denegar v. to reject; refuse

denodado, da adj. bold

denostar v. to insult; abuse

denotar v. to denote

densidad f. density

denso, sa adj. thick; dense

dentadura f. denture

dental adj. dental

dentellear v. to bite; nibble

dentera f. unpleasant tingling in the teeth; jealousy; envy

dentífrico m. toothpaste

dentista m., f. dentist

dentro adv. within; inside

denuedo m. courage; bravery

denuesto m. insult

denunciar v. to denounce

deparar v. to supply

departamento m. office; department; section

departir v. to converse; talk

dependencia f. dependence

depender v. to depend

deplorar v. to deplore

deponer v. to depose; put aside

deportación f. deportation

deportar v. to exile; deport

deporte m. sport

depositar v. to bank; deposit

depósito m. deposit

depravación f. corruption

depravado, da adj. corrupted

depravar v. to deprave

deprecar v. to implore

deprecatorio, ria adj. imploring

depreciar v. to depreciate

depredar v. to pillage

depresión f. slump; depression;

hollow
deprimido *adj.* depressed
deprimir *v.* to depress
derecho, cha *adj.* right; upright
derivar(se) *v.* to derive
dermatología *f.* dermatology
derramar(se) *v.* to overflow; to spill
derribar *v.* to overthrow; to knock down
derrochar *v.* to waste; squander
derroche *m.* squandering
derrotar(se) *v.* to defeat
desacoplar *v.* disconnect
desafiar *v.* to defy
desafío *m.* challenge
desagradar *v.* to displease
desahuciar *v.* to evict; deprive of hope
desaire *m.* slight
desalentar *v.* to discourage
desanimar(se) *v.* dismay
desánimo *m.* discouragement; depression
desaprobar *v.* disapprove
desarreglar(se) *v.* disarrange
desarreglo *m.* disorder
desarrollar(se) *v.* to unfold; to develop
desarrollo *m.* development
desasosiego *m.* unrest
desastre *m.* disaster
desatar(se) *v.* to undo
desatento, ta *adj.* inattentive; impolite
desatino *m.* blunder
desayunar(se) *v.* to have breakfast
desayuno *m.* breakfast
descalificar *v.* to disqualify
descansar *v.* to rest
descanso *m.* rest
descarado, da *adj.* brazen
descargar(se) *v.* to unload
descendente *adj.* downward
descender *v.* to descend
descifrar *v.* to decipher
descolorar(se) *v.* fade
descomponer(se) *v.* to decompose
desconcertar(se) *v.* to baffle; disconcert

desconfiar *v.* to distrust
desconocer *v.* to disavow; pass by; ignore
descontento *m.* discontent
descontinuar *v.* to discontinue
descortés *adj.* impolite
descoser(se) *v.* to come apart
describir *v.* to describe
descripción *f.* description
descubrir *v.* to find; discover
descuidado, da *adj.* careless; thoughtless
descuidar *v.* to neglect; to overlook
desde *prep.* since; from
desdeñar *v.* to disdain
desdicha *f.* unhappiness
deseable *adj.* eligible
desear *v.* hope; wish; desire
desechar *v.* to reject
desembocar *v.* to land
desembolsar *v.* disburse
desencorvar *v.* to unbend
desenlace *m.* ending
deseo *m.* desire; wish
desertar *v.* to defect
desertor, ra *m. f.* deserter
desesperar *v.* to despair
desfalcar *v.* to embezzle
desfigurar *v.* to blemish; disfigure
desfile *m.* parade
desgarrar(se) *v.* to tear
desgaste *m.* wear and tear; erosion
desgracia *f.* misfortune
desgraciado, da *m. f.* unfortunate
deshacer(se) *v.* to undo; destroy
deshelar(se) *v.* to thaw
deshidratación *f.* dehydration
deshonra *f.* disgrace; dishonor
deshonrar *v.* to dishonor
desigual *adj.* unequal
desinflar *v.* to deflate
desinterés *m.* disinterest
desistir *v.* to desist
desleal *adj.* disloyal
deslizar(se) *v.* to glide; slide
deslumbrar *v.* to blind
deslustrar(se) *v.* to tarnish
deslustre *m.* tarnish

desmayo *m.* swoon; fainting
desmigajar(se) *v.* to crumble
desnatar *v.* to skim
desnudar(se) *v.* to undress
desnudo, da *adj.* nude; bare
desnutrición *f.* malnutrition
desobedecer *v.* to disobey
desocupado, da *adj.* free; vacant; idle
desodorizar *v.* to deodorize
desolación *f.* desolation
desorden *m.* mess
desorganizar *v.* to disorganize
despacio *adv.* slowly
despachar *v.* to dispatch; send off
despedir(se) *v.* to dismiss; to see off
despeinado, da *adj.* unkempt
desperdiciar *v.* to waste; squander
despertar(se) *v.* to awaken; wake up
despierto, ta *adj.* awake
desplegar(se) *v.* to unfold
despojar(se) *v.* to strip; dispossess
desposar(se) *v.* to marry
despreciable *adj.* vile; worthless
despreciar(se) *v.* to scorn
después *adv.* after; later
desterrar *v.* to banish; exile
destetar(se) *v.* to wean
destilar *v.* to distill
destreza *f.* dexterity; skill
destrucción *f.* destruction
destruir *v.* to destroy
desunir *v.* to disunite
desvanecer(se) *v.* vanish
desvergonzado, da *adj.* unabashed
desviar(se) *v.* to divert; wander; detour
detallado, da *adj.* elaborate; detailed
detallar *v.* to itemize
detalle *m.* detail
detective *m.* sleuth
detención *f.* arrest; detention
detener(se) *v.* to arrest; stop
deteriorar(se) *v.* to decay
determinar *v.* to decide

detestar *v.* to hate
detrás *adv.* aback; behind
deuda *f.* debt
devanar *v.* to wind
devastar *v.* to devastate
devoción *f.* devotion
devolver *v.* to refund; return
devorar *v.* to devour
día *m.* day
diablo *m.* devil
diácono *m.* deacon
diafragma *m.* diaphragm
diagnosticar *v.* to diagnose
diagrama *m.* diagram
dialecto *m.* dialect
diamante *m.* diamond
diario *adj.* daily
dibujante *m. f.* cartoonist
dibujar *v.* to sketch; draw
diccionario *m.* dictionary
diciembre *m.* December
dictador *m.* dictator
dictar *v.* to dictate
dicho *m.* remark; saying
diecinueve *adj.* nineteen
dieciocho *adj.* eighteen
dieciséis *adj.* sixteen
diecisiete *adj.* seventeen
diente *m.* tooth
diez *adj.* ten
difamar *v.* to defame
diferencia *f.* difference
diferente *adj.* different
diferir *v.* to differ; delay; postpone
difícil *adj.* hard; difficult
difunto, ta *adj.* deceased
difuso, sa *adj.* widespread
digerir *v.* to digest
digestión *f.* digestion
dígito *m.* digit
dignidad *f.* dignity
dilatar(se) *v.* to dilate
diligente *adj.* diligent
diluir *v.* to dilute
diluviar *v.* to pour (rain)
dimensión *f.* dimension
dinastía *f.* dynasty
dinero *m.* money
dios *m.* god
diosa *f.* goddess
diplomacia *f.* diplomacy

dirección f. direction
directamente adv. straight
directo, ta adj. straight
dirigir(se) v. to lead; control
discernir v. to discern
disciplina f. to discipline
disciplinar v. discipline
disco m. record
discrepar v. to disagree
discreto, ta adj. discreet
disculpa f. excuse
disculpar v. to excuse
discusión f. discussion
discutir v. to argue
diseminar v. to spread
diseñar v. to design
disfraz m. costume
disfrazar v. to disguise
disfrutar tr. to enjoy
disfrute m. benefit; enjoyment
disgustar(se) v. to annoy
disgusto m. displeasure; disgust
disimular tr. cover up, to dissemble
disipar tr. to waste; to dissipate
dislocar tr. to dislocate
dislocación f. dislocation
dislocar(se) v. to dislocate
disolver(se) v. to dissolve; to separate
dispersar(se) v. to disperse; scatter
disponer(se) v. to get ready
dispuesto, ta adj. willing
disputa f. dispute; quarrel
disputar v. to fight; quarrel; dispute
distante adj. distant, far
distar v. to be distant; to be far
distinguir v. to distinguish
distraer(se) v. to divert; distract
distribuir v. to distribute
distrito m. district
disturbio m. disturbance; commotion
disuadir v. to dissuade
diván m. couch
divergir v. to diverge
diversión f. amusement
diverso, sa adj. varied; different
dividir(se) v. to split; to divide; to cut

divino, na adj. divine
división tr. to percieve
divorciar(se) v. to divorce
doblar(se) v. fold; double
doblez m. crease, fold
doce adj. twelve
docena f. dozen
docente adj. instructional; educational
dócil adj. meek; docile
docto adj. learned
doctor ra m. & f. doctor
doctrina f. teaching; doctrine
documento tr. document
dolencia f. complaint, ailment
dólar m. dollar
doler(se) v. to pain; hurt
dolor m. ache; pain
dolorido da adj. aching, sore, painful
doloroso sa adj. painful
doma f. breaking, taming
domar tr. to break, to tame
doméstico, ca adj. domestic
domicilio m. residence; domicile
dominación f. domination
dominar tr. to dominate; to master
domingo m. Sunday
don m. present, gift
donaire m. cleverness
donante m. donor
donar v. to donate, to give
dónde adv. where
dondequiera adv. anywhere
doña f. Mrs.
dorado adj. golden
dormido da adj. asleep
dormir(se) v. to sleep
dormitorio m. bedroom; dormitory
dos adj. two; second (of month); m. two
dragón m. dragon
dramático, ca adj. dramatic
droga f. drug
ducha f. shower
ducharse v. to shower
dudar v. to hesitate; doubt
dueña f. owner; mistress; chaperone

dulce *m.* candy
duodécimo, ma *adj.* twelfth
duplicar(se) *v.* to duplicate
duquesa *f.* duchess
duradero, ra *adj.* durable
durante *prep.* during
duro, ra *adj.* stiff; hard

E

ébano *m.* ebony
ebriedad *f.* inebriation
ebrio, ria *m.* drunk
ecléctico, ca *adj.* eclectic
eclipsar *v.* eclipse
eclipse *m.* eclipse
eco *m.* echo
ecología *f.* ecology
economía *f.* economy
economizar *v.* to economize
ecuación *f.* equation
ecuador *m.* equator
ecuánime *adj.* impartial
ecuatorial *adj.* equatorial
eczema *m.* eczema
echada *f.* toss
echar(se) *v.* to throw; cast away
edad *f.* age
edición *f.* edition
edicto *m.* edict
edificar *v.* to edify
editar *v.* to edit
editor, ra *m. f.* editor; publisher
editorial *m.* editorial; publisher
educación *f.* education
educar *v.* to instruct; teach; train;
   educate
efebo *m.* adolescent
efectividad *f.* effectiveness
efecto *m.* result; impact; effect
efectuar *v.* to contrive; effect
eficacia *f.* efficacy
eficiencia *f.* efficiency
eficiente *adj.* efficient
efusión *f.* effusion
efusivo, va *adj.* effusive
ego *m.* ego
egresar *v.* graduate
ejecución *f.* execution
ejecutar *v.* to execute
ejecutivo, va *adj.* executive
ejemplar *adj.; m.* example;

exemplary
ejemplificar *v.* exemplify
ejemplo *m.* example
ejercer *v.* to exercise
ejercicio *m.* drill;
   exercise; practice
ejército *m.* army
él *art. m.* he
elaborar *v.* to elaborate
elástico, ca *adj.* elastic
elección *f.* election
electo, ta *adj.* elect
electorado *m.* electorate
electricidad *f.* electricity
electrificar *v.* to electrify
electrocución *f.* electrocution
electrocutar *v.* to electrocute
electrón *m.* electron
elefante *m.* elephant
elegancia *f.* grace
elegante *adj.* elegant
elegido, da *adj.* chosen
elegir *v.* to choose; elect
elemental *adj.* elementary;
   essential; elemental
elevación *f.* elevation
elevado, da *adj.* high
elevar(se) *v.* to elevate; lift
eliminar *v.* to eliminate
elipse *f.* ellipse
elíptico, ca *adj.* elliptical
elíxir *m.* elixir
elocuencia *f.* eloquence
elocuente *adj.* eloquent
elogiar *v.* to eulogize
elucidar *v.* to elucidate
eludir *v.* to elude
ella *pron., f.* she
ellas *pl. pron., f.* them; they
ello *pron.* it
ellos *pl. pron., m.* them; they
emanar *v.* to emanate
emancipar *v.* to emancipate
embajada *f.* embassy
embajador, ra *m. f.* ambassador
embalsamar *v.* to embalm
embarazada *adj.* pregnant
embarazo *m.* embarrassment;
   pregnancy
embarcar(se) *v.* to embark
embarque *m.* shipment
embastar *v.* to tack; quilt

embeber v. to wet; absorb
embellecer v. to embellish
embestir v. to attack
emblanquecer v. to bleach
emblema m. emblem
embolia f. embolism
emborrachar(se) v. to get drunk
emboscar v. to ambush
embotado, da adj. dull
embotar v. to dull
embotellar v. to bottle
embravecer v. to infuriate
embriagar(se) v. to intoxicate
embrión m. embryo
embrollar v. to embroil
emergencia f. emergency
emigrado m. emigrant
emigrar v. to emigrate
emisario, ria m. f. emissary
emisión f. issue
emitir v. to give off; emit
emoción f. feeling; emotion
emocionar v. to affect
emotivo, va adj. emotional
empalmar v. to splice; join
empapar(se) v. to drench; wet
empapelado m. lining
empapelar v. line with paper
emparedado m. recluse;
captive; prisoner; sandwich
empatar v. to tie
empate m. impediment; draw;
connection
empecinado, da adj. obstinate
empecinar(se) v. to be obstinate
empellar v. to push
empeño m. patron; pledge; in-
sistence
empeorar(se) v. to become worse
emperador m. emperor
emperatriz n.f. empress
emperatriz f. empress
empero conj. however
empezar v. to start; begin
empírico, ca adj. empirical
emplastar v. to hamper; plaster
emplasto m. poultice; plaster
empleado, da m. f. employee
empleador, ra m. f. employer
emplear(se) v. to employ
empleo m. job; work
empiumar v. to feather

empobrecido, da adj. impover-
ished
emprender v. to begin
empresa f. company; business
empresario, ria m. f. director;
promoter
empujar v. to thrust;
push
empuje m. push
emulación f. emu-
lation
emulsión f. emulsion
en prep. in
enajenable adj. alienable
enajenación f. alienation
enajenar v. to alienate
enardecer v. to ignite
encabezamiento m. heading;
caption
encabezar v. to enroll; head
encajar v. to force; insert
encallecer v. to develop a corn
or callous
encandilar v. to excite; stir;
dazzle; blind
encantado, da adj. happy; de-
lighted
encantador, ra adj. charming;
enchanting
encantar v. to charm; enchant
encanto m. enchantment; charm
encapotado, da adj. cloudy;
cloaked
encapotar v. to become overcast
encaramar v. to elevate; raise;
promote
encarar v. to confront
encargar v. to advise; place in
charge; request
encargo m. assignment; task;
job; request
encarnación f. incarnation
encarnar v. to heal; mix; embody
encarnizado, da adj. bloody
encarrilar v. to guide
encefalitis f. encephalitis
encendedor m. lighter
encender(se) v. to ignite
encerar v. to polish
encerrar(se) v. to confine
encierro m. closing; seclusion;
enclosure

encima *adv.* above
encima de *adv.* upon
encinta *adj.* pregnant
encocorar *v.* to annoy
encoger *v.* to shrink; contract; become smaller
encogimiento *m.* shrinkage; contraction
encolar *v.* to glue
encomendar(se) *v.* to entrust; commend
encomiar *v.* to extol
enconar *v.* to irritate; anger
encontrar(se) *v.* to find; encounter
encorvar *v.* to curve; bend
encrucijada *f.* intersection
encuadernar *v.* to bind
encuadrar *v.* to frame
encubrir *v.* to hide
encuentro *m.* meeting; collision; encounter
encuesta *f.* inquiry; survey; poll
encumbrar *v.* to honor; lift; raise
encurtir *v.* to preserve
enchilada *f.* enchilada
enchufar *v.* to couple; connect; merge
enchufe *m.* plug; connection; socket
endeble *adj.* weak
endémico, ca *adj.* endemic
enderezar *v.* to direct; straighten
endiablado, ga *adj.* diabolical
endibia *f.* endive
endosable *adj.* endorsable
endosante *m. f.* endorser
endosar *v.* to endorse
endoso *m.* endorsement
endulzar *v.* to make sweet
endurecer(se) *v.* toughen
enemigo, ga *m. f.* enemy
enemistad *f.* animosity
energía *f.* energy
enégico, ca *adj.* energetic
enero *m.* January
enervación *f.* enervation
enervar *v.* to weaken
enfadar *v.* to annoy; make angry
énfasis *m.* stress; emphasis
enfermar *v.* to become ill
enfermedad *f.* sickness

enfermero, ra *m. f.* nurse
enfermo, ma *adj.* ill
enfervorizar *v.* to encourage; enliven
enfilar *v.* to string; point; direct
enfocar(se) *v.* to focus
enfrente *adv.* in front of
enfriar(se) *v.* to cool
enfurecer *v.* to make furious; infuriate
enganchar *v.* to hook
enganche *m.* hook
engañadizo *adj.* credulous
engañar *v.* to fool; deceive
engaño *m.* mistake; trick; error; fraud
engañoso, sa *adj.* tricking; deceitful; deceiving
engarzar *v.* to curl; mount; thread
engaste *m.* mounting
engendrar *v.* to breed
engendro *m.* fetus; monster
engolado, da *adj.* arrogant
engolletado, da *adj.* proud
engomar *v.* to glue
engorde *m.* fattening (cattle)
engorroso, sa *adj.* troublesome
engranar *v.* to link; connect
engrandecer *v.* to praise; increase; heighten; augment; be promoted; exaggerate
engrapadora *f.* stapler
engrasado, da *adj.* lubricated
engrase *m.* lubricant
engreído, da *adj.* arrogant
engrosar *v.* to swell; enlarge
enhacinar *v.* to heap
enhebrar *v.* to connect; string; link
enhilar *v.* to arrange; guide; thread; order
enigmático, ca *adj.* enigmatic
enjambrar *v.* to swarm
enjambre *m.* swarm
enjugar *v.* to settle; dry
enjuiciar *v.* to examine; indict; judge
enjundia *f.* fat; grease; vitality
enlace *m.* liaison; link; junction; connection
enlardar *v.* to baste
enlazar *v.* to connect; rope; lace;

lasso
enloquecer v. to make insane; drive crazy
enlosador m. tiler
enlucir v. to plaster
enlutar v. to sadden; darken
enmendable adj. amendable
ennegrecer v. to darken
ennoblecer v. to ennoble
enojar(se) v. to anger one
enojo m. annoyance
enojoso, sa adj. annoying
enorme adj. very large; enormous
enormemente adv. enormously
enramada f. arbor; bower
enrasar v. to smooth; level
enredador, ra m. gossip
enredar(se) v. to mesh; mix
enredo m. muddle; snarl; mess
enriquecer(se) v. to enrich
enriscar v. to lift
enrojecer v. to turn red; make red; redden
enrolar v. to recruit; enlist
enrollar v. to involve; entangle; roll
enroscar v. to twist; curl
ensalada f. salad
ensaladera f. bowl for salad
ensalzar v. to exalt
ensamblar v. to connect
ensanchar v. to extend; broaden; expand
ensanche m. expansion
ensayar v. to practice; train
ensayo m. test; essay
ensenada f. inlet
enseñanza f. teaching; education
enseñar v. to instruct; tell; teach
ensimismado, da adj. pensive
ensimismamiento m. vanity; pensiveness
ensombrecer v. to eclipse; darken
ensordecer v. to make deaf
ensuciar(se) v. to make soiled
ensueño m. daydream; illusion
entablado m. floor; platform
entallar v. to engrave; carve; groove

entender(se) v. to understand
entendimiento m. understanding
enteramente adv. totally; entirely
enterar(se) v. to learn
entereza f. fortitude; integrity
enterizo, za adj. entire; in one piece
entero, ra adj. whole; entire
entidad f. concern; entity
entierro m. funeral; burial; grave; internment; buried treasure
entintado m. inking
entintar v. to ink
entomología f. entomology
entonar v. to modulate; in tone
entonces adv. then
entorno m. environment
entorpecer v. to deaden; obstruct; dull
entrada f. entrance
entrampar v. to snare; trick; entangle
entrante adj. coming; next
entrañable adj. beloved; close; dear
entrar v. to go into; enter
entre prep. among; between
entrecano, na adj. graying
entrecortar v. to interrupt
entrega f. delivery
entregar(se) v. to deliver to
entrenador m. coach
entrenar v. to train
entretallar v. to impede; carve; engrave
entretener(se) v. to entertain
entrever v. to surmise
entrevero m. jumble
entrevistar v. to interview
entubar v. to put a tube into
entuerto m. injustice
enturbiar v. to cloud
entusiasmar v. to enthuse
entusiasmo m. enthusiasm
enumeración f. enumeration
enumerar v. to enumerate
enunciación f. enunciation
enunciar v. to enunciate
envasar v. to package; bottle
envase m. packaging; container
envergar v. to fasten sails
enviado m. envoy

enviar v. to send
envidia f. envy
envidiar v. to envy
envidioso, sa adj. envious
envío m. dispatch; package; sending
envoltura m. wrapper
envolvente adj. enveloping
envolver(se) v. to wrap up
enyesar v. to plaster
enzima f. enzyme
eón m. eon
epicentro m. epicenter
épico f. epic
epidemia f. epidemic
epidémico adj. epidemic
epiglotis f. epiglottis
epilepsia f. epilepsy
epílogo m. epilogue
episodio m. episode
epitelio m. epithelium
época f. age; time period
equidad f. equity
equilátero, ra adj. equilateral
equilibrado adj. well-balanced; reasonable
equilibrar v. to balance
equilibrio adj. equilibrium
equilibrista f. acrobat
equino, na adj. equine
equipaje m. baggage
equipar v. to equip
equiparar v. to compare
equipo m. team
equitativo, va adj. fair
equivocado, da adj. being wrong
equivocar(se) v. to make a mistake
equívoco, ca adj. equivocal
erbio m. erbium
erecto, ta adj. erect
erguir v. to lift up
erigir v. to erect
erosión f. erosion
erótico adj. erotic
erradicar v. to uproot; eradicate
errado adj. mistaken; miscalculation
errante adj. errant
errar(se) v. to wander; miss; roam; fail

erróneo adj. erroneous
error m. error
eructo m. burp
erudición f. erudition
erupción f. eruption
esa adj. & f. that
ésa pron. & f. that one
esbelto, ta adj. slender
esbozo m. outline
escabel m. footstool; stool
escabroso, sa adj. rough; rugged
escala f. range; ladder; scale
escalar v. climb; scale
escalera f. stairs; staircase
escalfar v. to poach
escalonar v. to stagger
escapar(se) v. to escape; get away
escaso, sa adj. scarce
escena f. scene; scenery
esclavizar v. to put into slavery
esclavo, va m. f. slave
escoba f. broom
escoger v. to decide; choose
esconder(se) v. to hide
escorpión m. scorpion
escribir v. to write
escuchar v. to listen
escuela f. school
esculpir v. to carve
escultura f. sculpture
ese adj. m. that
ése pron. that one
esencial adj. essential
esforzar(se) v. to strive for
esfuerzo m. exertion; attempt
esmalte m. enamel
esmeralda f. emerald
eso pron. neut. that
ésos pron. neut. pl. those
esófago m. esophagus
espaciar(se) v. to spread out
espacio m. space
espada f. sword
espagueti m. spaghetti
espalda f. back
espasmo m. spasm
espástico, ca adj. spastic
especial adj. special
especialidad f. speciality

especializar(se) v. to specialize
especificar v. to specify
espécimen m. specimen
espectador, ra m. f. witness; observer
espejo m. mirror
espera f. wait
esperar v. to hope; wait
espiar v. to spy
espina f. spine; thorn
espinazo m. backbone
espinilla f. shinbone; blackhead; pimple
espiral adj. spiral
espirar v. to exhale
espléndido, da adj. splendid
esplendor m. splendor
espontáneo, a adj. spontaneous
esposa f. wife; pl. handcuffs
esposo m. husband
esqueleto m. skeleton
esquí m. ski
esquiar v. to ski
esquina f. corner
esta adj., f. this
ésta pron., f. this
establecer(se) v. to settle; establish
estación f. station; season
estadio m. stadium
estado m. state
estallar v. to explode
estampar v. to stamp
estampida f. stampede
estancar(se) v. to stagnate
estandarte m. standard
estar v. to lie; be
estatua f. statue
estatura f. stature
este m. east
éste pron. & adj. this
esterilidad f. sterility
estibar v. to stow; load
estilo m. style
estimar(se) v. to estimate
estimular v. to stimulate
estirar v. to stretch
estómago m. stomach; belly
estorbar v. to block; impede
estornudar v. to sneeze
estornudo m. sneeze
estrangular v. to choke

estrategia f. strategy
estratificar(se) v. to stratify
estrechar(se) v. to narrow
estrella f. star
estrellar(se) v. to smash into
estremecer(se) v. to shake
estricto, ta adj. strict
estropajo m. mop
estructura f. form; structure
estruendo m. thunder; clatter
estudiante m., f. student
estudiar v. to study
estudio m. studio
estufa f. stove
estupendo, da adj. stupendous
estúpido, da adj. stupid
eterno, na adj. eternity
etiqueta f. label
euforia f. euphoria
evacuación f. evacuation
evacuar v. to evacuate
evadir v. to avoid; dodge
evaluación f. evaluation
evaporación f. evaporation
evaporar(se) v. to evaporate
evasión f. evasion
evidencia f. evidence
evidente adj. obvious
evitar v. to shun; evade; avoid; dodge
evocar v. to evoke
evolución f. evolution
exactamente adv. exactly
exageración f. exaggeration
exagerar v. to exaggerate
examen m. test; quiz
examinar(se) v. to examine
excavación f. excavation
exceder(se) v. to surpass
excelencia f. excellence
excelente adj. excellent
excepto adv. unless
excitar(se) v. to arouse
exclamación f. exclamation
exclamar v. to exclaim
excluir v. to exclude
exclusión f. exclusion
excusa f. excuse
excusar v. to excuse
exhalar v. to exhale
exigir v. to require

existir v. to exist

expansión f. expansion

expender v. to expend

experiencia f. experience

experimentar v. to experiment

experto m. expert

explicación f. explanation

explicar(se) v. to explain

exploración f. exploration

explorar v. to explore

exportación f. export

exportar v. to export

expresar(se) v. to tell; express

expresión f. expression

expulsar v. to put out; expel

extender(se) v. to expand out

exterior adj. exterior

extranjero, ra m. f. alien

extraño, ña adj. odd; strange

extremo, ma adj. extreme

F

fábrica f. mill; factory

fabricación f. manufacture

fabricar v. to manufacture

fábula f. fiction; fable

fabulosamente adv. fabulously

fabuloso, sa adj. fabulous

facción f. feature; faction

faceta f. facet

fácil adj. simple; easy; docile

facilidad f. to chance; facility

facilitar v. to expedite; facilitate

factible adj. feasible

factor m. factor

factoría f. foundry; factory

facturación f. invoicing

facturar v. to invoice

facultad f. power; faculty

facultar v. to empower

facha f. appearance

faisán m. pheasant

faja f. sash, band

fajadura f. bandaging; swadling

fajar v. belt; wrap

falaz adj. deceptive

falda f. skirt

fálico, ca adj. phallic

falsedad f. untruth; lie

falsificar v. to misrepresent; falsify

falso, sa adj. dishonest

falta f. fault; shortage; flaw; want; lack

faltar v. to fail; need

falto adj. wanting; wretched; short

fallar v. to fail

fallo m. judgment; void; ruling

fama f. fame

famélico, ca adj. famished

familia f. family

familiar adj. familiar; casual; familial

famoso, sa adj. well-known; famous

fanal m. lighthouse; lantern

fanatizar v. to fanaticize

fanfarrón, na adj. showy; bragging

fango m. mud

fangosidad f. muddiness

fantasear v. daydream

fantasía f. fantasy

fantástico, ca adj. bizarre, fanciful

farándula f. show business

faraón m. pharaoh

fardo m. bale, pack

faringe f. pharynx

farmacéutico m. pharmacist

farmacia f. pharmacy

faro m. beacon; light; lighthouse

farol m. light; lantern

farsa f. farce

fascinación f. fascination

fascinante adj. fascinating

fascinar v. to intrigue; fascinate

fascista m. f. fascist

fastidiar(se) v. to hassle; annoy; bother

fastidio m. annoyance; repugnance

fastidioso adj. annoying; tedious; bothersome

fasto m. splendor

fastosidad f. splendor

fatal adj. fatal

fatalidad f. fatality; fate

fatalmente adv. unhappily; wretchedly; fatally

fatiga f. to fatigue

fatigar(se) *v.* fatigue; tire
fatigoso, sa *adj.* tiring; fatigued; tired
fato *m.* fool
fauna *f.* fauna
favor *m.* favor
favorable *adj.* favorable
favorecer *v.* to favor; help another; support
favorito, ta *adj.* favorite
fe *f.* trust; faith
febrero *m.* February
febril *adj.* hectic
fécula *f.* starch
fecundidad *f.* fertility
fecha *f.* date
fechar *v.* to date
federación *f.* federation
federal *adj.* federal
federalista *adj.* federalist
federar *v.* to federate
felicidad *f.* bliss, happiness; felicity
felicitación *f.* congratulation
felicitar *v.* to congratulate
felino, na *adj.* feline
feliz *adj.* happy
felpo, pa *f.* plush
felposo *adj.* plush
felpudo *m.* rug
femenino, na *adj.* feminine
feminista *adj. m. f.* feminist
fémur *m.* femur
fenecer *v.* to pass away; settle; finish
fenobarbital *m.* phenobarbital
fenol *m.* phenol
feo, a *adj.* ugly
feria *f.* fair; market
feriado, da *adj.* holiday
ferino, na *adj.* ferocious; fierce
fermentación *f.* fermentation
fermentar *v.* ferment
ferocidad *f.* ferocity
feroz *adj.* fierce
férreo *adj.* iron
ferrocarril *m.* railway
fértil *adj.* rich
fertilizante *adj.* fertilizing
fertilizar *v.* to fertilize
férvido *adj.* fervid
fervor *m.* fervor

festejar *v.* to celebrate; entertain; court
festín *m.* feast
festival *m.* festival
festivo, va *adj.* merry; festive; witty
fetal *adj.* fetal
fetiche *m.* fetish
fetidez *f.* fetidness
feto *m.* fetus
feudal *adj.* feudal
feudalismo *m.* feudalism
fiable *adj.* dependable
fiador, ra *m. f.* bailsman; guarantor
fianza *f.* bail; security
fiar *v.* to entrust; guarantee
fiasco *m.* fiasco
fibroma *m.* fibroma
fibroso, sa *adj.* stringy; fibrous
ficción *f.* fiction
ficticio, cia *adj.* fictitious
ficha *f.* chip; token
fidedigno, na *adj.* trustworthy
fideicomiso *m.* trust
fidelidad *f.* accuracy; fidelity
fiebre *f.* fever
fiel *adj.* true; loyal; honest; faithful; trustworthy
fieltro *m.* felt
fiereza *f.* ferocity; deformity; fierceness
fiesta *f.* feast; party
figura *f.* shape; figure; character
figuración *f.* figuration
figurado, da *adj.* figurative
figurar(se) *v.* to figure
figurativo, va *adj.* figurative
fijador *m.* fixative
fijamente *adv.* firmly; fixedly
fijar(se) *v.* to determine; set
fijo, ja *adj.* permanent; set; steady; fixed
fila *f.* row; file; tier
filamento *m.* filament
filántropo *m.* philanthropist
filatelista *m. f.* philatelist
filigrana *f.* filigree
filmar *v.* to film
fílmico, ca *adj.* movie; film
filo *m.* edge
filología *f.* philology

filosofía f. philosophy
filósofo m. philosopher
filtración f. filtration
filtrar(se) v. to strain; filter
filtro m. filter
fin m. finish
final adj. ending; last; end; final
finalidad f. finality
finalista m.f. finalist
finalizar v. to conclude; finish
finalmente adv. finally
finca f. land; farm
fineza f. politeness; fineness; affection
fingir(se) v. to pretend; sham
finito, ta adj. finite
fino, na adj. acute; fine; elegant; delicate
firma f. firm; signature
firmamento m. firmament
firmar v. to sign something
firme adj. hard; strong; firm
fiscalizar v. to investigate; oversee; snoop
físico, ca adj. physical
fisiología f. physiology
fisiólogo m. physiologist
fisión f. fission
fístula f. fistula
fisura f. fissure
flaco, ca adj. skinny; gaunt
flagelado, da adj. flagellate
flagrante adj. flagrant
flamear v. to flame
flanco m. side
flaquear v. to weaken
flauta f. flute
flautín m. piccolo
flautista m. f. flutist
flebitis f. phlebitis
flecha f. arrow
flema f. phlegm
flete m. cargo; freight
flexibilidad f. flexibility
flexible adj. flexible
flexor adj. flexor
flojedad f. laziness; debility
flojera f. carelessness; laziness
flojo, ja adj. limp; weak; lazy
flor f. blossom; flower; bloom
florecer v. to bloom; prosper
floreo m. flourish

florista m., f. florist
flotar v. float
fluctuación f. fluctuation
fluctuar v. fluctuate
fluido, da adj. fluid
fluir v. flow
foco m. focus
folículo m. follicle
follaje m. foliage
folleto m. brochure
fomentar v. to encourage
fontanero m. plumber
forjar v. to forge
forma f. shape; form
formación f. formation
formalidad f. formality
formar(se) v. to make; shape
fortalecer(se) v. fortify
fortaleza f. fortress
fortuito, ta adj. fortuitous; accidental
fortuna f. fortune; luck; fate
forzar v. strain; force
fósil m. fossil
foto f. picture; photograph
fotografía f. photography
fracasar v. to fail
fracción f. fraction
fractura f. break; fracture
fracturar(se) v. to fracture
frágil adj. frail
francamente adv. frankly
francés, sa adj. French
franco, ca adj. open; candid
franqueza f. frankness
frase f. phrase; sentence
fraternidad f. fraternity
fraude m. deception; fraud
frecuencia f. frequency
frecuente adj. frequent
fregar v. to wash; scrub
freír(se) v. to fry
frenar v. to brake
frente f. front; forhead
fresco, ca adj. fresh
fricción f. friction
frío, a adj. cold; frigid
frontal adj. frontal
frontera f. border; limit
frotar(se) v. to rub; chafe
fruncir v. to gather; pleat; purse lips

frustración *f.* frustration
frustrar(se) *v.* to frustrate
fuego *m.* fire
fuente *f.* spring; fountain
fuera *adv.* outside; off
fuerte *adj.* sturdy; strong; *m.* fort; fortress
fuerza *f.* power; force
fugarse *v.* to flee; run away; elope
fumar *v.* to smoke
fundación *f.* foundation; founding
fundar(se) *v.* to establish; found
fundir(se) *v.* to fuse; melt
furia *f.* fury
furioso, sa *adj.* furious
futbol *m.* soccer
futuro *m.* future

G

gabán *m.* topcoat
gabardina *f.* gabardine
gabinete *m.* boudoir; study; studio
gacela *f.* gazelle
gaceta *f.* gazette
gacho, cha *adj.* floppy; bent
gafas *f.* eyeglasses
gaitero, ra *adj.* gaudy
gajo *m.* section; bunch
galáctico, ca *adj.* galactic
galanamente *adv.* elegantly
galanía *f.* elegance; charm
galante *adj.* gallant
galanteo *m.* flirting; courting another
galantería *f.* generosity; grace
galardonar *v.* to reward
galaxia *f.* galaxy
galeón *m.* galleon
galera *f.* galley
galería *f.* gallery
galimatías *m.* nonsense
galopante *adj.* galloping
galopar *v.* to gallop
galope *m.* gallop
galvanizar *v.* to galvanize
gallardía *f.* gallantry; grace; elegance
gallardo, da *adj.* graceful; brave

galleta *f.* cracker; cookie
gallina *f.* chicken; hen
gallinero *m.* henhouse
gallo *m.* cock; rooster
gama *f.* gamut
gambado, da *adj.* bowlegged
gambetear *v.* prance
gana *f.* longing; appetite
ganadero *m.* cattle breeder or dealer
ganado *m.* livestock
ganancia *f.* profit
ganar *v.* to earn; win
gancho *m.* hook
gandulería *f.* laziness
ganglio *m.* ganglion
gangoso, sa *adj.* nasal
gangrena *f.* gangrene
ganoso, sa *adj.* anxious
ganso *m.* goose
garabato *m.* grapnel
garaje *m.* garage
garantir *v.* to defend; guarantee
garatusa *f.* compliment
garbanzo *m.* chickpea
garbear *v.* to steal; rob; to put on airs
garbillo *m.* sieve; chaff
garboso, sa *adj.* graceful; generous
garfa *f.* claw
gargajear *v.* to spit
garganta *f.* neck
gárgara *f.* gargling
gargarizar *v.* to gargle
gárgola *f.* gargoyle
gargüero *m.* trachea
garra *f.* talon; claw
garrafal *adj.* enormous
garrapata *f.* mite; tick; chigger
garrapiñar *v.* to grab
garrón *m.* claw; paw of rabbit
garuar *v.* to drizzle
gas *m.* gas
gasa *f.* gauze
gasificar *v.* to gasify
gasolina *f.* gasoline
gastado, da *adj.* threadbare; exhausted
gastar *v.* to exhaust; spend; squander; wear
gástrico, ca *adj.* gastric

gastritis f. gastritis
gastronomía f. gastronomy
gastronómico adj. gastronomic
gatear v. to crawl; creep
gatillo m. hammer; trigger
gato m. cat
gatuno, na adj. catlike
gaucho m. gaucho
gaveta f. drawer
gaviota f. gull
gazapina f. brawl
gaznate m. windpipe; throat
géiser m. geyser
gelatina f. gelatin
gema f. gem
gemido m. groan
genealogía f. genealogy
generación f. generation
general m. general
generalidad f. generality
generalización f. generalization
generalizar v. to generalize
generativo, va adj. generative
genéricamente adv. generically
genérico, ca adj. generic
generosidad f. generosity
generoso, sa adj. fine; generous
genial adj. genial; inspired; pleasant
genio m. genius; disposition
genocidio m. genocide
genotipo m. genotype
gente f. nation; people
gentil adj. genteel; excellent; polite
gentío m. mob; crowd
genuino, na adj. real; true; genuine
geofísico, ca adj. geophysical
geografía f. geography
geógrafo, fa m., f. geographer
geología f. geology
geólogo m., f. geologist
geometría f. geometry
geranio m. geranium
gerente m., f. director
geriátrico, ca adj. geriatric
germanio m. germanium
germen m. germ
germinar v. to germinate
gerontología f. gerontology

gestación f. gestation
gesticulación f. gesture; grimace
gesticular v. to gesture
gibar v. to curve
gibón m. gibbon
gigante m. giant
gigolo m. gigolo
gimnasia f. gymnastics
gimnasta f., m. gymnast
gimotear v. to whine
ginecología f. gynecology
gingivitis f. gingivitis
girar v. to rotate; spin; gyrate
giratorio, ria adj. rotating
giro m. rotation; turn
giroscopio m. gyroscope
gitanesco, ca adj. gypsy-like
glaciación f. glaciation
glacial adj. glacial; icy
glaciar adj. glacial
gladiador m. gladiator
glándula f. gland
glasear v. to glaze
glaucoma m. glaucoma
global adj. global
globo m. globe
gloria f. glory
glorificación f. glorification
glorificar(se) v. glorify
glorioso, sa adj. glorious
glosa f. gloss; commentary
glosar v. to gloss; annotate
glosario m. glossary
glotis f. glottis
glucosa f. glucose
glutinoso, sa adj. glutinous
gobernación f. government
gobernar v. to govern
gobierno m. government
gola f. throat; gullet
golf m. golf
golfo m. gulf
golosina f. craving; delicacy; longing
golpe m. blow; hit
golpear v. to slug; hit; beat
golpetear v. to pummel; hit; pound; beat
goma f. rubber; gum; rubber band
gomoso, sa adj. gummy
góndola f. gondola

gondolero *m.* gondolier
gonococo *m.* gonococcus
gordo, da *adj.* fat
gorgoteo *m.* gurgle
gorila *m.* gorilla
goteo *m.* dripping
gozar *v.* to enjoy; rejoice
grabar *v.* to engrave
gracia *f.* kindness; generosity charm; pardon
gracioso, sa *adj.* funny; charming; amusing
grada *f.* step of a staircase
grado *m.* step; grade
gradual *adj.* gradual, bit-by-bit, imperceptible
grafito *m.* graphite
gramático, ca *adj.* grammatical
granate *m.* garnet
granítico, ca *adj.* granite-like
granjero, ra *m., f.* farmer
grapa *f.* staple
gratificar *v.* to gratify
grave *adj.* erious; important; grave
gregario, ria *adj.* gregarious
gris *adj.* grey
gritar *v.* to yell; cry
grito *m.* yell; scream
grosería *f.* coarseness; stupidity
grosero, ra *adj.* vulgar; coarse
grotesco, ca *adj.* grotesque
grueso, sa *adj.* fat; coarse
gruñir *v.* to grumble; grunt
grupo *m.* bunch; group
guante *m.* glove
guapetón, na *adj.* bold; flashy
guapeza *f.* daring; good looks
guapo, pa *adj.* flashy; good-looking
guarda *m. f.* custody; guard; watchman
guardar(se) *v.* to keep; guard
guardia *f.* guard
guardián, na *m., f.* guardian
guarnecer *v.* adorn; border; supply
gubernamental *adj.* governmental

guerra *f.* war
guerrear *v.* to fight
guía *m., f.* leader; guide
guiar *v.* to steer; guide
guitarra *f.* guitar
gusano *m.* worm
gustar *v.* to like
gusto *m.* zest; taste

H

haber *v.* to have
hábil *adj.* skillful
habilidad *f.* ability; skill
habitación *f.* habitation; lodging; room
habitar *v.* to dwell
habitual *adj.* habitual
habituar *v.* to habituate
habla *f.* speech
hablado, da *adj.* spoken
habladuría *f.* gossip; chatter
hablar *v.* to talk; speak
hace *adv.* ago
hacer(se) *v.* to act; become; force; compose
hacia *prep.* about; to
hacienda *f.* ranch; property; wealth
hacina *f.* pile
hacinar *v.* to pile up
hada *f.* fairy
hado *m.* fate
halagüeño, ña *adj.* promising; attractive; pleasing
halar *v.* to tow something
halcón *m.* falcon
halconería *f.* falconry
halconero *m.* falconer
hallar(se) *v.* to locate; find
hambre *f.* hunger
hambriento, ta *adj.* hungry; starved
hamburguesa *f.* hamburger
haraposo, sa *adj.* tattered
harén *m.* harem
hartar *v.* to annoy; stuff
hasta *prep.* till
hastiar *v.* to annoy; sicken
hebra *f.* filament; thread
hechicero, ra *m., f.* charmer; sor-

ceress; sorcerer
hechizo *m.* charm; spell
heder *v.* to stink; smell bad
hedor *m.* stink
helado *m.* ice cream
helar *v.* to freeze
helicóptero *m.* helicopter
helio *m.* helium
helipuerto *m.* heliport
hembra *f.* female; woman
hemofilia *f.* hemophilia
hemoglobina *f.* hemoglobin
hemorragia *f.* hemorrhage
hender(se) *v.* to crack
henil *m.* hayloft
heno *m.* hay
hepatitis *f.* hepatitis
herbario, ria *adj.* herbal; *m.* herbalist
hereditario, ria *adj.* hereditary
herencia *f.* heritage; inheritance; heredity
herida *f.* wound
herir *v.* to hurt; injure; wound
hermana *f.* sister
hermandad *f.* sisterhood; brotherhood; league
hermano *m.* brother
hermosear *v.* to beautify
hermoso, sa *adj.* beautiful
hernia *f.* hernia
heroico, ca *adj.* heroic
heroína *f.* heroine
herpes *m.* herpes
herrero *m.* blacksmith
herrín *m.* rust
herrumbrar *v.* to rust
hervor *m.* boiling
hesitación *f.* hesitation
hesitar *v.* to hesitate
hexágono *m.* hexagon
hibernación *f.* hibernation
hibernar *v.* to hibernate
híbrido *m.* hybrid
hidratación *f.* hydration
hidratar *v.* to hydrate
hidrocarburo *m.* hydrocarbon
hidrofobia *f.* hydrophobia
hidrógeno *m.* hydrogen
hidroterapia *f.* hydrotherapy
hidróxido *m.* hydroxide
hiedra *f.* ivy

hielo *m.* ice
hierba *f.* grass
higiene *f.* hygiene
higiénico, ca *adj.* hygienic
hija *f.* daughter
hijastra *f.* stepdaughter
hijastro *m.* stepson
hijo *m.* son
hilador, ra *m.,* *f.* spinner
hilar *v.* to spin
hilero *m.* current; stream
hilo *m.* filament; thread
himen *m.* hymen
himno *m.* hymn; anthem
hinchar *v.* to exaggerate; swell; blow up
hinojo *m.* fennel
hipérbola *f.* hyperbola
hipersensible *adj.* hypersensitive
hipertermia *f.* hyperthermia
hipnosis *f.* hypnosis
hipnotismo *m.* hypnotism
hipnotizar *v.* to hypnotize
hipocondría *f.* hypochondria
hipocresía *f.* hypocrisy
hipócrita *f.,* *m.* hypocrite
hipoteca *f.* mortgage
hipotecar *v.* to mortgage
hipotermia *f.* hypothermia
histeria *f.* hysteria
historia *f.* story; history
historial *adj.* historical
hocicar *v.* to smooch; nuzzle
hockey *m.* hockey
hoguera *f.* bonfire
hoja *f.* petal; leaf; sheet
hojoso, sa *adj.* leafy
holganza *f.* leisure
holocausto *m.* holocaust
hombre *m.* man
hombrera *f.* shoulder pad
hombrillo *m.* yoke
hombro *m.* shoulder
homicida *adj.* homicidal; *m.* *f.* murderer
homicidio *m.* homicide
hondo, da *adj.* intense; deep
hondonada *f.* gorge
honestidad *f.* honesty
hongo *m.* mushroom; fungus
honor *m.* honor
honorable *adj.* honorable

honradez f. honesty
honrado, da adj. honest
honroso, sa adj. honorable
hora f. time; hour
horcón m. pitchfork
horizontal adj. horizontal
horizonte m. horizon
hormigonera f. concrete mixer
hormona f. hormone
hornear v. to bake
hornero f., m. baker; ovenbird
hornillo m. portable stove
horno m. oven
horóscopo m. horoscope
horrendo, da adj. horrendous
horrible adj. awful; horrible
hórrido, da adj. horrid
horrificar v. horrify
horror m. terror; horror
hortícola adj. horticultural
horticultura f. horticulture
hospital m. hospital
hospitalizar v. to hospitalize
hostería f. hostel; inn
hostigar v. to harass; whip
hostil adj. hostile
hostilidad f. hostility
hotel m. hotel
hoy adv. today
hoya f. hole; pit; grave
hueco, ca adj. deep; hollow
huella f. print; footprint
huerta f. garden
huesa f. grave
huesudo, da adj. bony
huevo m. egg
huir(se) v. to flee; escape; avoid; run from
humanar v. to humanize
humanidad f. humanity
humanizar v. humanize
humano m. human
humear v. steam; smoke
humedad f. humidity
húmedo, da adj. humid
húmero m. humerus
humildad f. humility
humillación f. humiliation
humillante adj. humiliating
humo m. smoke
humorismo m. wit
humoso, sa adj. smoky

hundir v. to ruin; sink; plunge
huracán m. hurricane
hurgón m. poker; coal rake
hurón m. ferret
hurtar(se) v. to steal; take
hurto m. robbery
husmear v. to pry
husmeo m. prying

I

ibis f. ibis
icono m. icon
iconografía f. iconography
ictericia f. jaundice
ictiólogo m. ichthyologist
idea f. notion; thought; image; idea; picture
ideal adj.; m. ideal
idealista adj. idealistic; m. f. idealist
idear v. to invent; plan; design
idéntico, ca adj. identical
identidad f. identity
identificación f. identification
identificar v. to identify
idiomático, ca adj. idiomatic
idiota adj. idiotic; foolish; m. f. idiot
idolatrar v. to idolize
idolatría f. idolatry
ídolo m. idol
iglesia f. church
ignición f. ignition
ignominioso, sa adj. ignominious
ignorancia f. ignorance
ignorante adj. ignorant; unaware; uneducated
ignoto adj. undiscovered
igual adj. level; even; alike; like
igualamiento m. equalization
igualar v. to make equal; equate; smooth
igualdad f. equality
igualmente adv. too; equally
iguana m. iguana
ilación f. cohesiveness; connection
ilegal adj. unlawful; illegal;

against the law
ilegalidad f. illegality
ilegible adj. illegible
iletrado, da adj. illiterate
ilógico, ca adj. illogical
iluminación f. illumination
iluminar v. to light; illuminate
ilusión f. illusion
ilusorio, ria adj. illusory
ilustración f. illustration
ilustrador, ra adj. illustrative
ilustrar v. illustrate
ilustre adj. illustrious
imaginable adj. imaginable
imaginación f. imagination
imaginar(se) v. to think up;
conceive
imaginativo, va adj. imaginative
imanar v. to magnetize
imbecilidad f. imbecility
imitable adj. imitable
imitación f. imitation
imitar v. to imitate
impaciencia f. impatience
impaciente adj. impatient
imparcial adj. impartial
impartir v. to concede; grant
impasible adj. impassive
impecable adj. impeccable
impedimento m. impediment
impedir v. to deter; hinder
impensable adj. unimaginable;
unthinkable
imperar v. to reign
imperdonable adj. inexcusable
imperfección f. imperfection
imperial adj. imperial
impermeabilidad f. imperme-
ability
impermeable m. raincoat
impersonal adj. impersonal
impétigo m. impetigo
ímpetu m. energy; impetus
impetoso, sa adj. impetuous;
violent
implacable adj. implacable
implantar v. to implant
implicación f. implication; consequence
implicar v. to mean; implicate
implorar v. to invoke
imponer v. to charge; inspire;

inform
impopular adj. unpopular
importación f. importation
importancia f. authority; importance
importante adj. important
importunar v. to importune
importuno adj. inopportune
imposibilidad f. impossibility
imposible adj. impossible; difficult
impostor m. impostor
impotencia f. impotence
impracticable adj. unfeasible;
impracticable
impreciso, sa adj. imprecise
impregnar v. to impregnate
impresión f. impression
impresionante adj. impressive
imprevisto, ta adj. unexpected;
sudden
imprimir v. to stamp; print;
imprint
improbable adj. improbable;
doubtful
improductivo, va adj. unpro-
ductive
improvisación f. improvisation
impudencia f. impudence
impugnar v. to impugn
impulsar v. to drive; impel
impulsión f. impulse
impulso m. impulse
impunidad f. impunity
impureza f. impurity
impuro, ra adj. impure
inacción f. inaction
inactivo, va adj. inactive
inadecuado, da adj. inadequate
inadvertencia f. carelessness;
inadvertence
inalterable adj. unalterable
inane adj. pointless
inanidad f. inanity
inaplicable adj. inapplicable
inatención f. inattention
inatento, ta adj. inattentive
incapacidad f. incapacity
incapacitar v. incapacitate
incapaz adj. unable; incapable
incendio m. fire
incentivo m. incentive

incesto *m.* incest
incienso *m.* incense
incierto, ta *adj.* vague; uncertain; doubtful
incinerar *v.* to incinerate
incisión *f.* incision
incitar *v.* to urge; incite
inclemente *adj.* inclement
inclinación *f.* slant; inclination; slope
inclinar(se) *v.* to slant; sway; incline; persuade
incluir *v.* contain; include
inclusión *f.* inclusion
inclusivo, va *adj.* inclusive
incoherente *adj.* incoherent
incomible *adj.* inedible
incompatible *adj.* incompatible
incompleto, ta *adj.* incomplete
inconcluso, sa *adj.* inconclusive
inconstante *adj.* fickle
incorporal *adj.* incorporeal
incorporar *v.* to incorporate
incorrecto, ta *adj.* incorrect
incorrupto, ta *adj.* incorrupt
incrédulo, la *adj.* incredulous
increíble *adj.* incredible
incrementar *v.* to increase
incremento *m.* increase
increpar *v.* to reprimand
incriminar *v.* to incriminate
incrustar *v.* to encrust
incubación *f.* incubation
incubar *v.* to incubate
inculcar *v.* to inculcate
incurable *adj.* incurable
incurrir *v.* to incur
indecente *adj.* indecent
indecisión *f.* indecision
indeciso, sa *adj.* indecisive
indefenso, sa *adj.* defenseless
indeleble *adj.* indelible
indemne *adj.* unhurt
independizar *v.* to liberate
indeseable *adj.* undesirable
indicación *f.* sign; indication; direction
indicar *v.* to show; indicate
indiferente *adj.* indifferent
indigencia *f.* indigence
indigente *adj.* indigent

indigestión *f.* indigestion
indignar *v.* to infuriate
indigno, na *adj.* despicable
índigo *m.* indigo
indirecto, ta *adj.* hint; indirect
indiscreción *f.* indiscretion
indiscutible *adj.* indisputable
indistinto, ta *adj.* indistinct
individual *adj.* individual
individuo *m.* individual
indivisible *adj.* indivisible
indócil *adj.* indocile
indocilidad *f.* unruliness
indolencia *f.* indolence
indolente *adj.* indolent
indomable *adj.* uncontrollable; untamable
indómito, ta *adj.* untamable; indomitable
inducción *f.* induction
inducir *v.* to induce
indudable *adj.* certain
indulgente *adj.* indulgent
industria *f.* industry
industrial *adj.* industrial
industrializar *v.* to become industrialized
industrioso, sa *adj.* industrious
inefable *adj.* ineffable
ineficaz *adj.* ineffective
ineptitud *f.* ineptitude
inepto, ta *adj.* inept
inercia *f.* inertia
inerte *adj.* inert
inesperado, da *adj.* unexpected
inestable *adj.* unstable
inevitable *adj.* inevitable
inexistente *adj.* nonexistent; not existing
inexplorado, da *adj.* unexplored
infalible *adj.* infallible
infamar *v.* to slander
infamia *f.* infamy
infancia *f.* infancy
infante *m.* baby; infant
infantil *adj.* childish; baby
infarto *m.* infarction
infatuar *v.* to become conceited
infección *f.* infection
infeccioso, sa *adj.* infectious
infectar(se) *v.* infect
infeliz *adj.* wretched

inferencia f. inference
inferior adj. under; inferior
inferioridad f. inferiority
inferir v. to inflict; infer
infestar v. to infest
infiel adj. disloyal
infierno m. hell
infiltrar v. to infiltrate
ínfimo adj. worst; lowest
infinito adj., m. infinite
inflación f. inflation
inflamable adj. inflammable
inflamar v. to inflame
inflar v. to inflate
inflexible adj. rigid; unyielding
influencia f. influence
influenciar v. to influence
influjo m. influence; rise of the tide
información f. information
informal adj. informal
informar(se) v. to report; inform; find out
informe adj. formless
infortunio m. misfortune
infrarrojo, ja adj. infrared
infrecuente adj. infrequent
infructuoso, sa adj. fruitless
infundir v. to arouse
infusión f. infusion
ingeniería f. engineering
ingeniero m. engineer
ingenioso, sa adj. witty; clever
ingerir v. to ingest
ingestión f. ingestion
inglés, sa m. English
ingrato, ta adj. thankless
ingrediente m. ingredient
ingreso m. entrance; income
inhabilidad f. incompetence
inhalar v. to inhale
inherente adj. inherent
inhibir v. to inhibit
inhumano, na adj. inhuman
iniciación f. initiation
inicial adj. initial
iniciar v. to initiate
inicio m. beginning
inigualado, da adj. unequaled
inimitable adj. inimitable
injerir v. to insert
injerto m. transplant; graft

injuria f. injury
injusticia f. injustice
injusto, ta adj. unjust
inmaduro, ra adj. immature
inmemorial adj. immemorial
inmenso, sa adj. immense
inmensurable adj. immeasurable
inmersión f. immersion
inmigrar v. to immigrate
inmodesto, ta adj. immodest
inmolar v. to immolate
inmoral adj. immoral
inmortal adj. immortal
inmovible adj. immovable
inmóvil adj. immobile
inmundo, da adj. filthy
inmunidad f. immunity
inmunizar v. to immunize
inmutable adj. immutable
innovación f. innovation
innovar v. to innovate
inocencia f. innocence
inocente adj. innocent
inocular v. to inoculate
inocuo, cua adj. innocuous
inoperable adj. inoperable
inorgánico, ca adj. inorganic
inquietar v. to alarm
inquietud f. uneasiness
inquilino, na m., f. tenant
inquirir v. to probe
insano, na adj. insane; unhealthy
inscribir(se) v. to record; engrave
inscripción f. record; inscription
insecto m. insect
inseguro, ra adj. insecure
insensible adj. unfeeling; unconscious; insensible
inserción f. insertion
insertar v. to insert
insignia f. emblem
insincero, ra adj. insincere
insistente adj. insistent
insistir v. to insist
insolencia f. insolence
inspección f. inspection
inspirar v. to inspire
instrucción f. instruction
instruir(se) v. to teach; learn; instruct

insulina f. insulin
insultar v. to insult
intacto, ta adj. intact
inteligencia f. intellect; intelligence
inteligente adj. smart; intelligent
intensificar v. to intensify
interesar(se) v. to concern
interior m. inside
interno, na adj. inside
interrupción f. interruption
intervenir v. to mediate; intervene
íntimo, ma adj. intimate
introducción f. introduction
invadir v. to invade
invasión f. invasion
invención f. invention
inventar v. to contrive; think up; invent
investir v. to invest
invierno m. winter
ir(se) v. to depart; leave
irregular adj. irregular
isla f. island
izquierdo, da adj. left

J

jabalí m. boar
jabalina f. javelin
jabón m. soap
jabonado m. wash; laundry
jabonar v. to lather up
jabonero, ra m., f. soapmaker
jaca f. nag; pony
jacarero, ra adj. lively
jaco m. nag
jactancia f. arrogance; bragging; boast
jactancioso, sa adj. arrogant
jactarse v. to brag
jade m. jade
jadear v. to gasp for air
jadiar v. to hoe
jaguar m. jaguar
jalar v. to pull on
jalea f. jelly
jalear v. to urge one
jaleo m. racket; uproar
jalonar v. to mark with poles
jamás adv. never ever; never

again
jamba f. door jamb
jamelgo m. nag
jamón m. ham
jaque m. check (chess)
jaquear v. to check
jarabe m. syrup
jaranear v. to carouse
jarca f. acacia
jardín m. garden
jardinera f. gardener
jardinero m. gardener; outfielder (baseball)
jarra f. mug; pitcher
jarro m. flagon
jarrón m. vase
jaspe m. jasper
jaula f. cell; cage
jazmín m. jasmine
jefa f. master; boss
jefe m. head; boss; master
jemiquear v. to whine
jengibre m. ginger
jerarquía f. hierarchy
jeremías m., f. complainer
jerga f. jargon; slang
jerigonza f. gibberish
jeringar v. to pester; inject
jeringazo m. injection
jeroglífico m. hieroglyph
jersey m. sweater
jifia f. swordfish
jinda f. fright
jinete m. equestrian; horseman
jinetear v. to ride a horse
jipar v. to hiccup
jira f. excursion
jirafa f. giraffe
jocosidad f. joke; wit
jocoso, sa adj. jocular
jocundidad f. jocundity
jofaina f. washbowl
jornada f. trip; journey
jornal m. wage
joroba f. hump
jorobar v. to annoy; bother
jorrar v. to haul; pull a net
joven adj. young; juvenile; youthful; m. f. youth
jovial adj. jovial
joya f. gem; jewel
joyera f. box for jewelry

joyería f. jewelry store
joyero m. jeweler
jubilado, da m., f retired one
jubilar(se) v. to retire
jubileo m. jubilee
júbilo m. joy
jubiloso, sa adj. joyful
judía f. bean
juego m. play; game
jueves m. Thursday
juez m. judge
jugar v. to play
juguetear v. play
juguetón, na adj. playful
juicio m. verdict; judgment
julio m. July
junco m. bulrush; junk
junio m. June
junta f. union; council; board
juntamente adv. together
juntar(se) v. to connect; join
junto adv. together
jurado m. jury
jurar v. to vow; swear; curse
jurista m. f. jurist
justamente adv. fairly
justicia f. justice
justificar v. to warrant
justo, ta adj. fair
juvenil adj. youthful
juventud f. youth
juzgar v. to try; judge

K

kilo m. kilogram
kilociclo m. kilocycle
kilogramo m. kilogram
kilométrico, ca adj. kilometric
kilómetro m. kilometer
kilovatio m. kilowatt
kirsch m. cherry brandy
kummel m. cumin brandy

L

la def. article the
laberinto m. labyrinth
labia f. eloquence
labio m. lip
labor f. work
laborable adj. pertaining to working; working
laboral adj. pertaining to labor
laborar v. to work
laboratorio m. laboratory
laborear v. to work
laborioso, sa adj. arduous
labrado, da adj.
    plowed; cultivated; wrought
labrador, ra adj. farm-
    ing m. f. farmer;
    peasant
labranza f. farmland;
    farm
labrar v. to carve; work; plow;
    cultivate; tool
laca f. shellac; lacquer; hair spray
lacayo m. valet; attendant; aide;
    servant
laceración f. laceration
lacerar v. to injure; lacerate
lacería f. want; toil; poverty;
    needy
lacio, cia adj. limp; straight
lacónico, ca adj. laconic
lacre m. a sealing wax
lacrimógeno, na adj. tear produc-
    ing
lacrimoso, sa adj. tearful; sad;
    sorrowful
lactación f. nursing
lactancia f. lactation
lactar v. to suckle
láctico, ca adj. lactic
lactosa f. lactose
ladear v. to tilt
ladeo m. inclination
ladera f. slope
ladino, na adj. astute
lado m. room; side; next to;
    beside; along side
ladrar v. to snarl at something;
    to growl
ladrillo m. brick
ladrón m. robber
ladronería f. theft
lagartija f. a small lizard
lagarto m. lizard
lago m. lake
lágrima f. tear
lagrimear v. to tear; weep; cry
lagrimoso, sa adj. tearful; watery
laguna f. lagoon

laical *adj.* lay
laja *f.* slab of stone
lamedura *f.* licking
lamentable *adj.* lamentable
lamentación *f.* lamentation
lamentar *v.* to be sorry for; regret something
lamento *m.* lament
lamentoso, sa *adj.* mournful
lamer *v.* to lap up
lametada *f.* lick
lamido, da *adj.* polished
laminación *f.* lamination
laminar *v.* to laminate
lámpara *f.* lamp
lamparilla *f.* little or small lamp
lamparón *m.* stain; large lamp
lampiño, ña *adj.* hairless
lana *f.* wool
lanado, da *adj.* fleecy
lance *m.* argument; move; occurrence
lancear *v.* to lance
lanceta *f.* lancet
lancha *f.* boat
lanchero *m.* boatman
lanchón *m.* barge
lanero, ra *adj.* woolen
languidecer *v.* to languish
languidez *f.* feebleness; lethargy
lánguido, da *adj.* languid
languor *m.* languor
lanolina *f.* lanolin
lanoso, sa *adj.* woolly
lanza *f.* spear
lanzada *f.* wound due to a lance
lanzamiento *m.* throwing
lanzar *v.* to hurl; fire; release; vomit; throw; shoot
lápida *f.* tombstone
lapidario, ria *adj.* concise; lapidary
lápiz *m.* pencil
lapso, sa *m.* interval; lapse
laquear *v.* to varnish
lardo *m.* fat of bacon
largar *v.* to let go; dismiss; release; hurl; throw
largo, ga *adj.* lengthy; long; abundant
largor *m.* length
largueza *f.* length; generosity

laringe *f.* larynx
laringitis *f.* laryngitis
larva *f.* larva
larval *adj.* larval
las *pron.* them; *art., pl. f.* the
láser *m.* laser
lasitud *f.* lassitude
laso, sa *adj.* weak; limp
lástima *f.* compassion; shame; pity
lastimadura *f.* wound
lastimar *v.* to hurt; offend; injure
lastimero, ra *adj.* pitiful
lastimoso, sa *adj.* pitiful
lata *f.* can; tin can; pest
latear *v.* to bore; talk too much
latente *adj.* latent
lateral *adj.* lateral
látido *m.* beating; throbbing; beat
latiente *adj.* throbbing
latiguear *v.* to whip; crack the whip
latitud *f.* breadth; extent; width; scope; latitude
latitudinal *adj.* latitudinal
lato, ta *adj.* extensive; lengthy
latón *m.* brass
latonero *m.* brassworker
latoso, sa *adj.* bothersome
latrocinio *m.* theft
laudable *adj.* laudable; praiseworthy
laude *f.* tombstone
laudo *m.* verdict; decision
laurel *m.* bayleaf; laurel
laureo, a *adj.* laurel
lava *f.* lava
lavable *adj.* washable
lavada *f.* washing, wash
lavadero *m.* laundry
lavado *m.* wash; cleaning
lavador *m.* washer
lavanda *f.* lavender
lavandero, ra *m. f.* launderer
lavaplatos *m.* dishwasher
lavar *v.* to wash; clean
lavativa *f.* enema
laxar *v.* to slacken (bowels)
laxativo, va *adj.* laxative
lazar *v.* to rope
lazarino, na *adj.* leprous

lazo *m.* lasso; knot; trap; snare
le *obj. pron.* to him; for him
leal *adj.* faithful
lealtad *f.* loyalty
lección *f.* lesson
lector, ra *adj.* reading
lectura *f.* reading
lechada *f.* grout; whitewash
lechar *adj.* unweaned animal
leche *f.* milk
lecherío, ría *adj.* dairy; milky
lecho *m.* layer; bed
lechoso, sa *adj.* milky; *f.* papaya
lechuga *f.* lettuce
leer *v.* to read
legación *f.* legation
legado *m.* legacy
legajo *m.* file
legal *adj.* legal
legalidad *f.* legality
legalista *f.* legalist
legalización *f.* legalization
legalizar *v.* to legalize
legar *v.* to delegate; bequeath
legible *adj.* legible
legión *f.* legion
legislación *f.* legislation
legislador, ra *m. f.* legislator
legislatura *f.* legislative
lejos *adv.* far away
lengua *f.* language; tongue
león *m.* lion
leona *f.* lioness
leopardo *m.* leopard
les *pron.* for them; for you
letal *adj.* lethal
letra *f.* letter
levantar *v.* to lift up; erect
ley *f.* rule; law
liberación *f.* liberation
liberal *adj.* liberal
libertad *f.* freedom
libre *adj.* single; open; free
libro *m.* book
ligar *v.* to commit; bind
limitación *f.* limitation
limitado, da *adj.* limited
limitar *v.* to restrict; limit
limón *m.* lemon
limpiar *v.* to clear; clean
limpieza *f.* neatness; cleaning
limpio, pia *adj.* pure; clean

línea *f.* outline; line; boundary
lista *f.* list
listo, ta *adj.* ready
litro *m.* liter
liviano, na *adj.* faithless; light
lividez *f.* lividness
lívido, da *adj.* livid
lo *def. art. neut.* the; *pron.* him
loa *f.* praise
loable *adj.* praiseworthy
loar *v.* to praise
loba *f.* female wolf
lobo *m.* male wolf
lóbrego, ga *adj.* somber; dark
lóbulo *m.* lobe
locación *f.* leasing
local *adj.* local
localidad *f.* locality
localizar *v.* to find; locate
loción *f.* lotion
loco, ca *adj.* crazy; extraordinary
lograr *v.* to take; obtain
loro *m.* parrot
los *pron.* them; *art. m. pl.* the
lúcido, da *adj.* shining
lucir *v.* to illuminate; light
luego *adv.* later; then
luna *f.* moon
lunar *adj.* lunar
lustrar *v.* to shine
luz *f.* day; light

LL

llaga *f.* ulcer; injury; wound; sore
llagar *v.* to injure
llama *f.* blaze; llama
llamada *f.* knock; calling; call; gesture; lure
llamador, ra *m. f.* caller
llamamiento *m.* calling
llamar(se) *v.* to name; call; summon; call upon; telephone
llamarada *f.* outburst; flame; flare
llamativo, va *adj.* garish; striking; showy
llamear *v.* blaze
llaneza *f.* simplicity
llano, na *adj.* flat; even; level; simple
llanta *f.* tire
llanto *m.* cry

llave f. key; tap
llavero m. key ring
llegada f. arrival
llegar(se) v. to land; come; reach; arrive; amount
llenado m. filling
llenar(se) v. to stuff; fill; meet; fulfill
lleno, na adj. full; completely; fully
llevar(se) v. to bear; carry; wear; guide; take; conduct
llorar v. to weep; mourn
lloriquear v. to whimper
lloro m. weeping
lloroso, sa adj. sorrowful; tearful
llover v. to shower; rain
llovizna f. drizzle
lloviznar v. to sprinkle; drizzle
lluvia f. rain; rainfall
lluvioso, sa adj. rainy

M

macabro, bra adj. macabre funeral
macarrón m. macaroon pl. macaroni; pasta
maceración f. maceration
macerar v. to macerate
maceta f. flowerpot or holder
macilento, ta adj. lean; thin; emaciated
macizo, za adj. solid
mácula f. spot; stain
machaca f. pounder
machacar v. to beat; pound; bother
machacón, ona adj. tiresome; m. f. pest
machada f. stupidity
machado m. hatchet
machete m. machete
machetear v. to injure or cut with a machete
macho adj. manly; male; tough; virile
machucadura f. beating; bruising
machucar v. to beat; crush
madera f. timber; wood; lumber
maderada f. raft
maderería f. lumberyard

maderero, ra adj. timber
madero m. log
madrastra f. stepmother
madre f. mom; mother
madreselva f. honeysuckle
madriguera f. hole; burrow; lair
madrina f. bridesmaid; godmother; patroness
madrugar v. to anticipate; get up early
maduración f. ripening
madurador, ra adj. ripening
madurar v. to mature; ripen; maturate
madurez f. maturity; ripeness
maestre m. master
maestro, tra adj. expert; teacher; master, director, chief; ruler
magancería f. trickery
mágico, ca adj. magic
magistrado m. magistrate
magistral adj. imposing; masterful; magisterial
magnate m. magnate
magnesia f. magnesia
magnesio m. magnesium
magnético, ca adj. magnetic
magnetismo m. magnetism
magnificar v. to exalt; magnify; glorify
magnitud f. size; importance; magnitude
magnolia f. magnolia
mago, ga adj. magic; magical
magullar v. to batter
maíz m. corn
majadero, ra adj. foolish
majadura f. pounding
majar v. to pound; bother; mash
majestad f. grandeur; majesty
majo, ja adj. attractive; flashy; nice
mal adj. bad; evil; disease
mal adv. wrongly; badly
malabar m. juggling
malabarista m. juggler
malacostumbrado, da adj.

ill-mannered; having poor or bad habits; spoiled
malandrín, na *adj.* evil
malaria *f.* malaria
malaventura *f.* misfortune
malaventuranza *f.* misfortune
malbaratar *v.* to squander
malcomer *v.* to eat badly or poorly
malcomido, da *adj.* underfed
malcontento, ta *adj.* unhappy; rebellious
malcriado, da *adj.* ill-bred
malcriar *v.* to spoil
maldad *f.* evil
maldecir *v.* to slander; curse
maldiciente *adj.* defaming; slandering; *m. f.* curser; slanderer
maldición *f.* curse
maldito, ta *adj.* wicked; bad
maleabilidad *f.* malleability
maleable *adj.* malleable
maleante *adj.* corrupting; wicked; hoodlum
malear *v.* to ruin; corrupt; pervert
maledicencia *f.* slander
maleficencia *f.* evil
malefico, ca *adj.* maleficent
malestar *m.* uneasiness; malaise
maleta *f.* suitcase; baggage; luggage
malevolencia *f.* malevolence
malformación *f.* malformation
malgastar *v.* to waste; squander
malhadado, da *adj.* unfortunate
malherir *v.* to injure
malhumorar *v.* to irritate; bother; annoy
malicia *f.* cunning; wickedness; slyness
malicioso, sa *adj.* malicious; cunning
malignidad *f.* malignancy
maligno, na *adj.* malignant
malmirado, da *adj.* disliked
malo, la *adj.* harmful; nasty; bad
malograr *v.* to fail; lose; waste
malogro *m.* failure
malparar *v.* to harm; damage
malquistar *v.* to estrange

malquisto, ta *adj.* unpopular
malsonante *adj.* harsh
maltratamiento *m.* mistreatment
maltratar *v.* to mistreat
malvado, da *adj.* wicked
malversador, ra *m.,* *f.* embezzler
malversar *v.* to embezzle
mamá *f.* mother
mamar *v.* to nurse; suck
mamelón *m.* nipple
manante *adj.* running
manar *v.* to flow
mancar *v.* to disable
mancilla *f.* blemish
mancillar *v.* to blemish
mancipar *v.* to enslave
manco, ca *adj.* one-armed; disabled
mancomunar *v.* to join together; combine
mancha *f.* blot; stain
manchar *v.* to stain; spot; soil
manda *f.* bequest
mandado *m.* errand; task; order
mandamiento *m.* command; order
mandar *v.* to leave; order
mandarina *f.* mandarin orange
mandato *m.* trust; command; order
mandíbula *f.* mandible
mando *m.* leadership; power
mandolín *m.* mandolin
mandria *adj.* timid; worthless; useless
mandril *m.* mandrill
manear *v.* to hobble (horses; cattle)
manejable *adj.* manageable
manejar *v.* to handle; manage; drive
manejo *m.* operation; handling; management
manera *f.* style; way; manner; type
manga *f.* strainer; hose; sleeve
manganeso *m.* manganese
mangar *v.* to swipe; mooch
mangosta *f.* mongoose
manguear *v.* to startle; loaf
manguera *f.* garden hose
manguita *f.* cover

maní *m.* peanut
manía *f.* habit; craze
maníaco, ca *adj.* maniac
manifestación *f.* manifestation
manifestar *v.* to reveal; manifest
manifiesto, ta *adj.* manifest
manilla *f.* bracelet; handcuff
manipulación *f.* manipulation
manipulador, ra *m.* manipulator
manipular *v.* to manipulate; manage
maniquí *m.* mannequin
mano *f.* hand
manojo *m.* handful; bunch
manosear *v.* to touch
manso, sa *adj.* mild; tame
manta *f.* shawl; blanket
manteca *f.* fat; lard; butter
mantel *m.* tablecloth
mantenencia *f.* support; maintenance
mantener *v.* to support; keep; feed; maintain
mantenimiento *m.* support; sustenance
mantequería *f.* creamery
mantequero *m.* dairyman
mantequilla *f.* butter
manto *m.* mantle; robe; cloak; cover
manual *adj.* manual
manufacturar *v.* to manufacture
manutención *f.* maintenance
manzana *f.* apple
manzanar *m.* apple orchard
manzano *m.* apple tree
maña *f.* dexterity; skill
mañana *f.* morning; *adv.* tomorrow
mapa *f.* map
mapache *m.* raccoon
maquear *v.* to varnish
máquina *f.* machine
maquinación *f.* machination
maquinador, ra *m., f.* schemer
maquinar *v.* to scheme
maquinista *m. f.* machinist
mar *m.* sea; tide
maratón *m.* marathon
maravilla *f.* marvel; astonishment; wonder
maravillar *v.* to astonish; be amazed
maravilloso, sa *adj.* marvelous
marca *f.* brand; mark; stamp; trademark
marcado, da *adj.* notable
marcador, ra *adj.* marking
marcar *v.* to stamp; mark; note
marcial *adj.* military; martial
marco *m.* mark; standard weight
marcha *f.* march; trek; speed; progress
marchar *v.* to run; walk; march
marchitar *v.* to weaken; wilt
marchito, ta *adj.* wilted
marear *v.* to sail; to bother
marejada *f.* groundswell
mareo *m.* dizziness
margarina *f.* margarine
margarita *f.* daisy
margen *m.* fringe; margin
marginar *v.* to marginate
maridar *v.* to wed
marido *m.* spouse; husband
marinar *v.* to marinate
marinería *f.* sailoring
marinero, ra *adj.* marine; seaworthy
marino, na *adj.* marine
mariposa *f.* butterfly
mariquita *f.* ladybug
mariscal *m.* marshal
marisco *m.* crustacean; shellfish
marital *adj.* marital
marítimo, ma *adj.* maritime
mármol *m.* marble
marqués *m.* marquis
marrano *adj.* filthy
marrar *v.* to fail; miss something
marrón *adj.* brown
marrullero, ra *m., f.* conniver
marsopa *f.* porpoise
marsupial *adj.* marsupial
martes *m.* Tuesday
martillar *v.* to hammer
martillo *m.* hammer
mártir *m., f.* martyr
martirio *m.* martyrdom
marzo *m.* March
mas *conj.* but; however
más *adv.* more
masacrar *v.* to massacre

masacre f. massacre
masaje m. massage
masajista m. f. masseur; masseuse
mascar v. to chew
máscara f. disguise; mask
mascarada f. masquerade
mascota f. mascot; pet
masculinidad f. masculinity
masculino, na adj. manly; male
masivo, va adj. massive
masticar v. to masticate; ruminate
mástil m. mast
mastoides adj. mastoid
mata f. shrub
matador, ra m., f. killer
matafuego m. fire extinguisher
matar v. to extinguish; kill; slaughter
matarife m. slaughterer; butcher
matasellos m. canceler (post office)
matemático, ca adj. mathematical
materia f. matter; subject
material adj. material
materialidad f. materiality
materialista adj. materialistic; m. f. materialist
maternal adj. maternal
maternidad f. maternity
materno, na adj. motherly
matinal adj. of the morning
matiz m. tint; hue
matizar v. to tint; blend
matrero, ra adj. shrewd
matriarcado m. matriarchy
matriarcal adj. matriarchal
matricidio m. matricide
matrícula f. list; roster; matriculation
matriculación f. registration
matricular v. to matriculate
matrimonial adj. matrimonial
matrimonio m. matrimony; marriage
matriz f. uterus
matrona f. matron
matronal adj. matronly
máximamente adv. chiefly
máxime adv. principally
máximo, ma adj. maximum; greatest

mayo m. May
mayonesa f. mayonnaise
mayor adj. greatest; larger; older
mayoría f. majority
mayoridad f. majority (legal age)
mayúsculo, la adj. important; capital
mazmorra f. dungeon
mazo m. bunch; mallet
me pron. me
mecánico, ca adj. mechanical; m. mechanic
mecanizar v. to mechanize
mecedora f. rocking chair
mecer v. to sway; rock
mecha f. match; wick
mechera f. shoplifter
mechón m. tuft
medalla f. medal
medallón m. medallion
media f. stocking; sock; average; half
mediador, ra m., f. mediator
medianoche f. midnight
mediar v. to intercede
medicación f. medication
medicar v. to medicate
medicina f. medicine
medicinal adj. medicinal
medicinar v. to cure or treat with medicine
médico, ca m., f. doctor
medida f. measurement
medieval adj. medieval
medio adj. middle; half
mediocre adj. mediocre
mediocridad f. mediocrity
mediodía m. noon
medir v. to weigh; measure
meditación f. meditation
meditar v. to meditate
médium m. medium
medrar v. to thrive; prosper
medroso, sa adj. timorous
médula f. medulla; marrow
medusa f. jellyfish
megáfono m. megaphone
megatón m. megaton
mejilla f. cheek
mejor adj. superior; better

mejora *f.* betterment
mejorar *v.* to make better
mejoría *f.* improvement
melancolía *f.* melancholy
melaza *f.* molasses
melindrería *f.* affectation
melocotón *m.* peach
melodía *f.* tune
melódico, ca *adj.* tuneful
melodrama *m.* melodrama
melón *m.* melon
melote *m.* residue of molasses
mellar *v.* to nick; chip
membrana *f.* membrane
memorable *adj.* memorable
memorar *v.* to recall
memoria *f.* remembrance; memory
memorial *m.* memorial; (law) brief
memorización *f.* memorization
memorizar *v.* to memorize
mención *f.* mention
mencionar *v.* to mention
menear *v.* to sway
mengua *f.* poverty; decline
menguado, da *adj.* decreased; timid
menguar *v.* to wane; diminish
meningitis *f.* meningitis
menopausia *f.* menopause
menor *adj.* lesser; least; less; younger
menos *adv.* least; less
menoscabar *v.* to impair; lessen
menoscabo *m.* damage; diminishing
menospreciable *adj.* despicable
menosprecio *m.* underestimation; contempt
mensaje *m.* message
mensajero, ra *adj.* messenger
mensual *adj.* monthly
mensura *f.* measurement
mensurar *v.* to measure
menta *f.* mint; peppermint
mentado, da *adj.* renowned
mental *adj.* mental
mentalidad *f.* mentality
mentar *v.* to mention
mente *f.* intellect; intelligence
mentir *v.* to lie

mentira *f.* falsehood; lie
mentiroso, sa *adj.* lying
mentor *m.* mentor
menudo, da *adj.* little
mercadeo *m.* marketing
mercado *m.* marketplace
mercante *adj.* merchant
mercantil *adj.* mercantile
mercantilismo *n.m.* comercialization
mercar *v.* to buy
merced *f.* gift; mercy
mercurial *adj.* mercurial
mercurio *m.* mercury
merecimiento *m.* worth
merienda *f.* snack
mérito *m.* value; worth
meritorio, ria *adj.* meritorious
mermar *v.* to diminish
mero, ra *adj.* pure; mere; simple
merodear *v.* to plunder; maraud
mes *m.* month
mesa *f.* table
mesón *m.* tavern
mesura *f.* moderation
metáfora *f.* metaphor
metal *m.* metal
metálico, ca *adj.* metallic
metalizar *v.* to metallize
metano *m.* methane
meteórito *m.* meteorite
meteoro *m.* meteor
meteorología *f.* meteorology
meteorologista *m., f.* meteorologist
meter *v.* to insert into; cause
metilo *m.* methyl
metódico, ca *adj.* methodical
método *m.* method
métrico, ca *adj.* metric
mezclador, ra *adj.* blending
mezclar *v.* to mingle; blend
mezquindad *f.* miserliness
mezquino, na *adj.* petty; wretched; miserly
mezquita *f.* mosque
mi *pron.* me
microbio *m.* microbe
microbiología *f.* microbiology
microfilme *m.* microfilm

micrófono *m.* microphone
microscopio *m.* microscope
miedo *m.* dread; fear
miedoso, sa *adj.* cowardly
miel *f.* honey
mielga *f.* alfalfa; plot for sowing
miembro *m.* member
mientras *adv.* meanwhile *conj.* while
miércoles *m.* Wednesday
mies *f.* grain; cereal
miga *f.* crumb; scrap
migración *f.* migration
migraña *f.* migraine
migratorio, ria *adj.* migratory
mil *adj.* thousand
milagro *m.* miracle
milagroso, sa *adj.* miraculous
milicia *f.* militia
miliciano, na *adj.* military
miligramo *m.* milligram
mililitro *m.* milliliter
milímetro *m.* millimeter
militar *m.* soldier
milla *f.* mile
millón *m.* million
mimar *v.* to fondle; pamper
mímico, ca *adj.* mimic
mimoso, sa *adj.* finicky; spoiled
mina *f.* mine
minador, ra *adj.* mining
minar *v.* to mine
mineral *adj.* mineral
mineralogista *m.* mineralogist
minería *f.* mining
miniatura *f.* miniature
miniaturista *m., f.* miniaturist
minifalda *f.* miniskirt
minimizar *v.* to minimize
mínimo, ma *adj.* least; minimal; minute
ministerial *adj.* ministerial
ministerio *m.* ministry
ministro *m.* minister
minorar *v.* to reduce
minoría *f.* minority
minoritario, ria *adj.* minority
minucioso, sa *adj.* minute
minúsculo, la *adj.* tiny; small; *f.* small letter; lower case
minuta *f.* record; note; menu

minuto *m.* minute
mío, a *adj.* mine
miope *adj.* myopic
miopía *f.* myopia
mira *f.* sight; intention
mirado, da *adj.* circumspect; cautious
mirador, ra *adj.* watching
mirar *v.* to watch; look at; observe
mirasol *m.* sunflower
miríada *f.* myriad
mirlo *m.* blackbird
misceláneo, a *adj.* miscellaneous
miserable *adj.* miserable; poor; miserly
miseria *f.* suffering; miserliness; misery
misil *m.* missile
misión *f.* mission
misional *adj.* missionary
mismo, ma *adj.* likewise; same thing
misterio *m.* mystery
misterioso, sa *adj.* mysterious
místico, ca *adj.* mystic
mistificar *v.* to mystify
mistura *f.* mixture
mitad *f.* half
mitigación *f.* mitigation
mitigar *v.* to mitigate
mito *m.* myth
mitón *m.* mitt
mitra *f.* miter
mixto, ta *adj.* mixed
mixtura *f.* mixture
mixturar *v.* to mix up
mobiliario, ria *adj.* movable property
moblaje *m.* household furniture
moblar *v.* to furnish
mocedad *f.* youth
moción *f.* motion
mocho, cha *adj.* blunt; flat
moda *f.* fashion
modelo *m.* model
moderación *f.* moderation
moderado, da *adj.* moderate
moderar *v.* to regulate; restrain
modernización *f.* modernization

modernizar *v.* to modernize
moderno, na *adj.* modern
modestia *f.* modesty
módico, ca *adj.* moderate
modificación *f.* modification
modificador, ra *adj.* modifying
modificar *v.* to modify
modistería *f.* shop for dresses
modo *m.* way; fashion; manner
modoso, sa *adj.* well-mannered
modulación *f.* modulation
mojar *v.* to drench; dip; wet
molde *m.* pattern; mold
moldear *v.* to shape
molecular *adj.* molecular
moler *v.* to grind
molestar *v.* to annoy; disrupt
molestia *f.* annoyance; trouble
molesto, ta *adj.* bothered; annoying
momento *m.* moment
mona *f.* female monkey
monasterio *m.* monastery
monitor *m.* monitor
mono *m.* male monkey
monstruo *m.* monster
monstruoso, sa *adj.* monstrous
montaña *f.* mountain
montar *v.* to mount
monumento *m.* monument
moral *f.* morale
moralidad *f.* morality
moralizar *v.* to moralize
morar *v.* to dwell; live
mórbido, da *adj.* morbid
moreno, na *adj.* brown; tawny
morfina *f.* morphine
morir *v.* to die; pass away
mortal *adj.* fatal; mortal
mortalidad *f.* mortality
mortorio *m.* mortuary; funeral
mosca *f.* fly
mosquito *m.* mosquito
mostaza *f.* mustard
mostrar *v.* to exhibit; appear; show
motor *m.* motor engine
mover *v.* to move
movimiento *m.* movement
muchacha *f.* girl
muchacho *m.* boy

mucho, cha *adj.* much; a lot
muerte *f.* death
muerto, ta *adj.* dead
mujer *f.* female; woman
múltiple *adj.* multiple
multiplicar *v.* to multiply
mundo *m.* world
municipal *adj.* municipal
muñeca *f.* wrist; doll
músculo *m.* muscle
música *f.* music
musical *adj.* musical
muslo *m.* thigh
muy *adv.* very; greatly

N

nabo *m.* turnip; mast
nacarino, na *adj.* nacreous
nacer *v.* to rise; be born; be conceived
nacido, da *adj.* born
naciente *adj.* recent; growing; initial; nascent
nacimiento *m.* hatching; origin; birth; spring
nación *f.* nation
nacional *adj.* domestic; national
nacionalidad *f.* nationality
nacionalizar *v.* to nationalize; naturalize
nada *pron.* no; not anything; none; nothing
nadador, ra *m., f.* swimmer
nadar *v.* to swim
nadie *pron.* no one; nobody
naipe *m.* playing card
nalga *f.* behind; buttocks
naranja *f.* orange
naranjero *m.* orange tree
naranjo *m.* orange tree
narcótico, ca *adj.* narcotic
narcotizar *v.* to narcotize
nariz *f.* nostril; nose
narración *f.* narration; narrative
narrador, ra *adj.* narrating
narrar *v.* to narrate
narrativo, va *adj.* narrative
natación *f.* swimming

natal *adj.* natal
natalidad *f.* natality
Natividad *f.* Nativity
nativo, va *adj.* inborn; native
nato, ta *adj.* born; natural of a place
natura *f.* nature
natural *adj.* native; innate; natural
naturaleza *f.* nature
naturalidad *f.* naturalness
naturalización *f.* naturalization
naufragar *v.* to shipwreck
náusea *f.* nausea
nausear *v.* to feel nauseous
náutico, ca *adj.* nautical
naval *adj.* naval
navegable *adj.* navigable
navegación *f.* navigation
navegar *v.* to sail
Navidad *f.* Christmas
navío *m.* vessel; boat
neblina *f.* fog
neblinoso, sa *adj.* foggy
nebulosidad *f.* haziness
necedad *f.* nonsense
necesario, ria *adj.* necessary
necesidad *f.* need; poverty; necessity
necesitado, da *adj.* poor; needy
necesitar *v.* to want; require; need
necio, cia *adj.* foolish; stubborn
necrología *f.* necrology
néctar *m.* nectar
nectarina *f.* nectarine
nefritis *f.* nephritis
negable *adj.* refutable
negación *f.* denial; refusal; negation
negar *v.* to refuse; deny; forbid
negatividad *f.* negativity
negligencia *f.* disregard; negligence
negociable *adj.* negotiable
negociación *f.* negotiation; transaction
negociar *v.* to deal; negotiate
negocio *m.* job; work; business; transaction

negro, a *adj.* black
negrura *f.* darkness
negruzco, ca *adj.* dark
nene, na *m., f.* baby
nenúfar *m.* water lily
neófito, ta *m., f.* neophyte
neón *m.* neon
neonato *m.* neonate
nervio *m.* nerve
nerviosidad *f.* nervousness
nervioso, sa *adj.* nervous
nerviosidad *f.* nervousness
neto, ta *adj.* simple; pure net
neumático, ca *adj.* pneumatic
neurocirugía *f.* neurosurgery
neurólogo *m.* neurologist
neurótico, ca *adj.* neurotic
neutonio *m.* newton
neutral *adj.* neutral
neutralidad *f.* neutrality
neutralizar *v.* to neutralize
neutro, a *adj.* neutral; neuter
neutrón *m.* neutron
nevado, da *adj.* snow-covered
nevar *v.* to snow
nevera *f.* ice box; refrigerator
nexo *m.* link
ni *conj.* neither; nor
nicotina *f.* nicotine
nicho *m.* niche; recess
nidal *m.* nest; nest box
nido *m.* nest; liar; den
niebla *f.* mist
nieta *f.* granddaughter
nieto *m.* grandson
nieve *f.* snow
nihilista *adj.* nihilistic
nilón *m.* nylon
nimbo *m.* halo; nimbus
nimio, a *adj.* insignificant
ninfa *f.* nymph
ninfea *f.* white water lily
ninfo *m.* dandy
ninguno, na *adj.* no; none
niñería *f.* childish
niñez *f.* infancy; childhood
niño, ña *m., f.* child
níquel *m.* nickel
niquelar *v.* to nickel
nítido, da *adj.* clear
nitrato *m.* nitrite
nitrito *m.* nitrite

nitrógeno *m.* nitrogen
nitroglicerina *f.* nitroglycerin
nivel *m.* height; standard
nivelar *v.* to make level
no *adv.* no; not
noble *adj.* honorable; noble
nobleza *f.* nobleness; nobility
noción *f.* notion
nocividad *f.* noxiousness
nocivo, va *adj.* noxious
nocturnal *adj.* of the night; nocturnal
nocturno, na *adj.* nightly
noche *f.* night
nódulo *m.* nodule
nogal *m.* walnut tree
nómada *adj.* nomadic
nombramiento *m.* nomination; naming
nombrar *v.* to name; nominate
nombre *m.* name
nomenclatura *f.* nomenclature
nómina *f.* roll; payroll
nominación *f.* nomination
nominal *adj.* nominal
nominar *v.* to nominate
non *adj.* uneven; odd
nonada *f.* trifle
nono, na *adj.* ninth
norma *f.* rule
normal *adj.* normal
normalidad *f.* normality
normalización *f.* normalization
normalizar *v.* to normalize
noroeste *m.* northwest
norte *m.* north
nos *pron.* us
notable *adj.* outstanding; notable
notar *v.* to observe; note
notificar *v.* to notify
noveno, na *adj.* ninth
noventa *adj.* ninety
novia *f.* girlfriend; bride
novio *m.* boyfriend; groom
nubosidad *f.* cloudiness
nuca *f.* nape
nuestro, tra *adj.* our
nueve *adj.* nine; ninth (of month); *m.* nine
nuevo, va *adj.* new
número *m.* number

nunca *adv.* not ever; never
nutrir *v.* to nourish; feed

Ñ

ñame *m.* a type of yam
ñapa *f.* tip; bonus
ñaque *m.* junk
ñeque *m.* vigor; *adj.* strength
ñoñería *f.* insipidity
ñoñez *f.* prudery
ñoño, ña *adj.* insipid; fussy

O

o *conj.* or
oasis *m.* oasis
obcecadamente *adv.* blindly
obcecar *v.* to blind
obedecer *v.* to obey
obediencia *f.* obedience
obediente *adj.* obedient
obertura *f.* overture
obesidad *f.* obesity
óbice *m.* obstacle
obispo *m.* bishop
objeción *f.* objection
objetar *v.* to object
objetivar *v.* to objectify
objetividad *f.* objectivity
objetivo, va *adj.* objective
objeto *m.* theme; object
oblicuo, cua *adj.* oblique
obligación *f.* responsibility; obligation
obligar *v.* to force; oblige
oblongo, ga *adj.* oblong
oboe *m.* oboe
obra *f.* work; labor
obrar *v.* to act; work
obrero, ra *adj.* working
obscenidad *f.* obscenity
obsceno, na *adj.* obscene
obsequio *m.* present; gift; kindness
observación *f.* observation
observador, ra *adj.* observant; *m. f.* observer
observancia *f.* observance
observar *v.* to watch; observe
obsesión *f.* obsession
obsesionar *v.* to obsess about

something
obseso, sa *adj.* obsessive
obstaculizar *v.* to hinder;
  obstruct
obstáculo *m.* obstacle
obstante *adj.* obstructing
obstar *v.* to hinder; obstruct
  something
obstinación *f.* obstinacy
obstrucción *f.* obstruction
obstruir *v.* to obstruct
obtención *f.* obtaining
obtener *v.* to get; have; obtain
obtuso, sa *adj.* obtuse
obviar *v.* to clear away; obviate
obvio, via *adj.* obvious
ocasión *f.* cause; occasion; circumstance
ocasionar *v.* to cause; provoke;
  occasion
occidental *adj.* occidental
occipital *adj.* occipital
océano *m.* ocean
ocio *m.* leisure; idleness
octavo, va *adj.* eighth
octogésimo, ma *adj.* eightieth
octagonal *adj.* octagonal
octubre *m.* October
oculista *m., f.* oculist
ocultamente *adv.* secretly
ocultar *v.* to conceal; silence;
  hide
ocultismo *m.* occultism
oculto, ta *adj.* concealed;
  occult
ocupación *f.* trade; occupation;
  job
ocupado, da *adj.* occupied
ocupante *adj.* occupying
ocupar *v.* to fill; to occupy; to
  employ; pay attention to something
ocurrencia *f.* occurrence
ocurrir *v.* to happen; take
  place; occur
ochenta *adj.* eighty
ocho *adj.* eight; eighth (of
  month); *m.* eight
oda *f.* ode
odalisca *f.* odalisque
odiar *v.* to loathe; hate
odio *m.* loathing; hatred

odioso, sa *adj.* odious
odisea *f.* odyssey
oeste *m.* west
ofender *v.* to hurt; offend
ofensa *f.* offense
ofensivo, va *adj.* offensive
ofensor, ra *adj.* offending
ofertar *v.* to tender; offer
oficial *m.* officer
oficialidad *f.* officers
oficiante *m.* officiant
oficina *f.* office
oficinista *m., f.* office clerk
oficio *m.* work; office; occupation
oficioso, sa *adj.* obliging;
  diligent
ofrecimiento *m.* offering
ofrenda *f.* offering
ofrendar *v.* to give an
  offering for
oftalmología *f.* ophthal-
  mology
oftalmólogo *m.* ophthal-
  mologist
ofuscación *f.* confusion; dazzling
ofuscar *v.* to bewilder; blind
oído *m.* ear
oír *v.* to listen; hear; attend
ojal *m.* buttonhole
ojeada *f.* glimpse; glance
ojeriza *f.* grudge
ojo *m.* eye
ojota *f.* a type of sandal
oleada *f.* big wave
oleaje *m.* waves; swell
oler *v.* to smell
olfato *m.* sense of smell
olfatorio, ria *adj.* olfactory
oliva *f.* olive
olivar *m.* olive grove
olivo *m.* olive tree
olmo *m.* elm tree
olor *m.* smell; odor
oloroso, sa *adj.* fragrant
olvidado, da *adj.* forgetful;
  ungrateful; forgotten
olvidar *v.* to omit; forget;
  leave out
olvido *m.* forgetfulness;
  oblivion
olla *f.* kettle; pot

ombligo m. navel
omisión f. omission
omitir v. to omit
ómnibus m. omnibus
onanismo m. onanism
once adj. eleven
onceno, na adj. eleventh
oncología f. oncology
ondear v. to flutter; ripple
ondulación f. undulation
ondular v. to undulate
oneroso, sa adj. onerous
ónix f. onyx
onza f. ounce
onzavo, va adj. eleventh
opa adj. foolish
opacidad f. opacity
opaco, ca adj. opaque
ópalo m. opal
opción f. option
opcional adj. optional
ópera f. opera
operación f. operation; surgery
operante adj. operating
operar v. to operate
operativo, va adj. operative
opinión f. opinion
opio m. opium
oponer v. to oppose
oportunamente adv. opportunely
oportunidad f. chance
oportunista adj. opportunistic
oportuno, na adj. opportune;
  fitting
oposición f. opposition
opositor, ra m., f. opponent
opresión f. oppression
opresivo, va adj. oppressive
opreso, sa adj. oppressed
oprimido, da adj. oppressed
oprimir v. to press; oppress
oprobio m. disgrace; shame
oprobioso, sa adj. disgraceful
optar v. to select; opt
óptico, ca adj. optical
optimista adj. optimistic
óptimo, ma adj. optimal
optómetra m., f. optometrist
optometría f. optometry
opuesto, ta adj. contrary;
  opposite
opulencia f. opulence

ora conj. now; then
oración f. oration; speech; sentence; prayer
oráculo m. oracle
oral adj. oral
orangután m. orangutan
orar v. to pray; speak
oratorio, ria adj. oratorical
orbe m. orb
orden m. order
ordenación f. ordination;
  ordering
ordenada f. ordinate
ordenar v. to command; order;
  arrange; put into order
ordeñar v. to milk
ordinal adj. ordinal
ordinariez f. commonness
ordinario, ria adj. ordinary;
  usual; uncouth; coarse
orear v. to ventilate; air
orfanato m. orphanage
orfelinato m. orphanage
orgánico, ca adj. organic
organismo m. organism
organista m., f. organist
organizar v. to organize
órgano m. organ
orgullo m. conceit; pride
orientación f. orientation
oriental adj. oriental
orientar v. to orient
orificio m. opening; orifice
origen m. source; origin
original adj. authentic; original;
  new
originalidad f. originality
originar v. to originate
orilla f. edge
orillar v. to edge
orín m. rust; urine
orinal m. urinal
orinar v. to urinate
orlar v. to edge; trim
ornamental adj. ornamental
ornamentar v. to ornament;
  decorate
ornamento m. ornament
ornar v. to embellish
ornitología f. ornithology
oro m. gold
orquesta f. orchestra

orquestación f. orchestration
orquestal adj. orchestral
orquestar v. to orchestrate
orquídea f. orchid
ortiga f. nettle
ortodoxo, xa adj. orthodox
ortografía f. orthographic
ortopédico, ca adj. orthopedic
oruga f. caterpillar
orujo m. residue
os pron. you
osadía f. audacity
osado, da adj. daring
osamenta f. bones; skeleton
osar v. to dare
oscilación f. wavering; swinging
oscilar v. to oscillate; swing
oscurecer v. to dim; obscure; shade
oscurecimiento m. darkening
oscuridad f. haziness; obscurity
oscuro, ra adj. unclear; dark; obscure
osificar v. to ossify
ósmosis f. osmosis
oso m. bear
ostensible adj. ostensible
ostentación f. ostentation
ostentar v. to flaunt; show
ostra f. oyster
ostracismo m. ostracism
otear v. to survey; spy; scan
otoñal adj. autumnal
otoño m. autumn
otorgar v. to give
otro, ra adj. other
ovación f. ovation
ovacionar v. to give another an ovation
oval adj. oval
óvalo m. oval
ovario m. ovary
oveja f. female sheep; ewe
overtura f. overture
ovillo m. snarl; ball (wool; silk)
ovino, na m. ovine
ovulación f. ovulation
ovular v. ovulate
oxidación f. oxidation
oxidar v. to oxidize
óxido m. oxide

oxigenado, da adj. oxygenated
oxigenar v. to give oxygen to; oxygenate
oxígeno m. oxygen
oyente adj. listening; m. f. listener
ozono m. ozone

P

pabellón m. banner; pavilion
pabilo m. candle wick
pábulo m. pabulum; support
pacer v. to graze
paciencia f. patience
paciente adj. patient
pacificación f. pacification
pacificador, ra m., f. pacifier
pacificar v. to pacify
pacífico, ca adj. pacific
pacifista adj. pacifist
pacho, cha adj. unruffled
pachorra f. sluggishness
padecer v. to bear; suffer; endure
padrastro m. stepfather
padre m. dad; father
padrillo m. stallion
padrino m. godfather
paga f. payment
pagadero, ra adj. payable
pagano, na adj. pagan
pagar v. to pay; repay
página f. page
paginar v. to paginate
pago, ga adj. paid
país m. land; country
paisaje m. landscape (painter; artist)
paisajista f. landscape painter
paja f. straw
pajar m. barn; straw loft; haystack
pajarera f. cage for birds
pajarería f. bird store
pájaro m. bird
pala f. blade; spade; shovel
palabra f. word; promise
palabreo m. chatter
palaciego, ga adj. magnificent; palatial
palacio m. palace

palada f. shovelful
paladear v. to relish; savor
paladio m. palladium
palafrenero m. groom
palanca f. shaft; lever; crowbar
palangana f. washbasin
palco, n.m. box
palear v. to shovel
paleontología f. paleontology
paleta f. trowel; palette; small shovel
paliativo, va adj. palliative
palidez f. pallor
pálido, da adj. pallid; pale
palito m. small stick; cocktail stirrer
paliza f. thrashing
palma f. palm tree; palm (of hand)
palmado, da adj. palm-shaped
palmar m. palm grove
palmeado, da adj. palm-shaped; webbed (feet)
palmear v. to applaud
palmera f. palm tree
palmo m. span; measure of length
palmotear v. to applaud
palo m. pole; handle; timber; mast; stick
paloma f. pigeon; dove
palomita f. small dove; (de maíz) popcorn
palote m. drumstick
palpable adj. palpable
palpar v. to feel
palpitación f. palpitation
palpitante adj. palpating
palpitar v. to palpitate; beat
paludismo m. malaria
palurdo, da m. f. boor; uncouth; peasant
pampa f. pampa
pan m. bread
pana f. corduroy
panadería f. bakery
panadero, ra m., f. baker
panal m. honeycomb
páncreas m. pancreas
pancreático, ca adj. pancreatic
panda f. panda
pandemonio m. pandemonium

pandero m. large tambourine
pandilla f. gang
panfleto m. pamphlet
pánico, ca m., adj. panic; panicky; m. panic
panorama f. panorama
panorámico, ca adj. panoramic
pantalones m. slacks; pants
pantalla f. movie screen; lampshade
pantano m. marsh
panteón m. pantheon; graveyard
pantera f. panther
pantomima f. pantomime
pantorrilla f. calf (of leg)
paño m. cloth
pañoleta f. scarf; fichu
pañolón m. shawl
pañuelo m. kerchief; handkerchief
papa f. potato
papagayo m. parrot
papal adj. papal
papar v. to swallow soft food
papaya f. papaya
papel m. paper
papelero, ra adj. paper
papeleta f. file card; slip; form
papera f. goiter
papila f. papilla
papiro m. papyrus
paquete m. packet; pack; package
paquetería f. elegance; small goods shop
par adj. paired; equal
para prep. for; to; towards
parábola f. parable
parabrisas m. windshield
paracaídas f. parachute
parado, da adj. stopped; stationary; idle
paradoja f. paradox
paradójico, ca adj. paradoxical
parafina f. paraffin
paraguas m. umbrella
paraíso m. paradise
paraje m. area
paralelo m. parallel
parálisis f. paralysis
paralización f. paralyzation
paralizar v. to paralyze

paramédico, ca *adj.* paramedical
parámetro *m.* parameter
paranoia *f.* paranoia
paranoico, ca *adj.* paranoid
parapléjico, ca *adj.* paraplegic
parar *v.* to halt; check; stop
parasítico, ca *adj.* parasitic
parásito, ta *adj.* parasitic
parasol *m.* parasol
parcela *f.* parcel
parcial *adj.* partial
parcialidad *f.* partiality
pardo, da *adj.* brown
parear *v.* to pair
parecer *m.* view; appearance
parecido, da *adj.* similar; alike
pared *f.* wall
parejo, ja *adj.* equal; smooth; alike
parentela *f.* relatives
parentesco *m.* kinship
paréntesis *m.* parenthesis
paridad *f.* parity
paritario, ria *adj.* joint; equal
parlamentario, ria *adj.* parliamentary
parlamento *m.* parliament
parlar *v.* to chatter
parloteo *m.* chatter
paro *m.* work stoppage (protest)
parodia *f.* parody
parodiar *v.* to parody
parodista *m., f.* parodist
paroxismo *m.* paroxysm
parpadear *v.* to blink
párpado *m.* eyelid
parque *m.* park
parquedad *f.* moderation
parqueo *m.* parking
parra *f.* grapevine
párrafo *m.* paragraph
parricidio *m.* parricide
parroquial *adj.* parochial
parsimonia *f.* moderation; circumspection
parte *f.* share; part
partera *f.* midwife
partición *f.* partition
participación *f.* participation
participar *v.* to inform; take part
partícipe *adj.* participating

partícula *f.* particle
particular *adj.* particular; special
particularidad *f.* peculiarity
particularmente *adv.* particularly
partidista *adj.* of a party
partida *f.* leaving; departure
partido *m.* party; divided
partir *v.* to depart; leave; split; divide
partitivo, va *adj.* partitive
partitura *f.* score
pasadizo *m.* passage
pasado *m.* past
pasador *adj.* passing
pasaje *m.* passage; corridor
pasaporte *m.* passport
pasar *v.* to elapse; occur; happen; pass
pasatiempo *m.* pastime
pase *m.* pass; permit
paseo *m.* stroll; outing
pasión *f.* passion
paso *m.* footstep; pace
pasta *f.* paste
pastel *m.* cake; pie
pasteurizar *v.* to pasteurize
pasteurización *f.* pasteurization
pasto *m.* pasture; grass
pata *f.* foot; leg; paw; female duck
patada *f.* kick
patata *f.* potato
patear *v.* to kick
patentar *v.* to register
patente *adj.* patent; evident; obvious
paternal *adj.* paternal
paternidad *f.* paternity
patillas *f.* sideburns
patín *m.* skate
patinar *v.* to skate
patio *m.* patio
pato *m.* duck
patología *f.* pathology
patólogo, ga *m., f.* pathologist
patriarca *m.* patriarch
patriota *m., f.* patriot
patriótico, ca *adj.* patriotic
patrocinar *v.* to patronize
patrón, na *m. f.* patron saint; master; employer; boss
patronal *adj.* management

patronato *m.* trust; foundation; employer's association
patrullar *v.* to patrol
paulatino, na *adj.* gradual
pausa *f.* interruption; pause
pauta *f.* rule; example
pavada *f.* foolishness; flock of turkeys
pavimentación *f.* paving
pavimento *m.* pavement
pavo *m.* turkey
pavor *m.* terror
pavura *f.* terror
payaso *m.* clown
paz *f.* peace
pazguato, ta *adj.* foolish
pecar *v.* to sin
pecera *f.* aquarium
pectina *f.* pectin
pectoral *adj.* pectoral
peculiar *adj.* peculiar
peculiaridad *f.* peculiarity
peculio *m.* peculium; private money
pecunia *f.* money; cash
pechar *v.* to pay (tax)
pecho *m.* breast; chest
pedal *m.* pedal
pedaleo *m.* pedaling
pedantería *f.* pedantry
pedazo *m.* bit; piece
pedernal *m.* flint
pedestal *m.* pedestal
pedestre *adj.* pedestrian
pediatría *f.* pediatrics
pedículo *m.* peduncle
pedigree *m.* pedigree
pedir *v.* to order; beg; ask for
pedregoso, sa *adj.* rocky; stony
pedrisca *f.* hailstorm
pedúnculo *m.* peduncle
pegadizo, za *adj.* catching
pegajoso, sa *adj.* catching; adhesive
pegar *v.* to glue; attach; stick
peinado *m.* hairdo; hair style
peine *m.* comb
pelado, da *adj.* bare; bald
peladura *f.* peeling
pelagra *f.* pellagra
pelar *v.* to peel; cut

peleador, ra *adj.* fighting; quarrelsome
pelícano *m.* pelican
película *f.* film; movie
peligro *m.* danger
peligroso, sa *adj.* dangerous
pelo *m.* fur; hair
pelota *f.* ball; jai alai game
peltre *m.* pewter
peluca *f.* wig
peludo, da *adj.* shaggy; hairy
pelvis *f.* pelvis
pellizcar *v.* to pinch; nibble
pellón *m.* long fur robe or saddle pad
pena *f.* anxiety; penalty; distress; sorrow
penacho *m.* crest; tuft of feathers
penado, da *adj.* grieved
penalizar *v.* to penalize
penar *v.* to punish
pendenciar *v.* to quarrel; argue
pender *v.* to hang; dangle
pendiente *adj.* hanging; pending
penetrable *adj.* penetrable
penetración *f.* penetration
penetrar *v.* to pierce; penetrate
penicilina *f.* penicillin
península *f.* peninsula
penique *m.* penny
penitencia *f.* penitence; penance
penitente *adj.* penitent
penoso, sa *adj.* grievous; wearing
pensamiento *m.* thought; pansy
pensante *adj.* thinking
pensar *v.* to think; think about
pensativo, va *adj.* thoughtful
pensionar *v.* to pension
pentotal *m.* pentothal
peña *f.* circle; group
peñascoso, sa *adj.* rocky
peor *adj.* worse
pepino *m.* cucumber
péptico, ca *adj.* peptic
pequeño, ña *adj.* tiny; small; little
pera *f.* pear
peral *m.* pear tree

percepción f. perception
perceptivo, va adj. perceptive
percibir v. to sense; receive
percudir v. to dull; tarnish
percusión f. percussion
percutir v. to percuss
percha f. hanger; prop
perder v. to waste; lose
pérdida f. waste; loss
perdido, da adj. missing;
  wasted
perdiz f. partridge
perdón m. pardon
perdonar v. to remit; excuse;
  pardon
perdurar v. to last
perecer v. to perish; die
peregrinación f. pilgrimage
perejil m. parsley
perenne adj. perennial
pereza f. laziness
perezoso, sa adj. lazy
perfección f. perfection
perfeccionar v. to make something perfect
perfeccionista adj. perfectionist
perfecto, ta adj. perfect
pérfido, da adj. unfaithful;
  treacherous
perfilar v. to profile
perforación f. perforation
perforador, ra adj. perforating
perforar v. to perforate
perfumar v. to perfume
perfume m. perfume
perfumería f. perfumery
pericardio m. pericardium
pericia f. skill
perico m. parakeet
perímetro m. perimeter
periódicamente adv. periodically
periódico m. periodical; newspaper
periodismo m. journalism
periodista m., f. journalist
período m. period
perístole f. peristalsis
periquito m. parakeet
periscopio m. periscope
peritoneo m. peritoneum
perjudicar v. to harm
perjudicial adj. harmful

perjurio m. perjury
perla f. pearl
permanecer v. to remain; stay
permanente adj. permanent
permisible adj. permissible
permisivo, va adj. permissive
permiso m. consent; permit
permitir v. to allow; give; permit
permutar v. to exchange
pernicioso, sa adj. pernicious
perno m. pin; bolt; spike
pero conj. but; yet
peroné m. fibula
peróxido m. peroxide
perpetración f. perpetuation
perpetuar v. to perpetuate
perplejidad f. perplexity
perplejo, ja adj. perplexed
perro m. dog
persecución f. persecution;
  chase
perseguir v. to follow; hound;
  pursue
persiana f. Venetian blind
persignar v. to cross
persistencia f. persistence
persistir v. to persist
persona f. person
personal adj. personal
personalidad f. personality
personalizar v. to personalize
personificación f. personification
perspectiva f. perspective
persuadir v. to persuade
persuasión f. persuasion
persuasivo, va adj. persuasive
pertenecer v. to belong
perteneciente adj. pertaining
pertinencia f. relevancy
pertinente adj. relevant
pertrechar v. to equip; supply
perturbación f. disturbance
perturbar v. to upset
perversidad f. perversity
perversión f. perversion
pervertido, da adj. perverted
pesadilla f. nightmare
pesado, da adj. dull; heavy;
  boring
pesar v. to weigh; grieve
pesca f. fishing; catch
pescadería f. fish market

pescadilla *f.* whiting
pescado *m.* fish (when caught)
pescador *m.* fisherman
pescar *v.* to fish
pesebre *f.* manger
pesimista *adj.* pessimistic; *m.
f.* pessimist
peso *m.* weight; monetary unit
pesquero, ra *adj.* fishing
pestaña *f.* eyelash
pestañear *v.* to wink; blink
pestañeo *m.* winking; blinking
peste *f.* plague
pétalo *m.* petal
petición *f.* petition
pétreo, a *adj.* rocky
petrificar *v.* to petrify
petróleo *m.* petroleum
petulancia *f.* arrogance
petulante *adj.* arrogant
petunia *f.* petunia
pez *m.* fish (alive)
pianista *m., f.* pianist
piano *m.* piano
piar *v.* to chirp; peep
picante *adj.* spicy hot; biting
picar *v.* to sting; to chip;
to bite
picaresco, ca *adj.* mischievous
pícaro, ra *adj.* wicked; sly
picazón *f.* itching
pico *m.* spout; beak
picor *m.* itching
picotear *v.* to pick; peck
pictórico, ca *adj.* pictorial
pie *m.* foot
piedra *f.* stone
piel *f.* fur; skin
pierna *f.* leg
pieza *f.* piece
pifiar *v.* to miscue; jeer
pigmentar *v.* to pigment
pigmeo *adj.* pygmy
pijama *m.* pajamas
pilar *m.* pillar
pileta *f.* sink; swimming pool
pilotar *v.* to pilot
piloto *m.* pilot
pillar *v.* to plunder; to catch
someone doing something
pimentón *m.* paprika
pimienta *f.* pepper

pimpante *adj.* spruced; graceful;
poised
pináculo *m.* pinnacle
pinar *m.* pine grove
pincel *m.* brush
pinchadura *f.* puncture
pinchar *v.* to puncture
pinchazo *m.* puncture
pingüino *m.* penguin
pino *m.* pine
pintar *v.* to paint
pinto, ta *adj.* speckled
pintor, ra *m., f.* painter
pintoresco, ca *adj.* picturesque
pintura *f.* painting; paint
piña *f.* pine cone; pineapple
piojo *m.* louse
piola *f.* cord
pipa *f.* barrel
pipermín *m.* peppermint
pip eta *f.* pipette
piqueta *f.* pick; pick ax
piquete *m.* picket; small cut
piramidal *adj.* pyramidal
pirámide *f.* pyramid
pirata *m.* pirate
pirita *f.* pyrites
pirueta *f.* pirouette
pisada *f.* footprint; step
pisar *v.* to walk upon
piscina *f.* swimming pool
piso *m.* story; flat; floor
pisón *m.* tamper
pisotear *v.* to trample
pista *f.* runway; trail; track
pistacho *m.* pistachio
pistola *f.* pistol
pistón *m.* piston
pitido *m.* whistling
pitillo *m.* cigarette
pito *m.* whistle
pitón *m.* python; budding horn
or antler
pitonisa *f.* pythoness
pivote *m.* pivot
placa *f.* plaque; badge; license
plate
placebo *m.* placebo
placenta *f.* placenta
placer *m.* pleasure;
gratification
plácido, da *adj.* placid

plagar v. to plague; infest
plan m. scheme; plan
plancha f. sheet; iron; flat iron
pianchado, da adj. ironed
  (clothes)
planchar v. to iron
planear v. to plan
planeta m. planet
planetario, ria adj. planetary m.
  planetarium
planicie f. plain; level ground
planificación f. planning
planificar v. to plan
plano adj. level; flat
planta f. plant
plantación f. plantation
plantar v. to plant
plantear v. to start; expound
planido m. lament
plasma m. plasma
plasmar v. to mold
plástico, ca adj. plastic
plastificar v. to shellac something; to plasticize
plata f. silver; money
plataforma f. platform
plátano m. banana; plantain
platear v. to silver-plate
platero m. silversmith
platicar v. to talk
platino m. platinum
plato m. dish; plate
platónico, ca adj. platonic
plausible adj. plausible
playa f. beach
playero, ra adj. beach
plegable adj. collapsible; folding
plegado, da m. folding; folded
plegar v. to fold; bend; pleat
pleuresía f. pleurisy
plisado m. pleat
plomero m. plumber
plomo, ma adj. leaden
pluma f. pen; feather
plural adj. plural
pluralidad f. plurality
pluralizar v. to pluralize
plutonio m. plutonium
población f. population; village;
  town
poblado m. settlement; inhabited
  place

poblar v. to populate
pobre adj. poor
pobreza f. poverty
poción f. potion; concoction
poco adv. little
podar v. to prune
poder v. to be able; can
poderío m. power
podiatra m. podiatrist
poema m. poem
poesía f. poetry
poeta m. poet
poético, ca adj. poetical
poetisa f. poetess
poker m. poker (card game)
polar adj. polar
polarización f. polarization
polarizar v. to polarize
polen m. pollen
policía m. f. constable; police
policial adj. police; detective
  (novel)
polifonía f. polyphony
polígono m. polygon
polilla f. moth
polinización f. pollination
polinomio m. polynomial
pólipo m. polyp
política f. policy; politics
político, ca adj. political
politizar v. to politicize
polo m. pole; polo (sport)
poltrón, na adj. lazy; idle
polución f. pollution; contamination
polvo m. powder; dust
pólvora f. powder (explosive)
pollo m. chicken
pomada f. pomade
pompa f. pomp
pomposidad f. pomposity
pomposo, sa adj. pompous
ponche m. punch (drink)
poncho m. poncho
ponderable adj. ponderable
ponderar v. to consider
poner v. to place; don; put
pontifical adj. pontifical
pontificar v. to pontificate
ponzoñoso, sa adj. poisonous;
  venomous
populacho m. populace; rabble

popular *adj.* popular
popularidad *f.* popularity
popularizar *v.* to popularize
popurrí *m.* potpourri
póquer *m.* poker (card game)
por *prep.* from; via; for
porcentaje *m.* percentage
porcentual *adj.* percentage
porción *f.* part; portion
porche *m.* porch
porfiado, da *adj.* stubborn
porosidad *f.* porosity
poroso, sa *adj.* porous
porque *conj.* because
porqué *m.* reason; cause; motive
portal *m.* porch
portalón *n.m.* gate
portátil *adj.* portable
portentoso, sa *adj.* marvelous
porvenir *m.* future
posar *v.* to rest; lodge; pose
posdata *f.* postscript
poseer *v.* to have; possess
poseído, da *adj.* possessed
posesión *f.* ownership; possession
posesivo, va *adj.* possessive
poseso, sa *adj.* possessed
posfecha *f.* postdate
posibilidad *f.* possibility
posibilitar *v.* to make; something possible
posible *adj.* possible
posición *f.* place; status; position
positivo, va *adj.* positive
posponer *v.* to postpone
posta *f.* slice; relay team
postal *adj.* postal
poste *m.* post; pillar
postergación *f.* postponement
postergar *v.* to postpone
posterior *adj.* posterior
posterioridad *f.* posteriority
postizo, za *adj.* artificial; detachable
postoperatorio, ria *adj.* postoperative
postor *m.* bidder
postrar *v.* to debilitate; humiliate
postre *m.* dessert

postremo, ma *adj.* final
postrero, ra *adj.* final
postura *f.* posture
potable *adj.* potable
potasio *m.* potassium
pote *m.* pot; jug; a kind of stew
potencia *f.* potency
potencial *adj.* potential
potente *adj.* potent; powerful
potrear *v.* to annoy; frolic
potrero *m.* pasture
potrillo *m.* colt; horse (in gym)
potro *m.* colt
práctica *f.* custom; practice
practicante *n.m.f.* medical assistant
practicar *v.* to practice
práctico, ca *adj.* practical
pradera *f.* meadowland; large prairie
prado *m.* meadow; field
preámbulo *m.* preamble
precario, ria *adj.* precarious
precaución *f.* precaution
precavido, da *adj.* cautious
precedente *adj.* preceding
preceder *v.* to precede; go before
precepto *m.* precept
preceptor, ra *m.*, *f.* tutor
preciado, da *adj.* precious
precintado, da *adj.* sealed
precintar *v.* to stamp; bind with straps
precio *m.* fare; cost; price
preciosidad *f.* beauty
precioso, sa *adj.* precious
precipitación *f.* precipitation; haste; rush
precipitar *v.* to hasten
precisamente *adv.* precisely
precisar *v.* to set; to explain
precisión *f.* precision
precocidad *f.* precocity
precognición *f.* precognition
preconcebir *v.* to preconceive
preconizar *v.* to recommend something; praise
precóz *adj.* precocious
predecesor, ra *m. f.* predecessor
predecir *v.* to foretell
predestinación *f.* predestination

predeterminar v. to predetermine
prédica f. sermon
predicado m. predicate
predicar v. to preach
predicción f. prediction
predilecto, ta adj. favorite
predio m. property
predisponer v. to predispose
predisposición f. predisposition
predominante adj. predominant
predominar v. to prevail
predominio m. predominance
preescolar adj. preschool
prefabricado, da adj. prefabricated
prefabricar v. to prefabricate
prefacio m. preface
prefectura f. prefecture
preferente adj. preferable
preferentemente adv. preferably
preferido, da adj. preferred
preferir v. to prefer
pregonar v. to divulge; proclaim
pregunta f. question
preguntar v. to ask; question
prehistoria f. prehistory
prehistórico, ca adj. prehistoric
prejuzgar v. to prejudge
preludio m. prelude
prematuro, ra adj. premature
premeditación f. premeditation
premeditadamente adv. deliberately
premeditar v. to premeditate
premiar v. to reward
premio m. prize; award
premisa f. premise
premonición f. premonition
premura f. urgency
prenatal adj. prenatal
prenda f. token; guarantee; jewel
prender v. to catch; apprehend; switch on (radio, light)
prensa f. press; newspaper; clamp
prensar v. to press
prenupcial adj. prenuptial
preñez f. pregnancy
preocupación f. concern
preocupar v. to mind; preoccupy

preparar v. to ready; fix; prepare
preponderante adj. preponderant
preposición f. preposition
prepotencia f. prepotency
prepotente adj. prepotent
prepucio m. prepuce
presa f. victim; capture; prey
prescindencia f. omission
prescindible adj. nonessential
prescindir v. to ignore
prescribir v. to prescribe
presencia f. presence
presenciar v. to witness
presentación f. presentation
presentar v. to introduce; feature
presente adj. current
preservación f. preservation
preservar v. to preserve
preservativo, va adj. preservative; prophylactic
presidencia f. presidency
presidencial adj. presidential
presidenta f. president
presidente m. president
presidiario m. convict
presidio m. prison
presidir v. to preside
presión f. pressure
presionar v. to press
prestación f. services
préstador, ra adj. lending
prestamente adj. quickly
préstamo m. loan
prestar v. to loan; lend
presteza f. promptness
prestigio m. prestige
prestigioso, sa adj. prestigious
presto, ta adj. prompt
presumible adj. presumable
presumir v. to presume
presunción f. presumption
presuntoso, sa adj. presumptuous
presuponer v. to presuppose
presuposición f. presupposition
presurizar v. to pressurize
pretencioso, sa adj. pretentious
pretender v. to attempt; to pretend
pretendiente m. claimant; pretender; suitor

pretensión f. pretension; desire
pretensioso, sa adj. pretentious
prevalecer v. to prevail
prevaleciente adj. prevailing
prevaler v. to prevail
prevención f. prevention
prevenir v. to prepare; prevent
preventivo, va adj. preventive
previamente adv. previously
prez m. glory
prima, mo f., m. cousin
primario, ria adj. primary
primate m. primate
primavera f. spring
primero, ra adj. prime; first
primitivo, va adj. primitive
primoroso, sa adj. delicate; exquisite
princesa f. princess
principado m. principality
principal adj. leading; master; principal
principalmente adv. principally
príncipe m. prince
principiante, ta adj. beginning
principiar v. to begin
principio m. beginning
pringoso, sa adj. greasy
prioridad f. priority
prisa f. haste; rush
prisión f. prison
prisionero, ra m., f. prisoner
prisma m. prism
pristino, na adj. pristine; original
privado, da adj. private
privatizar v. to privatize
privilegio m. privilege
probabilidad f. probability
probable adj. probable
probar v. to prove; try
probidad f. probity
problema m. problem
problemático, ca adj. problematic
probo, ba adj. upright
procedimiento m. procedure
procesar v. to prosecute
procesión f. procession
proceso m. process; trial
proclamación f. proclamation
proclamar v. to announce; proclaim

procreación f. procreation
procrear v. to produce; procreate
prodigar v. to waste; lavish
pródigo adj. prodigal; lavish; spendthrift
prodigioso, sa adj. marvelous
producción f. turnout; production
producir v. to yield; produce
productividad f. productivity
productivo, va adj. productive
producto m. product
profanar v. to disgrace
profesar v. to teach; to profess (a faith)
profesión f. vocation; job; profession
profesional adj. professional
profesor, ra m., f. professor; teacher
profilaxis f. prophylaxis
profundidad f. profundity
profundo, da adj. profound; deep
profusión f. profusion
profuso, sa adj. profuse
programa m. program
programación f. programming
programar v. to program
progresar v. to progress
progresión f. progress
progresista adj. progressive
progreso m. progress
prohibición f. prohibition
prohibido, da adj. forbidden
prohibir v. to prohibit something
prohibitivo, va adj. prohibitive
proliferación f. proliferation
proliferar v. to proliferate
prolífico, ca adj. prolific
prólogo m. prologue
prolongado, da adj. prolonged
prolongar v. to lengthen
promedio m. average
promesa f. vow; promise
prometedor, ra adj. promising
prometer v. to promise
prominente adj. prominent
promisorio, ria adj. promissory
promoción f. promotion
promocionar v. to promote
promovedor, ra adj. promoter;

promoting
promover v. to promote
prono, na adj. prone
pronombre m. pronoun
pronominal adj. pronominal
pronosticar v. to predict
prontitud f. promptness
pronto, ta adj. prompt; adv. soon
pronunciación f. pronunciation
pronunciar v. to pronounce
propagación f. propagation
propalar v. to divulge
propender v. be inclined
propenso, sa adj. prone
propiedad f. estate; property
propina f. gratuity
propio, pia adj. proper
proponedor, ra adj. proposing
proponer v. to intend; propose
proporción f. proportion
proporcional adj. proportional
proposición f. motion; proposition; proposal
propósito m. purpose; intention
propuesta f. proposal
propugnar v. to advocate
propulsar v. to push; reject
propulsión f. propulsion
prorratear v. to prorate
prorrogar v. to extend
prosa f. prose
prosaico, ca adj. prosaic
proscribir v. to proscribe
proscripción f. proscription
prospecto m. prospectus
prosperar v. to thrive; to prosper
prosperidad f. prosperity
próspero, ra adj. prosperous
próstata f. prostate
prostitución f. prostitution
protección f. protection
protector, ra adj. supporting; protective
proteger v. to defend; protect
proteína f. protein
protesta f. protest
protestar v. to protest; profess faith
protesto m. protest (of a bill)
protón m. proton
prototipo m. prototype

protozoario m. protozoan
provecho m. profit; benefit
provechoso, sa adj. profitable
proveer v. to cater; fill; to supply; provide
providencial adj. providential
provisión f. provision
provocación f. provocation
provocar v. to incite; provoke; antagonize
próximo, ma adj. near
prudencia f. prudence
psicología f. psychology
publicación f. publication
publicar v. to publish
público m. public
pueblo m. nation; town; population
puerta f. entrance; door
pues conj. then; for
pulgar m. thumb
pulir v. to shine; polish
pulmón m. lung
punta f. point
punto m. dot; point
puro, ra adj. pure
púrpura f. purple

Q

quantum m. quantum
que pron. that; whom
qué adj. what; which
quebrada f. gap; ravine; stream
quebradizo, za adj. fragile
quebrado, da adj. rough; broken; bankrupt
quebradura f. rupture; fracture; crack; split
quebrajar v. to crack
quebrantador, ra adj. crushing; breaking
quebrantamiento m. cracking; deterioration; breaking
quebrantar v. to crush; break; weaken
quebranto m. sorrow; loss; poor health
quebrar v. to break
quedamente adv. calmly
quedar v. to stay; be; remain
quedo, da adj. calm

quejarse v. to complain; whine
quejido m. groan
quejoso, sa adj. complaining
quema f. burning
quemadero m. incinerator
quemado, da adj. burnt; burned out
quemador, ra adj. burning
quemar v. to heat up; burn
quemazón f. burning; itching
querella f. lament; quarrel
querellante adj. complainant; plaintiff
querer v. to desire; to want m. love; affection
querido, da adj. beloved
queso m. cheese
quiebra f. crack; fissure; bankruptcy
quién pron. who
quieto, ta adj. quiet
química f. chemistry
químico, ca adj. chemical
quince adj. fifteen
quinto, ta adj. fifth
quitar v. to forbid; remove; take away

R

rábano m. radish
rabí m. rabbi
rabia f. rabies; anger; fury
rabiar v. to have rabies; get angry
rabino m. rabbi
rabioso, sa adj. furious
rabo m. stem; tail
racial adj. racial
racimo m. bunch; cluster
ración f. allowance; ration
racional adj. rational
racionalidad f. rationality
racionalista adj. rationalistic
racionalizar v. to rationalize
racionar v. to ration
racha f. gust (of wind)
rada f. bay; inlet
radar m. radar
radiación f. radiation
radiactividad f. radioactivity
radiactivo, va adj. radioactive

radiador m. radiator
radial adj. radial
radiante adj. radiant
radiar v. to radiate
radical adj. radical
radio m. radio; radius
radiodifundir v. to broadcast
radiografía f. radiography
radiograma f. radiogram
radiología f. radiology
radiólogo, ga m., f. radiologist
radioscopia f. radioscopy
raer v. to scrape; become threadbare
raid m. raid
raído, da adj. worn out
raja f. splinter; crack
rajado, da adj. cracked
rajadura f. crack
rajar v. to sliver; crack
ralo, la adj. thin; sparse
rallar v. to grate
rama f. branch; bough
ramada f. grove; branches; arbor
ramal m. branch (railway, mountain range)
rambla f. boulevard; dry ravine
ramificación f. ramification
ramificarse v. to branch
ramillete m. cluster; bouquet (flowers)
ramo m. bouquet; bunch
ramonear v. to graze
rampa f. ramp
rana f. frog
rancidez f. rancidity
rancio, cia adj. rancid
rancho m. farm
rapacidad f. rapacity
rapar v. to crop; shave
rápidamente adv. rapidly
rápido, da adj. fast; express; rapid
rapsodia f. rhapsody
rapto m. abduction; kidnapping; rapture
raqueta f. racket
raquitismo m. rickets
raramente adv. rarely
rareza f. rarity
raro, ra adj. rare; bizarre; odd
rasar v. to graze; skim

rascacielos m. skyscraper
rascadura f. scratch; scrapping
rascar v. to scrape; scratch
rascazón f. itch
rasgadura f. tear; rip
rasgar v. to tear; rip; strum(string instrument)
rasgo m. feature; trait
rasgón m. tear; rip
rasguñar v. to scratch
rasguño m. scratch
raso, sa adj. level; flat
raspador m. scraper; eraser
raspadura f. rasping; dark hardened sugar
raspante adj. abrasive
raspar v. to scratch; scrape
rastra f. trail; rake
rastrear v. to trail; track
rastrillo m. rake
rasura f. shaving
rasurar v. to shave
rata f. rat
ratero, ra m., f. petty thief; pickpocket
ratificación f. ratification
ratificatorio, ria adj. ratifying
rato m. while
ratón m. mouse
raya f. stripe; line
rayar v. to rule; streak
rayo m. beam; ray
rayón m. rayon
raza f. race; breed
razón f. cause
razonable adj. rational; reasonable
razonar v. to reason
reacción f. reaction
reaccionar v. to react
reactivación f. reactivation
reactivar v. to reactivate
readaptación f. readaptation
readaptar v. to readapt
reafirmar v. to reaffirm
reajustar v. to readjust
reajuste m. readjustment
real adj. true; real; royal
realeza f. royalty
realidad f. reality

realista adj. realistic
realizable adj. attainable
realizador, ra adj. fulfilling
realizar v. to accomplish; fulfil; realize
realzar v. to enhance
reanimar v. to reanimate
reanudación f. resumption
reanudar v. to resume; renew
reaparecer v. to reappear
reata f. rope
reavivar v. to revive; rekindle
rebaja f. reduction; discount
rebajar v. to reduce
rebanada f. slice
rebanar v. to slice
rebaño m. flock
rebelarse v. to rebel; to revolt
rebelde adj. rebel
rebelión f. revolt
reborde m. edge; flange
rebotar v. to bounce
rebuzno m. braying
recabar v. to request; obtain
recado m. message
recaer v. to relapse
recalcar v. to squeeze
recalentar v. to reheat
recapacitar v. to reconsider
recapitulación m. recapitulation
recapitular v. to recapitulate
recargar v. to overload; reload
recaudar v. to collect
recaudo m. collection; precaution
recelar v. to suspect
recelo m. jealousy; mistrust; suspicion
receloso, sa adj. suspicious
recepción f. reception
recepcionista m., f. receptionist
receptáculo m. receptacle
receptividad f. receptivity
receptivo, va adj. receptive
recesión f. recession
recetar v. to prescribe
recibidor, ra adj. receiving
recibimiento m. reception
recibir v. to accept; to receive
recibo m. receipt
reciclar v. to recycle
recién adv. recently

reciente *adj.* recent
recientemente *adv.* recently
recio, cia *adj.* severe; strong
reciprocar *v.* to reciprocate
reciprocidad *f.* reciprocity
recitación *f.* recitation; recital
recitar *v.* to recite
reclamación *f.* complaint; claim
reclamador, ra *adj.* claiming
reclamar *v.* to reclaim; to complain
reclinar *v.* to rest on
recluir *v.* to imprison; confine
reclusión *f.* imprisonment
recluso *m.* recluse; confined; prisoner
recluta *f.* recruitment; *m.* recruit
reclutamiento *m.* recruitment
reclutar *v.* to recruit
recobrar *v.* to regain; recover
recobro *m.* recovery
recodo *m.* bend; twist; turn
recogedor, ra *adj.* collecting
recoger *v.* to collect; gather; shorten
recogido, da *adj.* withdrawn
recogimiento *m.* retirement; withdrawal into oneself
recolección *f.* collection; harvest; crop
recolectar *v.* to gather
recomendable *adj.* recommendable
recomendación *f.* recommendation
recomendar *v.* to recommend
recompensa *f.* to reward
recompensar *v.* to compensate
reconciliación *f.* reconciliation
reconciliar *v.* to reconcile
reconfortar *v.* to comfort
reconocer *v.* to acknowledge
reconocido, da *adj.* grateful; acknowledged
reconquistar *v.* to recover
reconsiderar *v.* to reconsider
reconstituir *v.* to reconstitute
reconstrucción *f.* reconstruction
reconstruir *v.* to reconstruct
recontar *v.* to recount
recopilación *f.* compilation

recopilador *m.* compiler
recopilar *v.* to compile
recordación *f.* remembrance
recordar *v.* to remember
recorrer *v.* to travel; go through
recortar *v.* to reduce; to trim
recreación *f.* recreation
recrear *v.* to recreate
recreativo, va *adj.* recreational
recreo *m.* recreation
recriminación *f.* recrimination
recrudecimiento *m.* worsening
rectal *adj.* rectal
rectamente *adv.* justly
rectangular *adj.* rectangular
rectángulo *m.* rectangle
rectificación *f.* rectification
rectificar *v.* to rectify
rectitud *f.* honesty
recto, ta *adj.* right; upright
recubrir *v.* to cover
recuento *m.* recount
recuerdo *m.* memory; remembrance
reculada *f.* backing up
recuperación *f.* recovery
recuperar *v.* to recover
recurrente *adj.* recurrent
recurrir *v.* to turn; resort to
recurso *m.* remedy; resource
recusación *f.* rejection
recusar *v.* to refuse
rechazamiento *m.* rejection
rechazar *v.* to reject; rebuff
rechazo *m.* rejection
rechifla *f.* hissing
rechiflar *v.* to hiss
redacción *f.* writing; editing
redactar *v.* to edit; write
redada *f.* roundup; catch; haul
redecilla *f.* mesh; small net; hairnet
redención *f.* redemption
redil *m.* sheepfold
redimir *v.* to redeem; to exempt
rédito *m.* revenue; profit; interest
redituar *v.* to yield
redoblar *v.* to double; to repeat
redoble *m.* roll
redondez *f.* roundness
redondo, da *adj.* round
reducción *f.* reduction

reducido, da *adj.* reduced
reducir *v.* to shorten; to reduce
reductor, ra *adj.* reducing
redundancia *f.* redundancy
redundante *adj.* redundant
redundar *v.* to overflow; result in
reelegir *v.* to reelect
reembolsable *adj.* reimbursable
reembolsar *v.* to reimburse
reembolso *m.* reimbursement
reemplazar *v.* to replace
reemplazo *m.* substitution
reencarnación *f.* reincarnation
reestructuración *f.* restructuring
reestructurar *v.* to restructure
refectorio *m.* refectory
referencia *f.* reference
referente *adj.* referring
referir *v.* to refer; tell
refinado, da *adj.* refined
refinamiento *m.* refinement
refinar *v.* to refine
refinería *f.* refinery
reflejar *v.* to speculate; to reflect
reflexión *f.* reflection
reflexivo, va *adj.* reflective
reforma *f.* reform
reformación *f.* reformation
reformar *v.* to reform
reformatorio, ria *adj.* reformative
reformista *adj.* reformist
reforzado, da *adj.* reinforced
reforzar *v.* to reinforce
refracción *f.* refraction
refractar *v.* to refract
refrenar *v.* to restrain
refrescante *adj.* refreshing
refrescar *v.* to refresh
refresco *m.* refreshment
refrigeración *f.* refrigeration
refrigerador *m.* refrigerator
refrigerar *v.* to refrigerate
refrito, ta *adj.* refried
refuerzo *m.* reinforcement
refugiado, da *m. f.* refugee
refugio *m.* shelter; refuge
refulgente *adj.* refulgent
refunfuñar *v.* to grumble
refunfuño *m.* grumble
refutación *f.* rebuttal
refutar *v.* to rebut
regalado, da *adj.* easy; delicate;

dirt cheap
regalar *v.* to give away
regaliz *m.* licorice
regalo *m.* present; gift
regañar *v.* to argue
regar *v.* to water; irrigate; sprinkle; scatter
regazo *m.* lap
regeneración *f.* regeneration
regenerar *v.* to regenerate
regentar *v.* to direct; govern; manage
régimen *m.* regimen
regimentar *v.* to regiment
regio, gia *adj.* regal; magnificent
región *f.* area; region
regional *adj.* regional
regionalismo *m.* regionalism
regir *v.* to govern
registrador, ra *adj.* registering; *m.* registrar, inspector
registrar *v.* to record; register
registro *m.* search; registration; registry; register
regla *f.* rule; ruler (for lines)
reglamentación *f.* regulation
reglamentar *v.* to regulate; to adjust
reglar *v.* to regulate; draw lines on
regocijo *m.* joy
regodeo *m.* pleasure
regresar *v.* to return
regresión *f.* regression
regresivo, va *adj.* regressive
regreso *m.* return
reguero *m.* trail; stream
regulación *f.* regulation
regulador *m.* regulator
regular *adj.* regular
regularidad *f.* regularity
regurgitación *f.* regurgitation
regurgitar *v.* to regurgitate
rehabilitación *f.* rehabilitation
rehabilitar *v.* to rehabilitate
rehacer *v.* to remake
rehogar *v.* to cook slowly without water
rehuir *v.* to avoid
rehusar *v.* to refuse
reimprimir *v.* to reprint
reina *f.* queen

reinado *m.* reign
reinante *adj.* ruling
reinar *v.* to reign
reino *m.* kingdom
reír(se) *v.* to laugh
relación *f.* account; relation
relajación *f.* relaxation
relajar *v.* to relax
relatividad *f.* relativity
relevar *v.* to relieve
religión *f.* religion
religioso, sa *adj.* religious
reloj *m.* watch; clock
remediar *v.* to cure
remendar *v.* to mend; to repair
remisión *f.* remission
remolcar *v.* to tow
remontar *v.* to remount
remoto, ta *adj.* faraway
remover *v.* to remove
rencor *m.* spite; bitterness;
resentment
rencoroso, sa *adj.* spiteful
rendido, da *adj.* submissive;
exhausted; devoted (admirer)
rendir *v.* to yield; surrender
renombre *m.* renown
renovación *f.* renovation
renovado, da *adj.* renewed
renovar *v.* to renovate; reform
renunciar *v.* to surrender; waive;
renounce
reorganización *f.* reorganization
reparación *f.* repair
reparar *v.* to mend; repair
repartir *v.* to share; apportion
repasar *v.* to review; revise
repercusión *f.* repercussion
repetición *f.* repetition
repetir *v.* to repeat
réplica *f.* answer; replica; copy
replicar *v.* to reply; respond;
contradict
reposado, da *adj.* quiet; rested
reposición *f.* reposition
representacion *f.* representation
representar *v.* to represent
reproche *m.* rebuke
reproducción *f.* reproduction
república *f.* republic
repulsar *v.* to reject
requerir *v.* to want; require;

court; woo
resbalar *v.* to slip; slide; go
astray
rescatar *v.* to rescue
rescate *m.* rescue
resentimiento *m.* resentment
reserva *f.* reserve
reservación *f.* reservation
reservar *v.* to reserve
resfriar *v.* to catch a cold; cool
resguardo *m.* protection; security; amulet
residencia *f.* residence
residencial *adj.* residential
residente *m., f.* resident
residir *v.* to live; reside
resignación *f.* resignation; patience
resistencia *f.* endurance; resistance
resistir *v.* to oppose; resist
resolución *f.* resolution
resolver *v.* to settle; solve;
resolve
respaldo *m.* back (of seat);
endorsement; backing
respectivo, va *adj.* respective
respecto *m.* respect; consideration
respetable *adj.* respectable
respeto *m.* respect
respiración *f.* respiration
respirar *v.* to inhale and exhale;
breathe
responder *v.* to reply; respond
responsable *adj.* responsible
respuesta *f.* answer
restaurante *m.* restaurant
resto *m.* remainder
resultado *m.* issue; result
resultar *v.* to result
resurrección *f.* resurrection
retención *f.* retention
retener *v.* to keep; retain
retirado, da *adj.* retired
retirar *v.* to retire
retornar *v.* to return
retracción *f.* retraction
retractar *v.* to recant
retrato *m.* portrait
reumático, ca *adj.* rheumatic
reunión *f.* meeting; reunion

reunir v. to gather; collect; meet
revelación f. revelation
revelar v. to develop (photos); reveal
reverso m. reverse
revisar v. to review; inspect
revisión f. revision; inspection
revocar v. to repeal; revoke
revolución f. revolution
revolucionario, ria adj. revolutionary
revolver v. to stir up; mix; disarrange
rey m. king
rezar v. to pray
ribetear v. to hem
rico, ca adj. wealthy
ridículamente adv. ridiculously
ridículo, la adj. ridiculous
riesgo m. danger; risk
rifle m. rifle
rígido, da adj. stiff; rigid
riguroso, sa adj. severe; strict
rima f. rhyme
rincón m. corner
río m. river
riqueza f. riches
risa f. laughter
ritual m. ritual
rival m. rival
rivalidad f. rivalry
robar v. to steal
roble m. oak
robo m. robbery
robusto, ta adj. hardy; strong
rodear v. to circle; ring
rodilla f. knee
rogar v. to request; pray; beg
rojo, ja adj. red
romántico, ca adj. romantic
romper v. to smash; break
ropa f. clothing
rosa f. rose
rosado, da adj. pink
rotación f. rotation
rubí m. ruby
rubio, bia adj. blonde
rudimental adj. rudimentary
rueda f. wheel
ruido m. sound; rattle; noise

ruinar v. to ruin
rumbo m. direction; ostentation
rumor m. rumor
ruptura f. rupture
rural adj. rural
rutina f. routine; habit; custom

S

sábado m. Saturday
saber v. inform; know to
sable m. saber
sabor m. flavor; taste
sabroso, sa adj. delightful
sacar v. to pull out; get out
sacerdocio m. priesthood
sacerdote m. priest
sacerdotisa f. priestess
saco m. bag; jacket; sports coat
sacrificar v. to sacrifice
sacro, cra adj. sacred
sacudir v. to beat; tug; shake
sal f. salt
salado, da adj. salted; salty; witty; unlucky
salamandra f. salamander
salida f. exit; solution
salir v. get out; leave
saliva n. saliva
salsa f. sauce
saltador m. jumper
saltar v. to jump; leap; bounce
salto m. jump; waterfall
salud f. health
saludable adj. healthy
saludar v. salute
salvación f. salvation
salvar v. to avoid; save
salvo, va adj. safe
sandía f. watermelon
sanear v. to make right; make healthy
sangrar v. to bleed
sangre f. blood
sangriento, ta adj. bloody
sano, na adj. unharmed; wholesome; healthy
santo, ta adj. blessed
sapiente adj. wise

sapo *m.* toad
sarcástico, ca *adj.* sarcastic
sátira *f.* satire
satisfacer *v.* to satisfy
sazonado, da *adj.* flavorful
sazonar *v.* to season
se *pron.* herself; oneself; your self; himself
secadora *f.* clothes or hair dryer
secar *v.* to dry
sección *f.* section
secesión *f.* secession
seco, ca *adj.* dried
secreción *f.* secretion
secretaria *f.* secretary
secreteo *m.* whispering
secreto *m.* secret
sector *m.* sector
sectorial *adj.* sectorial
secuaz *adj.* following; under- ling; henchman
secuela *f.* consequence
secuencia *f.* sequence
secuestrar *v.* to kidnap
secuestro *m.* kidnapping
secular *adj.* secular
secularizar *v.* to secularize
secundar *v.* to second
secundario, ria *adj* secondary
sed *f.* thirst
seda *f.* silk
sedante *adj.* sedative
sedar *v.* to soothe; to sedate
sedativo, va *adj.* sedative
sedentario, ria *adj.* sedentary
sedición *f.* sedition
sediento, ta *adj.* thirsty
sedimento *m.* sediment
sedoso, sa *adj.* silky
seducción *f.* seduction
seductivo, ra *adj.* seductive
segador, ra *adj.* seductive
segar *v.* to mow; harvest
seglar *adj.* secular; lay
segmentación *f.* segmentation
segmento *m.* segment
segregación *f.* segregation
segregacionista *adj.* segre- gationist
segregar *v.* to segregate
seguido, da *adj.* consecutive
seguir *v.* to chase; follow

según *prep.* according to
segundo, da *adj.* second
segur *m.* sickle
seguramente *adv.* surely
seguridad *f.* safety
seguro, ra *adj.* sure; certain
seis sixth (of month); *m.* sing
selección *f.* selection
seleccionar *v.* to select
selectivo, va *adj.* selective
selecto, ta *adj.* select
selva *f.* woods; forest
sellar *v.* to stamp
sello *m.* stamp
semana *f.* week
semanal *adj.* weekly
semanario, ria *adj.* weekly
semántico, ca *adj.* semantic
sembrador, ra *adj.* sowing
sembrar *v.* to sow
semejante *adj.* similar
semejanza *f.* similarity
sementar *v.* to seed
semestral *adj.* semiannual
semestre *m.* semester
semiautomático, ca *adj.* semiau- tomatic
semicircular *adj.* semicircular
semicírculo *m.* semicircle
semifinalista *adj.* semifinalist
semilla *f.* seed
seminario *m.* seminary
senado *m.* senate
senador *m.* senator
sencillamente *adv.* simply
sencillez *f.* simplicity
sencillo, lla *adj.* simple; easy
senda *f.* path; trail
senil *adj.* senile
seno *m.* cavity; hollow
sensación *f.* sensation
sensato, ta *adj.* sensible
sensible *adj.* sentimental
sensitivo, va *adj.* sensitive
sentar *v.* to sit
sentencia *f.* sentence
sentenciar *v.* to sentence
sentencioso, sa *adj.* sententious
sentido, da *adj.* heartfelt
sentimental *adj.* sentimental
sentimiento *m.* sentiment
sentir *v.* to feel; to sense; to

experience
seña *f.* signal; sign
señal *f.* sign
señalar *v.* to point; to determine
señalizar *v.* to put up signs
señero, ra *adj.* solitary
señor *adj.* Mr.; Mister
señorío *m.* domain; solemnity
señorita *f.* lady; girl
señorito *m.* boy; young man
señuelo *m.* trap; bait
separación *f.* separation
separadamente *adv.* separately
separado, da *adj.* separated
separar *v.* to divide
separatista *adj.* separatist
sepelio *m.* burial
séptico, ca *adj.* septic
septiembre *m.* September
séptimo, ma *adj.* seventh
septuagésimo, ma *adj.* seventieth
sepultar *v.* to bury
sepulto, ta *adj.* buried
sepultura *f.* burial
sequedad *f.* dryness
sequía *f.* drought
ser *v.* to be; come from
serafín *m.* angel
serenar *v.* to calm
serenata *f.* serenade
serenidad *f.* serenity
serio, ria *adj.* serious
serpiente *f.* snake
servicio *m.* help; service
servilleta *f.* napkin
servir *v.* to serve
sesión *f.* session
sexto, ta *adj.* sixth
si *conj.* if
sí *adv.* yes
siempre *adv.* forever; always
siervo *m.* servant; serf
siesta *f.* nap in the afternoon
siete *adj.* seventh (of month); *m.* seven
siglo *m.* century
siguiente *adj.* next
silbato *m.* whistle
silenciar *v.* to silence
silencio *m.* silence
silencioso, sa *adj.* silent

silo *m.* silo
silla *f.* chair
simbolizar *v.* to symbolize
símbolo *m.* symbol
simetría *f.* symmetry
similar *adj.* similar
similitud *f.* similarity
simpático, ca *adj.* pleasant
simple *adj.* simple
simplicidad *f.* simplicity
simplificar *v.* to simplify
sin *prep.* without
sincronía *f.* synchrony
síndrome *m.* syndrome
sinfonía *f.* symphony
sino *conj.* but
sintetizar *v.* to synthesize
síntoma *m.* symptom
síquico, ca *adj.* psychic
sirviente *m.* servant
sitio *m.* place
situación *f.* situation
soborno *m.* bribery
sobrar *v.* to surpass; exceed
sobre *prep.* over; on; above
sobrellevar *v.* to bear
sobrenombre *m.* nickname
sobrentender *v.* to understand
sobresalir *v.* to project; stand-out
sobretodo *m.* coat; over coat
sobrevivir *v.* to survive
sobrina *f.* niece
sobrino *m.* nephew
social *adj.* social
sociedad *f.* society
sociología *f.* sociology
sociológico, ca *adj.* sociological
sociólogo, ga *m.*, *f.* sociologist
socorrer *v.* to aid
socorro *m.* aid
sodio *m.* sodium
sofá *m.* sofa
sofisma *m.* sophism
sofista *adj.* sophistic
sofisticación *f.* sophistication
sofisticado, da *adj.* sophisticated
sofocación *f.* suffocation
sofocador, ra *adj.* suffocating
sofocar *v.* to suffocate; to suppress
soga *f.* rope

soja f. soybean
sojuzgar v. to subjugate
sol m. sun
solamente adv. only
solano m. the east wind
solar adj. solar
solarium m. solarium
solaz m. relaxation
soldado m. soldier
soldador m. solderer
soldadura f. soldering
soldar v. to join
soleado, da adj. sunny
solecismo m. solecism
soledad f. loneliness
solemne adj. solemn
solemnidad f. solemnity
solevantar v. to lift
solicitación f. request
solicitante m., f. petitioner
solicitar v. to ask for; request
sólido, da adj. solid
solista m. f. soloist
solista f. soloist
soliviantar v. to irritate
soliviar v. to lift something
solo adj. alone
solsticio m. solstice
soltar v. to let go; loosen
soltero, ra adj. single
soluble adj. soluable
solución f. solution
solucionar v. to solve
solvencia f. solvenct
solventar v. to resolve
solvente adj. solvent
somático, ca adj. somatic
somatización f. somatization
somatizar v. to somatize
sombra f. shade
sombrear v. to shade
sombra f. shade
sombrar v. to shade
sombrero m. hat
sonar v. to sound
soñeto m. sonnet
sonido m. sound
sonreír v. to smile
sonrisa f. smile
soñar v. to dream
sopa f. soup
soportar v. support

soprano m. soprano
sorprender v. to surprise
sosiego m. quietness
soso, sa adj. dull; insipid
sospechar v. to suspect
sostenedor, ra m. f. supporter
sostener v. to uphold; support
sótano m. basement
Sr. abbr. señor, m. Mr.
Sra. abbr. señora, f. Mrs.
su, sus adj. her; his; its; your
suavidad f. smoothness
subastar v. to auction
subir v. to raise; go up; come up
súbito adj. hasty; sudden
sublevar v. to revolt
substancia f. substance
substancial adj. substantial
substanciar v. to substantiate
substitución f. substitution
substituir v. to substitute
surtido m. selection; supply
surtidor, ra m. supplier
surtir v. To supply something
suspender v. to interrupt
suspensión f. suspension
suspicacia f. distrust
susurrar v. to murmur to
  whisper
susurro m. whisper
sutileza f. sublety
suturar v. to suture a wound
suyo adj. their; her; his; your

T

taba f. bone of the ankle
tabacal m. field for tobacco
tabaco m. tobacco
tabaquería f. tobacco shop
taberna f. tavern
tabla f. table; board; plank; chart
tableado m. box pleats
tableta f. tablet; small plank
tacón m. heel
tacto m. touch
tafetán m. taffeta
taimado, da adj. crafty
tajada f. slice; profit
tal adj. such
talega f. bag; sack; wealth
talento m. talent

talentoso, sa *adj.* talented
talón *m.* heel
talla *f.* size; height
tallar *v.* to carve
talle *m.* figure; shape
tallo *m.* stem
tamaño ña *adj.* very big
también *adv.* too; also
tambor *m.* drum
tamboril *m.* little drum
tampoco *adv.* nor; neither
tan *adv.* as
tangible *adj.* tangible
tango *m.* tango
tantear *v.* to consider; test
tanto, ta *adj.* so many
tapar *v.* to cover; block something
tapete *m.* small carpet; doily
tapón *m.* cork
taquigrfía *f.* stenography
taquígrafo, fa *m.,f.* stenographer
tarde *f.* afternoon
tarea *f.* homework
tarjeta *f.* card
tasación *f.* appraisal
tasajear *v.* to jerk beef
tauromaquia *f.* bullfighting
taxi *m.* taxi
taxidermia *f.* taxidermy
taza *f.* bowl; cup
te *pron.* you
teatro *m.* theater
técnico, ca *adj.* technical
tecnología *f.* technology
techo *m.* ceiling; roof
tedioso, sa *adj.* tedious
tejer *v.* to knit
telefonazo *m.* telephone call
teléfono *m.* telephone
telefoto *m.* telephoto
telegrafía *f.* telegraphy
telescopico, ca *adj.* telescopic
telescopio *m.* telescope
televisión *f.* television
televisor *m.* television set
temblar *v.* to tremble
temblor *m.* earthquake
temer *v.* to be afraid of
temor *m.* fear
temperamental *adj.* temperamental

temperamento *m.* temperament; nature; weather
temperar *v.* to calm
tempestad *f.* storm
temple *m.* mood; temper
templo *m.* temple
temporada *f.* season
temporáneo, a *adj.* temporary
temprano, na *adj.* early
tendencia *f.* tendency
tender *v.* spread out
tendido, da *adj.* spread out
tenedor *m.* fork; holder; bearer
tener *v.* to contain; have; keep
tenis *m.* tennis
tensión *f.* tension
teñir *v.* to dye
teorético, ca *adj.* theoretical
teoría *f.* theory
tequila *f.* tequila
terapéutico, ca *adj.* therapeutic
tercero, ra *adj.* third
terminal *adj.* terminal
terminar *v.* to complete; end
término *m.* ending
terminología *f.* terminology
terraza *f.* terrace
terrenal *adj.* earthly
territorio *m.* territory
terror *m.* terror
testificar *v.* to testify
testigo *m.* one who sees something; witness
testimonio *m.* testimony
texto *m.* textbook
ti *pron.* yourself
tía *f.* aunt
tiburón *m.* shark
tiempo *m.* weather; time
tienda *f.* store; shop
tiento *m.* caution; touch
tierra *f.* land; country
tigre *m.* tiger
tigresa *f.* tigress
timar *v.* cheat
timbrar *v.* to stamp
timbre *m.* doorbell; buzzer
tímido, da *adj.* timid
tinte *m.* dye
tío *m.* uncle
típico, ca *adj.* typical
tipo *m.* type; kind

tiranía f. tyranny
tirante adj. tight
tirar v. to throw
títere m. puppet
toalla f. towel
tobillo m. ankle
tobogán m. slide
tocar v. to ring; handle; touch
todavía adv. every; all; even still
tolerante adj. tolerant
toma f. intake; taking
tomar v. to have; take
tomate m. tomato
tonada f. tune; song
tonel m. barrel
tonificar v. to tone
tonto, ta m. f. fool
tópico m. topic
topógrafo m. topographer
toque m. beat; touch
torcer v. to sprain; bend; twist
torear v. to fight (bulls)
tormento m. torment
tornado m. tornado
tornillo m. screw
toro m. bull
torre f. tower; steeple; turret
tórrido, da adj. torrid
torta f. cake; torte
tortuga f. turtle
tostado, da adj. roasted; toasted
tostar v. to roast; toast
total adj. total
totalidad f. totality
tóxico adj. toxic
trabajador, ra m. f. worker
trabajar v. to work
trabajo m. job; work
trabar v. to fasten; bolt
tracción f. traction
tradición f. tradition
tradicional adj. traditional
traducir v. to express; translate
traer v. to carry; bring
tráfico m. traffic
tragar v. to devour; swallow
traje m. dress; suit
trajear v. to dress
tramar v. to scheme
tranquilidad f. tranquility
transformación f. transformation
transfusión f. transfusion

tránsito m. traffic
transitorio, ria adj. temporary
translúcido adj. translucent
transmitir v. to transmit
tras prep. behind; after
trasladar v. to transcribe; move
traslado m. transfer
traspasar v. to pierce; transfer;
  violate (law)
tratar v. to process; handle
trato m. treatment; deal
trauma m. trauma
traumático, ca adj. traumatic
travesura f. mischief
traza f. plan; looks
trazar v. to draw; trace
trece adj. thirteen
tregua f. rest; truce
treinta adj. thirty
treintavo, va adj., m. thirtieth
tremendo, da adj. terrible;
  horrible
tremor m. tremor
tren m. train
tres adj. three; third (of month);
  m. three
treceavo adj. thirteenth
triangular adj. triangular
tribulación f. tribulation
tributario, ria adj. tributary
trigo m. wheat
trilogía f. trilogy
trillizo, za f. m. triplet
trío m. trio
triplicación f. triplication
triplo, pla adj. triple
triste adj. miserable; sad
tristeza f. sorrow; sadness
triunfante adj. triumphant
trivial adj. trivial
trombón m. trombone
trompeta f. trumpet
tronar v. to thunder
troncha f. slice; cushy job
tropical adj. tropical
trópico m. tropic
tú pron. you
tuba f. tuba
tubo m. tube
tubular adj. tubular
tucán m. toucan
tulipá m. tulip

tumbar v. to knock out
tumor m. tumor
túnica f. tunic
turbación f. confusion
turbador, ra adj. disturbing
turbio, bia adj. cloudy; turbid; dishonest
turista m. f. tourist
turno m. turn
tuyo adj. yours

U

ubérrimo, ma adj. luxuriant
ubicación f. placing
ubicar v. locate
úlcera f. ulcer
últimamente adv. finally
último, ma adj. final; last
ultrajar v. to insult
ultraje m. insult; rape
ultravioleta adj. ultraviolet
umbilical adj. umbilical
un indef. art. an; a
uña f. fingernail
unánime adj. unanimous
undécimo, ma adj. eleventh
ungüento m. ointment
único, ca adj. single; sole
unidad f. unity
unido, da adj. united
unificación f. unification
unificar v. to unify
uniforme adj. even; uniform
unilateral adj. unilateral
unión f. joint; unity; syndicate
unir(se) v. to unite together
universal adj. worldwide
universidad f. university

V

vaca f. cow
vacación f. vacation
vaciar v. to void; empty
vacilar v. to falter; vacillate; fool around
vacío adj. empty; void
vacunación f. vaccination
vagar v. to roam; stray; wander
vago, ga adj. hazy; wandering; vague

vaho m. vapor
valentía f. courage; valor
valeroso, sa adj. valorous; brave
válido, da adj. good; valid
valiente adj. brave; valiant
valor m. valor; worth
valle m. valley
vanidad f. vanity
vano, na adj. vain
vapor m. steam
variable adj. variable
variación f. change; variation
variar v. to change; to vary
variedad f. variety
varón m. man; male
vascular adj. vascular
vaso m. vessel; glass; tumbler
vasto, ta adj. vast
vaticinar v. to predict
vecinamente adv. nearby
vecindad f. vicinity
vector m. vector
veda f. prohibition
vedar v. to suspend; prohibit
vegetación f. vegetation
vehículo m. vehicle
veinte adj. twenty; twentieth (of month); m. twenty
vejar v. ill-treat; abuse; to persecute; vex
vejiga f. bladder
velar v. to veil; guard; keep vigil
velocidad f. velocity
vena f. vein
vencer v. to conquer; beat
vencido adj. conquered
vender v. to sell
venenosidad f. poisonous
venerable adj. venerable
venir v. to come
ventana f. window
ventilación f. ventilation
ventoso, sa adj. windy
ventura f. happiness
ver v. to sight; see
verano m. summer
verbalmente adv. verbally
verbo m. verb
verdad f. truth
verídico, ca adj. true

verde *adj.* green
versión *f.* version
vertical *adj.* vertical
vestido *m.* clothing; dress; suit
vestir *v.* to attire; dress; clothe
vez *f.* time
vía *f.* means; way
viajar *v.* to journey; travel
viaje *m.* journey; trip
vial *adj.* traffic
vianda *f.* food
vibración *f.* vibration
vibrar *v.* to shake; vibrate
víctima *f., m.* victim
vida *f.* life
viejo, ja *adj.* aged; old
viento *m.* wind
viernes *m.* Friday
vigilante *adj.* watchful; vigilant
vigilar *v.* to guard
vigor *m.* strength; vigor
vigoroso, sa *adj.* forceful
vino *m.* wine
viñedo *m.* vineyard
violencia *f.* violence
violento, ta *adj.* violent
virulento, ta *adj.* virulent
viscosidad *f.* viscosity
visión *f.* vision
visitar *v.* to visit
vista *f.* sight; view
visual *adj.* visual
viuda *f.* widow
viudo *m.* widower
vivaz *adj.* lively
vívido, da *adj.* vivid
vivir *v.* to reside; live
vivo, va *adj.* vivid; lively
vocabulario *m.* vocabulary
vocación *f.* job; occupation
vocalización *f.* vocalization
volar *v.* to fly
voltear *v.* to turn over
volumen *m.* volume
voluntario, ria *adj.* voluntary
volver *v.* to turn; return; recur
vos *pron., m., f.* you
vosotras *pron., f. pl.* you
vosotros *pron., m. pl.* you
votar *v.* to vote
voz *f.* voice
vuestra *adj.* your

W

wat *m.* watt
welter *m.* *welterweight*
whisky *m.* whiskey

X

xenon *m.* xenon
xilófono *m.* xylophone
xilografía *f.* xylography

Y

y *conj.* and
ya *adv.* now; already
yarda *f.* yar
yate *m.* yacht
yema *f.* egg yolk; bud; fingertip
yermo *m.* wilderness
yerno *m.* son-in-law
yo *pron.* I
yugular *adj.* jugular
yute *m.* jute

Z

zafar(se) *v.* loosen; escape
zagal *m.* boy; lad
zamarro *m.* sheepskin
zambullida *f.* dive; plunge
zambullir *v.* to plunge into
zanahoria *f.* carrot
zanja *f.* trench; ditch
zapatero *m.* shoemaker
zapatilla *f.* slipper
zapato *m.* shoe
zar *m.* czar
zarzamora *f.* blackberry
zoco, ca *adj.* left-handed
zodíaco *m.* zodiac
zona *f.* zone
zoología *f.* zoology
zorra *f.* fox
zorro *m.* fox
zozobrar *v.* to founder; capsize
zumbar *v.* whir; buzz; tease; joke
zumo *m.* juice
zumoso, sa *adj.* juicy
zurcir *v.* to darn; mend

a *indef. article* una; un
aback *adv.* atrás
abacus *n.* ábaco
abandon *v.* abandonar
abase *v.* humillar; rebajar
abate *v.* degradar; reducir
abbey *n.* abadía
abbreviation *n.* abreviación; abreviatura
abdicate *v.* abdicar
abdomen *n.* abdomen
abduct *v.* secuestrar
aberration *n.* aberración
abet *v.* instigar; ayudar
abhor *v.* aborrecer
abide *v.* habitar; continuar
ability *n.* habilidad
abject *adj.* abyecto
abjure *v.* conjurar; rogar
able *adj.* capaz; competente
abnegate *v.* renunciar; negarse de
abnormal *adj.* anormal
aboard *adv. prep.* a bordo de
abode *n.* domicilio
abolish *v.* abolir
abominate *v.* abominar
aborigines *n.* aborígenes
abortion *n.* aborto
abound *v.* abundar
about *prep.* alrededor de; respecto a; a eso de
above *prep.* sobre; encima de; superior a
abrasion *n.* abrasión
abreast *adv.* de frente; a fondo
abridge *v.* abreviar; resumir
abroad *adv.* fuera de casa; en el extranjero
abrogate *v.* abrogar
abrupt *adj.* escarpado; abrupto; áspero
abscess *n.* absceso
abscond *v.* fugarse; ocu tarse; esconderse
absent *adj.* ausente
absolute *adj.* completo; absoluto
absolve *v.* absolver
absorb *v.* absorber
abstain *v.* abstenerse
abstemious *adj.* abstract;

abstemio *n.* extracio; re sumen
abstract *v.* abstraer
absurd *adj.* absurdo
abundant *adj.* abundante
abuse *v.* abusar de; insultar; maltratar; violar
abyss *n.* abismo; precipicio
academic *adj.* académico
academy *n.* academia
accede *v.* acceder; consentir
accelerate *v.* acelerar
accent *n.* acento; énfasis
accept *v.* aceptar; recibir; admitir; aprobar
access *n.* acceso
accessible *adj.* accesible
accessory *n.* accesorio; cómplice
accident *n.* accidente
acclaim *v.* aclamar
acclimate *v.* aclimatar
accolade *n.* acolada
accommodate *v.* acomodar
accompany *v.* acompañar
accomplice *n.* cómplice
accomplish *v.* cumplir; acabar
accord *n.* acuerdo; *v.* acordar; convenir
accordion *n.* acordeón
account *v.* explicar; *n.* cuenta; razón; narracion
accountable *adj.* responsable (de; ante)
accumulate *v.* acumular
accuracy *n.* exactitud; precisión
accurate *adj.* exacto; fiel
accuse *v,* acusar; culpar
accustom *v.* acostumbrar; habituar
acetic *n.* acético
acetone *n.* acetona
ache *n.* dolor persistente; *v.* doler
achieve *v.* llevar a cabo; realizar; lograr
acid *adj.* ácido
acknowledge *v.* reconocer; admitir; aceptar
acme *n.* cima; colmo
acne *n.* acné

acolyte *n.* acólito; monaguillo

acom *n.* bellota

acoustics *n.* acústica

acquaint *v.* enterar (de); familiarizarse (con)

acquaintance *n.* conocido; conocimiento

acquiesce *v.* consentir; aceptar; conformarse con

acquire *v.* adquirir; obtener

acquit *v.* absolver; exonerar

acre *n.* acre

acrid *adj.* acre; amargo

acrimony *n.* acrimonia

acrobat *n.* acróbata

across *prep., adv.* al otro lado; horizontalmente; a través de

act *n.* acción; hecho; acto; *v.* fingir; hacer; actuar

action *n.* acción; movimiento; desarrollo; trama; litigio

active *adj.* activo

actor *n.* actor

actress *n.* actriz

actual *adj.* real; presente

acuity *n.* agudeza

acumen *n.* perspicacia

acute *adj.* agudo; ingenioso

adage *n.* adagio

adamant *adj.* firme

adapt *v.* adaptar

add *v.* sumar; añadir

addition *n.* adición; suma

address *v.* dirigir (se a)

adept *n., adj.* experto

adequate *adj.* adecuado; apto

adhere *v.* adherirse; pegarse; cumplir

adhesive *adj.* adhesivo

adjacent *adj* adyacente

adjective *n.* adjetivo

adjoin *v.* juntar; estar contiguo

adjourn *v.* suspender

adjudge *v.* juzgar; sentenciar

adjust *v.* ajustar; adaptar

adjutant *n.* ayudante

adlib *v.* improvisar

administer *v.* administrar

administration *n.* administración

admire *v.* admirar

admissible *adj.* admisible; permitido

admission *n.* entrada; confesión; reconocimiento

admit *v.* confesar; admitir; reconocer

admonish *v.* amonestar; reprender

adobe *n.* adobe

adolescence *n.* adolescencia

adopt *v.* adoptar; aceptar

adore *v.* adorar

adorn *v.* adornar; engalanar

adrenaline *n.* adrenalina

adroit *adj.* hábil; diestro

adulation *n.* adulación

adult *adj.* adulto; maduro; *n.* persona mayor

adultery *n.* adulterio

advance *v.* avanzar; mejorar; adelantar

advantage *n.* ventaja; delantera

adventure *n.* aventura

adventuresome *adj.* aventurado

adverb *n.* adverbio

adversary *n.* adversario; trincante

adversity *n.* adversidad

advertise *v.* publicar; anunciar; divulgar

advice *n.* consejo; opinión; aviso

advise *v.* aconsejar; recomendar; avisar

advocate *v.* abogar

adz, adze *n.* azuela

aegis *n.* égida

aerate *v.* airear; ventilar; orear

aerial *adj.* aéreo

aesthete *n.* esteta

aesthetic *adj.* estético

afar *adv.* lejos; distante; desde lejos

affable *adj.* afable; cariñoso

affair *n.* asunto; negocio; aventura amorosa

affect *v.* afectar; influir en; impresionar

affection *n.* afección; cariño; afecto

affectionate *adj.* cariñoso

affidavit *v.* declaración jurada

affinity *n.* afinidad
affirm *v.* afirmar
affirmative *n.* afirmativo
affix *v.* añadir; fijar
affliction *n.* aflicción
affluence *n.* afluencia abundancia
affluent *adj.* afluente
afford *v.* tener medios para; dar
affront *v.* afrentar
afire *adj., adv.* ardiendo
aflame *adj., adv.* en llamas
afloat *adv.* a flote
afoul *adj., adv.* enredado
afraid *adj.* atemorizado
afresh *adv.* de nuevo; otra vez
aft *adj., adv.* en (a) popa
after *prep.* detrás de; después de
afterbirth *n.* secundinas
afternoon *n.* tarde
afterwards *adv.* después
again *adv.* otra vez; de nuevo
against *prep.* contra
agape *adj., adv.* boquiabierto
age *n.* edad
aged *adj.* viejo; envejecido
agency *n.* agencia; acción; departamento
agenda *n., pl.* orden del día
agent *n.* agente; representante
agglomerate *v.* aglomerar
aggrandize *v.* engrandecer
aggravate *v.* agravar; irritar; exasperar
aggregate *n.* agregado
aggression *n.* agresión
aggressive *adj* agressivo
aghast *adj.* horrorizado
agil *adj.* ágil
agility *n.* agilidad
agitate *v.* agitar; inquietar
aglow *adj.* fulgurante
agnostic *n., adj.* agnóstico
ago *adj.* hace; ha
agony *n.* agonía; angustia
agrarian *adj.* agrario
agree *v.* acordar; estar de acuerdo con
agreeable *adj.* agradable; conforme
agreement *n.* acuerdo; convenio
agriculture *n.* agricultura

aground *adj., adv.* encallado
ahead *adv.* de frente; adelante de
aid *v.* ayudar; auxiliar
ailment *n.* enfermedad; dolencia
aim *v.* aspirar; apuntar
air *n.* aire; aspecto
air conditioner *n.* acondicionador de aire
airplane *n.* avión
airport *n.* aeropuerto
airraid *n.* ataque aéreo
airy *adj.* ligero; alegre
aisle *n.* nave lateral; pasillo
ajar *adj., adv.* entreabierto
akin *adj.* semejante; con sanguíneo
alabaster *n.* alabastro
alacrity *n.* alacridad
alarm *n.* alarma
alarmist *n.* alarmista
albatross *n.* albatros
albeit *conj.* aunque
albino *n.* albino
albumin *n.* albúmina
alchemy *n.* alquimia
alcohol *n.* alcohol
ale *n.* cerveza
alee *adj.* a sotavento
alert *adj.* alerto
alfalfa *n.* alfalfa
alga *n.* alga
algebra *n.* algebra
alias *n.* alias
alib *n.* coartada; excusa
alien *n.* extranjero; forastero
alienate *v.* enajenar
alight *v.* bajar; desmontar
align *v.* alinear
alike *adj.* semejante
aliment *n.* alimento
alimentary *adj* alimenticio
alimony *n.* alimentos
alive *adj.* vivo; viviente; activo
alcalize *v.* alcalizar
all *adj., n.* todo
allay *v.* aliviar; aquietar
allegation *n.* alegación
allege *v.* alegar; declarar

alleged *adj.* supuesto; alegado
allegiance *n.* lealtad
allergy *n.* alergia
alleviate *v.* calmar; mitigar
alley *n.* callejuela
alliance *n.* alianza
alligator *n.* caimán; lagarto
allocate *v.* colocar
allocation *n.* reparto; colocación
allot *v.* asignar; distribuir; adjudicar
allow *v.* ceder; permitir
allowance *n.* ración; subvención; permisó
alloy *n.* aleación
allude *v.* aludir
allure *v.* tentar; fascinar
allusion *n.* alusión
alluvium *n.* derrubio
ally *n.* aliado; confederado
almanac *n.* almanaque
almighty *adj.* omnipotente
almond *n.* almendra
almost *adv.* casi
alms *n.* limosna
aloft *adv.* en alto
alone *adj.* solo
along *adv., con., prep.* a lo largo de
aloof *adv.* desde lejos
aloud *adv.* en voz alta; fuerte
alphabet *n.* alfabeto; abecedario
already *adv.* ya
also *adv.* también; además
altar *n.* altar
alter *v.* cambiar; alterar; modificar
alteration *n.* alteración; arreglo; cambio
altercation *n.* altercación
alter ego *n.* alter ego
alternate *v.* alternar
alternative *n.* alternativa
although *conj.* aunque
altimeter *n.* altímetro
alto *n.* alto; contralto
altogether *adv.* en total; del todo; por completo
aluminum *n.* aluminio
alumna *n., f.* graduada
alumnus *n.* graduado

always *adv.* siempre
am *abbr.* antemeridiano
amalgam *n.* amalgama
amalgamate *v.* amalgamar
amalgamate *v.* amalogamar
amass *v.* acumular; amontonar
amateur *n.* aficionado
amaze *v.* asombrar
amazement *n.* sorpresa; asombro
amazon *n.* amazona
ambassador *n.* embajador
amber *n.* ámbar
ambidextrous *adj.* ambidextro
ambiguity *n.* ambigüedad; doble sentido
ambiguous *adj.* ambiguo
ambition *n.* ambición; aspiración
ambitious *adj.* ambicioso
ambivalence *n.* ambivalencia
amble *v.* amblar; andar lentamente
ambulatory *adj.* ambulante
ambuscade *n.* emboscada
ameba *n.* amiba
ameliorate *v.* mejorar
amelloration *n.* mrjora
amen *int.* amén
amenable *adj.* dócil
amend *v.* enmendar; corregir
amends *n., pl.* compensación
amenity *n.* amenidad
American *adj.* americano
amethyst *n.* amatista
amiable *adj.* amable
amicable *adj.* amistoso
amid *prep.* en medio de; entre
amidships *adv.* en medio del navío
amiss *adv., adj.* impropiamente; mal
amnesty *n.* amnistía
among *prep.* en medio de
ample *adj.* abundante
amplify *v.* amplificar
amusement *n.* diversión; pasatiempo
an *indef. article* una; un; uno
ancestor *n.* antepasado
ancient *adj.* antiguo
and *conj.* y
angel *n.* ángel
angry *adj.* enfadado

animal n. animal
animate v. animar; dar vida a
animation n. animación
ankle n. tobillo
annihilate v. aniquilar
anniversary n. aniversario
announce v. anunciar; proclamar
announcement n. anuncio
annoyance n. fastidio; molestia; incomodidad
another adj., pron. otro; uno más
answer v. contestar; responder
ant n. hormiga
antagonize v. enemistar; provocar hostilidad
antelope n. antílope
anterior adj. anterior
antibiotic n. antibiótico
anticipate v. anticipar; esperar
anticipation n. anticipación; antelación
antique adj. antiguo
antisocial adj. antisocial
anxious adj. ansioso; inquieto; preocupado
any adj., pron. cualquier; cualquiera; alguno; algún
anybody pron. alguien
anyone pron. alguien; alguno
anything pron. algo
apartment n. apartamento
ape n. simio; antropoide
apologize v. disculparse
apparel n. ropa
appear v. parecer; aparecer
appearance n. apariencia; aspecto
appetite n. apetito
applaud v. aplaudir
apple n. manzana
application n. aplicación; solicitud de empleo
apply v. aplicar; solicitar empleo
appraise v. valorar; evaluar
approach v. aproximarse a
approval n. aprobación
approve v. aprobar
approximate v. aproximar(se)
April n. abril

aquarium n. acuario; pecera
architect n. arquitecto
architecture n. arquitectura
arctic adj. ártico
arena n. arena; estadio
argue v. argumentar; razonar
argument n. disputa; argumento
aristocrat n. aristócrata
arithmetic n. aritmética
arm n. brazo
armful n. brazado; brazada
around adv. alrededor; aproximadamente
arrangement n. arreglo; orden; convenio; adaptación
arrest v. detener; arrestar; capturar
arrive v. llegar; arribar
arrogant adj. arrogante; soberbio
art n. arte
articulate v. articular
articulation n. articulación
artificial adj. artificial
artist n. artista
artistic adj. artístico
as conj., adv. como
ascend v. subir; ascender
ascribe v. atribuir
ashamed adj. avergonzado
ask v. rogar; preguntar
asleep adj. dormido; adv. dormidamente
aspirin n. aspirina
assault v. asaltar; atacar
assemble v. juntar; reunir
assembly n. asamblea; reunión
assign v. asignar; designar
assignment n. asignación; tarea; deber
assist v. ayudar
assistance n. ayuda; asistencia
astonish v. asombrar
astonishment n. asombro
astrology n. astrología
at prep. a; en
athlete n. atleta
athletic adj. atlético
atom n. átomo
attach v. pegar; sujetar
attack v. atacar
attempt v. intentar; probar

attend v. asistir; cuidar
attention n. atención; cuidado
attract v. atraer
attraction n. atracción
audience n. público; auditorio; audiencia
audition n. audición
August n. agosto
aunt n. tía
author n. autor
authority n. autoridad
authorize v. autorizar
autobiography n. autobiografía
automatic adj. automático
avenge v. vengar; vindicar
avenue n. avenida
average adj. promedio; término medio
await v. esperar
awake v. despertar(se)
away adv. lejos; a distancia
awful adj. horrible; atroz; desagradable
awkward adj. tosco; torpe; desmañado

B

baboon n. babuino
babushka n. pañuelo para la cabeza
baby n. niño; bebé; nene
bachelor n. soltero
back n. espalda
backbone n. espinazo; espina dorsal
backer n. promotor; financidor
backgammon n. chaquete (juego)
backup n. suplente; reserva
backward adv. hacia atrás
bacon n. tocino; tocineta
bacterium n. bacteria
bad adj. malo
badge n. insignia; símbolo
baffle v. desconcertar; confundir
bag n. bolso; saco; cartera
baggage n. equipaje; maletas
bail v. dar fianza
bait n. carnada
bake v. cocer en horno
baker n. panadero

baking n. cocción al horno
balance n. equilibrio; saldo; contrapeso
bald adj. calvo
ball n. pelota; bola
ballerina n. bailarina (de ballet)
ballet n. ballet
balloon n. globo; balón
ballot n. balota; papeleta para votar
ban v. prohibir
banana n. plátano guineo; banana
bandage v. vendar
bandit n. bandido
banish v. desterrar; deportar
bank n. banco
banker n. banquero
baptism n. bautismo
bar v. excluir de; impedir que
barber n. peluquero; barbero
barbershop n. peluquería; barbería
bare adj. desnudo; v. desnudar
barely adv. apenas; simplemente
barge n. lanchón; gabarra
barium n. bario
bark v. ladrar; n. ladrido
barn n. granero; establo
barometer n. barómetro
baron n. barón
baroness n. baronesa
barrel n. barril
baseball n. béisbol
basic adj. básico
basket n. cesta; canasta
basketball n. baloncesto
bat v. golpear, n. maza; bate; murciélago
bath n. baño
bathe v. bañar(se)
battle v. luchar, n. ucha
bay n. bahía
be v. estar; ser
beach n. playa
beak n. pico (de ave)
beam n. rayo (luz); viga; tablón
bear n. oso
beat v. vencer; golpear
beautiful adj. hermoso

beauty *n.* belleza
because *conj.* porque; ya que
become *v.* hacer(se)
bed *n.* cama
bedroom *n.* alcoba; recámara; cuarto de dormir
bee *n.* abeja
beehive *n.* colmena
before *prep.* antes de; *adv.* delante
begin *v.* comenzar; empezar
beginning *n.* comienzo; principio
behavior *n.* comportamiento
behind *adv.* atrás; detrás; *prep.* detrás de; tras
being *n.* ser
believable *adj.* creíble
believe *v.* creer
bell *n.* cascabel; campana
belongings *n.* pertenencias
below *adv.* abajo; *prep.* debajo
belt *n.* cinturón
bench *n.* banco; banca; judio catura
beneath *prep.* debajo de
benediction *n.* bendición
beneficent *adj.* benéfico
beneficial *adj.* beneficioso
benefit *v.* beneficiar(se)
benevolence *n.* benevolencia
benevolent *adj.* benévolo
besides *prep.* además de
best *adj.* mejor; superior; óptimo
betray *v.* traicionar; delatar; revelar
better *adv.* mejor
between *adv.* en medio; *prep.* entre
beverage *n.* bebida
beyond *prep.* después de
Bible *n.* Biblia
bicycle *n.* bicicleta
bicyclist *n.* ciclista
big *adj.* grande
bike *n.* bicicleta
bill *n.* pico (de ave); cuenta (de banco, en restaurante); billete (dinero)
billboard *n.* cartelera
billiards *n.* billar

bind *v.* encuadernar; atar
biographic *adj.* biográfico
biography *n.* biografía
biology *n.* biología
biplane *n.* biplano
bird *n.* pájaro
birth *n.* nacimiento
birthday *n.* cumpleaños
bisect *v.* bisecar
bishop *n.* obispo
bit *n.* pizca; trocito
bite *v.* picar; morder
bitterness *n.* rencor
bizarre *adj.* raro
black *adj.* negro
blacken *v.* ennegrecer; difamar
blank *n., adj.* blanco
blanket *n.* manta; frazada; cobija
blast *v.* destruir; explotar; *n.* explosión; ráfaga
blemish *v.* manchar
bless *v.* bendecir
blind *v.* cegar; *adj.* ciego
blindness *n.* ceguera
bliss *n.* felicidad; gloria
block *n.* manzana; cuadra; bloque (madera); *v.* obstruir; bloquear
blockade *adj.* bloqueo
blockage *n.* obstrucción
blond *adj.* rubio
blood *n.* sangre
bloom *v.* florecer *n.* flor
blouse *n.* blusa
blow *v.* inflar; soplar
blue *adj.* azul
blunt *adj.* abrupto; rudo
board *n.* consejo; junta; mesa; comida; pensión
boat *n.* barco; bote
body *n.* cuerpo
bold *adj.* descarado; arrojado; intrépido; valiente
bone *n.* hueso
bony *adj.* huesudo
book *n.* libro
boom *n.* prosperidad repentina; estampido
boot *n.* bota
bore *v.* aburrir; taladrar; barrenar

born adj. nacido
borrow v. pedir prestado; apropiarse de
boss n. jefe
botany n. botánica
both adj. los dos; ambos
bottle n. botella
bough n. rama
boulevard n. avenida; bulevar
bounce v. rebotar
bound v. saltar
bounteous adj. abundante
bouquet n. ramo
boxer n. boxeador
boy n. chico; chiquillo; muchacho
bracket n. soporte; paréntesis
brake v. frenar
branch n. rama
brave adj. valiente
bread n. pan
break v. quebrar; romper
breakfast n. desayuno
breath n. respiración
bribe v. cohechar; sobornar
bridge n. puente
brief adj. breve; corto
bright adj. brillante; claro
brightness n. lustre; esplendor; luminosidad
brilliant adj. brillante; talentoso
bring v. traer
brisk adj. vigoroso
broken adj. roto; quebrado
bronze n. bronce
brook n. arroyo
broom n. escoba
brother n. hermano
brother-in-law n. cuñado
brow n. ceja
brown adj. moreno; castaño
bruise n. contusión; magulladura
brush n. cepillo
brutal adj. brutal
budget n. presupuesto
bug n. chinche; fanático
build v. construir
building n. edificio
bull n. toro
bullet n. bala

bump n. choque; protuberancia; chichón
bunch n. racimo
bureaucracy n. burocracia
bureaucrat n. burócrata
burglar n. ladrón
burglarize v. robar
burn v. incendiar
burnt adj. quemado
burst v. explotar
bus n. autobús
bush n. arbusto; matorral; maleza
business n. oficio; ocupación; negocio; comercio
but conj. pero
butter n. mantequilla
buy v. comprar
buyer n. comprador
by adv.,prep. cerca; cerca de; por

C

cab n. taxi
cabala n. cábala
cabbage n. col; repollo
cabdriver n. taxista
cabin n. cabaña; camarote
cabinet n. gabinete; armario
cabinetwork n. ebanistería
cable n. cable
cablegram n. cablegrama
cacao n. cacao
cachet n. sello de distinción
cactus n. cacto
cadaver n. cadáver
caddie n. portador de palos (golf)
cadet n. cadete
cadmium n. cadmio
caduceus n. caduceo
cafe n. café
cafeteria n. cafetería
caffeine n. cafeína
cage n. jaula
cake n. pastel; torta; bizcocho
calamine n. calamina
calamity n. calamidad
calcification n. calcificación
calcify v. calcificar
calcium n. calcio

calculate v. calcular
calculated adj. intencional
calculating adj. calculador
calculation n. cálculo
calculator n. calculadora
caldron n. caldera
calendar n. calendario
caliber n. calibre
calibrate v. calibrar
calico n. calico
caliper n. calibrador
caliph n. califa
calisthenics n. calistenia
call v. llamar
caller n. visitante
calligrapher n. calígrafo
calligraphy n. caligrafía
calling n. vocación
callous adj. calloso; duro; insensible
callow adj. inmaturo; inexperto
callus n. callo
calm v. calmar(se); n. calma
calmness n. tranquillidad
caloric adj. calórico
calorie n. caloría
calumniate v. calumniar
calyx n. cáliz
calvary n. calvario
cambium n. cámbium; cambio
camel n. camello
camellia n. camelia
cameo n. camafeo
camera n. cámara
camp v. acampar
campaign n. campaña
camper n. campista
camphor n. alcanfor
can v. poder
canary n. canario
cancel v. cancelar; suprimir; anular
cancellation n. cancelación
cancer n. cáncer
cancerous adj. canceroso
candescent adj. candente
candid adj. franco
candidacy n. candidatura
candidate n. candidato
candied adj. escarchado
candle n. cirio; vela
candleholder n. candelero

candy n. azucar cristalizada; caramelo; confite; bombón
cane n. caña; bastón
canine adj. canino
canned adj. enlatado
cannibal n. caníbal
cannon n. cañón
canoe n. canoa
cantaloupe n. una clase de melón
canteen n. cantina; cantimplora
canvas n. lona; lienzo; pintura
canyon n. cañón; desfiladero
cap n. tapa; gorra
capability n. capacidad
capable adj. capaz
capacity n. capacidad
caper n. cabriola; alcaparra
capillary n. vaso; capilar
capital n., adj. capital
capitalist n. capitalista
capitalistic adj. capitalista
capitalize v. capitalizar
capitally adv. admirablemente
capitol n. capitolio
capitulate v. capitular
caprice n. capricho
capsule n. cápsula
captain n. capitán
caption n. subtítulo (cine); encabezamiento; leyenda
captious adj. capcioso
captivate v. cautivar
captivation n. encanto; fascinación
captive adj. cautivo; prisionero; cautivado; fascinado
capture v. capturar
car n. coche; carro; auto
caramel n. caramelo
carat n. quilate
caravan n. caravana
carbide n. carburo
carbohydrate n. carbohidrato
carbon n. carbono
carbuncle n. carbunco
carburetor n. carburador
carcinogenic adj. cancerígeno
card n. tarjeta; naipe; carta (de baraja)
cardiac adj. cardíaco
cardinal adj. cardinal

cardiology n. cardiología

care v. cuidar; importarle a uno

career n. carrera; profesión

carefree adj. despreocupado; alegre

careful adj. cuidadoso

careless adj. espontáneo; descuidado

caress n. caricia

caretaker n. portero; cuidador; guardián

cargo n. carga; cargamento

caricature n. caricatura

carnal adj. carnal

carnival n. carnaval

carnivorous adj. carnívoro

carousal n. jarana; parranda

carousel n. carrusel; tiovivo; caballitos

carpentry n. carpintería

carpet n. alfombra; tapiz; tapete

carriage n. carruaje; coche; porte del cuerpo

carrier n. carrero

carrot n. zanahoria

carry v. lograr; llevar

cart n. carro; carreta; carretón

cartilage n. cartílago

cartload n. carretada

cartoon n. tira cómica; historieta

cartridge n. cartucho

carve v. esculpir; tallar; trinchar (slice food)

case n. caja; condición; caso; estuche

cash n. dinero efectivo

cashier n. cajero

cashmere n. cachemira; casimir

casino n. casino

cask n. barril; tonel

casserole n. cacerola

cassette n. casete

cast v. tirar; plancar; echar

castanets n. castañuelas

caste n. casta

castle n. castillo

casual adj. casual

casually adv. casualmente

casuistry n. casuística

cat n. gato

catabolism n. catabolismo

catalog n. catálogo

catalyst n. catalizador

catalytic adj. catalítico

catalyze v. catalizar

catapult n. catapulta

cataract n. catarata; salto de agua grande

catastrophe n. catástrofe

catastrophic adj. catastrófico

catatonic adj. catatónico

catch v. atrapar; coger

catcher n. receptor

catching adj. pegadizo; atrayente

catchy adj. capcioso

catechism n. catecismo

categoric adj. categórico

categorically adv. categoricamente

categorize v. categorizar

category n. categoría

caterpillar n. oruga

caterwaul v. chillar; maullar (gato)

catharsis n. catarsis

cathedral n. catedral

cathode n. cátodo

catnip n. nébeda; calamento

cattail n. espadaña

cattle n. ganado

cattleman n. ganadero

cauliflower n. coliflor

causation n. causalidad

causative adj. causante

cause n. razón; causa

causeway n. calzada

caustic adj. cáustico

cauterize v. cauterizar

caution v. advertir

cautionary adj. preventivo; amonestador

cautious adj. cauteloso; precavido

cavalry n. caballería

cave n. cueva; caverna; gruta

cavern n. caverna; antro; cueva

cavity n. cavidad; caries (de dientes)

cavort v. cabriolar; retozar; divertise

cease v. suspender; cesar;

dejar de
ceaseless adj. continuo
cedar n. cedro
cede v. ceder
ceiling n. techo interior; cielo raso
celebrant n. celebrante
celebrate v. celebrar
celebrated adj. célebre
celebration n. celebración
celebrity n. celebridad
celery n. apio
celestial adj. celestial
celibacy n. celibato
celibate adj. célibe
cell n. celda; célula
cellular adj. celular
cellulose n. celulosa
cement n. cemento
cemetery n. cementerio
censer n. incensario
censor n. censor
censorious adj. censurador
censure v. censurar
census n. censo
cent n. centavo
centaur n. centauro
center n. centro
centigrade adj. centígrado
centigram n. centigramo
centimeter n. centímetro
central adj. central
centralize v. centralizar(se)
centric adj. céntrico
centrifugal adj. centrífugo
century n. siglo
ceramic adj. cerámico
cereal n. cereal
cerebral adj. cerebral
cerebrum n. cerebro
ceremonial adj. ceremonial
ceremony n. ceremonia
certain adj. seguro; cierto
certainly adv. cierto
certainty n. certeza
certifiable adj. certificable
certificate n. certificado
certification n. certificacion
certified adj. certificado
certify v. certificar
certitude n. certidumbre
cessation n. cesación

chafe v. frotar; rozar
chair n. silla
chairman n. presidente (directiva, conferencia)
chairwoman n. presidenta
chalet n. chalet
chalk n. tiza; creta
chalkboard n. pizarra
challenge v. desafiar; retar
challenger n. desafiador; retador
chamberlain n. chambelán
chameleon n. camaleón
champ n. campeón
champion n. campeón
championship n. campeonato
chance n. oportunidad; casualidad
chancellor n. canciller
change v. transformar; cambiar
changeable adj. cambiable
changer n. cambiador
channel n. canal
chant n. canto
chapel n. capilla
chaperone n. chaperona; dama de compañia
chaplain n. capellán
chapter n. capítulo
character n. carácter
characteristic n. característica
characterize v. caracterizar
charcoal n. carboncillo; carbón de leña
charge v. pedir; cargar
charitable adj. caritativo
charity n. caridad
charm n. encanto; atractivo
charmer n. encantador
charming adj. encantador
chart v. trazar; cartografiar
charter n. reglamento; alquiler (barco, avión)
chase v. perseguir
chaste adj. casto
chasten v. castigar; disciplinar
chastise v. castigar; corregir; disciplinar
chat v. charlar
chatter v. charlar; parlotear
cheap adj. barato
cheapen v. degradar(se); abaratar(se); despreciar(se)

cheaply *adv.* barato
cheat *v.* engañar
cheater *n.* tramposo
cheating *adj.* tramposo
check *n.* cheque; cuenta; jaque (ajedrez)
checkbook *n.* chequera
checkered *adj.* a cuadros
cheek *n.* mejilla; cachete
cheep *n.* piada
cheer *v.* aplaudir; alentar; animar
cheerful *adj.* alegre; animado
cheerily *adv.* alegremente
cheerless *adj.* triste; melancólico
cheese *n.* queso
cheesecake *n.* quesadilla; bizcocho de queso
chef *n.* cocinero; jefe de cocina
chemical *n.* producto químico
chemist *n.* químico
chemistry *n.* química
chemotherapy *n.* quimioterapia
cherish *v.* abrigar; querer; apreciar
cherry *n.* cerezo; cereza
cherub *n.* querubín
cherubic *adj.* querúbico
chess *n.* ajedrez
chest *n.* pecho; cofre; baúl
chestnut *n.* castaña
chew *v.* masticar
chewing *n.* masticación
chicken *n.* pollo
chickpea *n.* garbanzo
chief *n.* jefe
chiffon *n.* chifón
child *n.* hijo; niño
childbirth *m.* parto
childish *adj.* aniñado
childlike *adj.* infantil
chili *n.* chile
chill *n.* frío; escalofrío
chilling *adj.* frío
chime *n.* carillón; campanilla
chimney *n.* chimenea
chimpanzee *n.* chimpancé

chin *n.* barbilla; barba
china *n.* porcelana china; vajilla
chip *n.* astilla; *v.* astillar
chipper *adj.* jovial
chiropractor *n.* quiropráctico
chirp *v.* gorjear
chisel *n.* cincel
chiseler *n.* cincelador
chivalry *n.* caballerosidad
chive *n.* cebollino
chloride *n.* cloruro
chlorine *n.* cloro
chlorophyll *n.* chorofila
chocolate *n.* chocolate
choice *adj.* selecto; *n.* preferencia
choir *n.* coro
choke *v.* ahogar; atorar; estrangular
cholera *n.* cólera
choleric *adj.* colérico
cholesterol *n.* colesterol
choose *v.* escoger; elegir
choosing *n.* selección
chop *v.* cortar; tajar
choral *n.* coral (música)
choreographer *n.* coreógrafo
chosen *adj.* escogido
chow *n.* comida
Christ *n.* Cristo
christen *v.* bautizar; dar nombre
christening *n.* bautismo
Christmas *n.* Navidad
chromatic *adj.* cromático
chrome *n.* cromo
chromium *n.* cromo
chromosome *n.* cromosoma
chronic *adj.* crónico
chronicle *n.* crónica
chronologic *adj.* cronológico
chronology *n.* cronología
chrysalis *n.* crisalida
churn *n.* compañero
chunk *n.* trozo
church *n.* iglesia
churchman *n.* clérigo; sacerdote; feligrés
churn *n.* mantequera
chute *n.* conducto; rampa; sumidero de agua
cicada *n.* cigarra

cider n. sidra
cigar n. puro; cigarro
cigarette n. cigarrillo; pitillo
cinch n. cincha; certidumbre
cinder n. carbonilla; escoria volcánica
cinema n. cine
cinematic adj. fílmico
cinnamon n. canela
circle n. ciclo; círculo
circuit n. circuito
circular adj. circular
circulate v. circular
circulation n. circulación
circumference n. circunferencia
circumnavigate v. circunnavegar
circumscribe v. circunscribir
circumstance n. circunstancia
circus n. circo
cirrus n. cirro
cistern n. cisterna
citadel n. ciudadela
citation n. citación; cita
cite v. citar
citizen n. ciudadano
citizenship n. ciudadanía
city n. ciudad
civic adj. cívico
civil adj. civil
civilian n. civil
civility n. civilidad
civilization n. civilización
civilize v. civilizar
claim v. demandar; reclamar; debatir
clairvoyant adj. clarividente
clam n. almeja
clamor n. clamor
clamorous adj. clamoroso
clamp n. abrazadera; grapa
clap v. aplaudir; palmotear
clapper n. badajo; matraca
clapping n. aplausos
claret n. clarete (vino)
clarification n. clarificación
clarify v. clarificar
clarinet n. clarinete
clarity n. claridad
clash v. entrechocarse; chocar; estar en conflicto
class n. clase
classic adj. clásico

classical adj. clásico
classicism n. clasicismo
classicist n. clasicista
classification n. clasificación
classified adj. clasificado
classify v. clasificar
clause n. cláusula
claustrophobia n. claustrofobia
clavicle n. clavícula
claw n. garra; pinza (de cangrejo)
clay n. arcilla; barro
clean v. limpiar
cleancut adj. bien definido; nétido; limpio; sano
cleaner n. limpiador; quitamanchas; tintorero
cleaning n. limpieza; desmonte
cleanse v. limpiar
cleanser n. limpiador
clear adj. despejado; claro; transparente
clearcut adj. claro
clearing n. claro
clearly adv. claramente
cleavage n. división; hendedura
cleaver n. cuchillo de carnicero
clergy n. clero
clerical adj. clerical
clerk n. oficinista; vendedor de tienda
clever adj. listo; ingenioso
cleverness n. inteligencia; ingenio; maña
client n. cliente
climactic adj. culminante
climate n. clima
climatic adj. climático
climax n. clímax; punto culminante
climb v. trepar
climber n. alpinista; montañista
climbing adj. trepador
clinic n. clínica
clinical adj. clínico
clinician n. profesional clínico
clip v. cortar con tijeras; recortar; juntar con grapas
clock n. reloj
clog n. traba; obstáculo; zueco; chanclo

clone *n.* clon
close *v.* cerrar
closed *adj.* cerrado; vedado
closely *adv.* atentamente; de cerca
closeout *n.* liquidación
closet *n.* armario; ropero
clot *n.* coágulo
cloth *n.* tela; paño
clothe *v.* vestir; cubrir; arropar
clothes *n.* ropa
clothing *n.* ropa
cloud *n.* nube
cloudy *adj.* nublado; encapotado
clout *n.* bofetada
clown *n.* payaso
club *n.* cachiporra; trébol; palo; club; círculo; peña
clue *n.* pista; indicio
clumsy *adj.* torpe; desmañado; desatinado
coach *n.* vagón; entrenador; coche
coal *n.* carbón; hulla; carbón de piedra
coarse *adj.* tosco; ordinario
coarsen *v.* engrosar; engruesara; vulgarizar
coast *n.* costa; litoral
coastal *adj.* costero; costeño; costanero
coat *n.* pelo de animal; pelaje; abrigo; gabán
coated *adj.* bañado; revestido
coating *n.* capa; baño
coattail *n.* faldón
coax *v.* engatusar; persuadir
coaxing *n.* engatusamiento
cob *n.* elote; mazorca de maíz; cisne macho
cobbler *n.* zapatero; remendón
cobra *n.* cobra
cobweb *n.* telaraña; cosa sutil
coccyx *n.* cóccix; coxis
cock *n.* gallo; macho de las aves
cockle *n.* berberecho; neguilla; candileja
cockpit *n.* gallera; cabina del piloto; cancha
cockroach *n.* cucaracha
cocktail *n.* coctel

cocoa *n.* cacao
coconut *n.* coco
code *n.* código; clave; compilación de leyes
codefendant *n.* coacusado
codfish *n.* bacalao
codify *v.* codificar
coefficient *n.* coeficiente
coerce *v.* coercer; forzar
coercion *n.* coerción; coacción
coexist *v.* coexistir
coextensive *adj.* coextenso
coffee *n.* café
coffer *n.* cofre; arca; caja (de caudales, valores)
coffin *n.* ataúd
cog *n.* diente (de rueda); pieza
cogitate *v.* meditar
cognac *n.* coñac
cognition *n.* cognición; conocimiento
cognizant *adj.* enterado; sabedor; informado
cohabit *v.* cohabitar
cohere *v.* adherirse
coherence *n.* coherencia
coherent *adj.* coherente
cohesion *n.* cohesión
coil *n.* rollo; carrete; bobina
coin *v.* acuñar; *n.* moneda
coincide *v.* coincidir
coincidence *n.* coincidencia
coincidental *adj.* coincidente; fortuito
cola *n.* cola
colander *n.* colador
cold *n.* frío; resfrío; *adj.* frío
coldblooded *adj.* impasible; cruel; despiadado
coldhearted *adj.* insensible; indiferente
colic *n.* cólico
coliseum *n.* coliseo
collaborate *v.* colaborar
collaborative *adj.* cooperativo
collaborator *n.* colaborador
collapse *v.* desplomarse; caerse
collapsible *adj.* plegable
collar *n.* cuello; collar; ceñir con collar
collate *v.* colacionar; cotejar

collateral *adj.* colateral
collect *v.* recoger; reunir; coleccionar; recaudar
collected *adj.* sosegado; calmado; completo
collection *n.* colección
collective *adj.* colectivo
collectivize *v.* colectivizar
college *n.* colegio; universided
collegian *n.* estudiante; universitario
collegiate *adj.* universitario; colegiado
collide *v.* chocar
colloquial *adj.* familiar
colloquium *n.* coloquio
colloquy *n.* coloquio; diálogo
collusion *n.* colusión
cologne *n.* colonia
colon *n.* colon (puntuación)
colonel *n.* coronel
colonial *adj.* colonial
colonialist *n.* colonialista
colonist *n.* colonizador; colono
colonization *n.* colonización
colonize *v.* colonizar
colonnade *n.* columnata
colony *n.* colonia
color *v.* colorear; *n.* color
coloration *n.* coloración
colored *adj.* coloreado; pintado
colorful *adj.* pintoresco; vivido
colorless *adj.* incoloro
colossal *adj.* colosal
colossus *n.* coloso
column *n.* columna
columnist *n.* columnista
coma *n.* coma
comb *v.* peinar, *n.* peine
combat *v.* combatar(se)
combination *n.* combinación
combine *v.* combinar
combustible *adj.* combustible
come *v.* llegar; venir
comedian *n.* comediante; cómico
comedy *n.* comedia
comet *n.* cometa
comfort *v.* consolar; confortar
comfortable *adj.* confortable; cómodo
comforter *n.* consolador; cobertura; colcha

comic *adj.* cómico
comical *adj.* cómico
coming *adj.* venidero
comma *n.* coma (puntuación)
command *n.* orden; *v.* mandar
commander *n.* comandante
commence *v.* comenzar
commencement *n.* comienzo; inauguración; día de graduación
commend *v.* encomendar; recomendar; clogiar
commendation *n.* recomendación; alabanza
comment *n.* comentario; observación
commentary *n.* comentario; observación
commentate *v.* comentar; narrar (deportes, ceremonies)
commerce *n.* comercio
commercial *adj.* comercial
commercialism *n.* comercialismo
commercialize *v.* comercializar
commiserate *v.* compadecerse
commissar *n.* comisario
commissary *n.* economato; comisario; delegado
commission *v.* comisionar; *n.* comisión
commit *v.* confiar
committal *n.* comprometimiento; reclusión; obligaciión; confinamiento
committee *n.* comité
commode *n.* cómoda; retrete
commodore *n.* comodoro
common *adj.* común
commonplace *adj.* ordinario
commotion *n.* tumulto; conmoción; desorden
communal *adj.* comunal
commune *v.* comunicarse; conversar con
communicable *adj.* comunicable
communicate *v.* comunicar(se)
communication *n.* comunicación
communicator *n.* comunicante
communion *n.* comunión
communistic *adj.* comunista
community *n.* comunidad

commutation n. conmutación
commutative adj. conmutativo
commute v. conmutar
compact adj. compacto
companion n. compañero
companionship n. compañerismo
company n. compañía
comparable adj. comparable
comparative adj. comparativo
compare v. comparar
compartment n. compartimiento
compass n. compás
compassion n. compasión
compassionate adj. compasivo
compatible adj. compatible
compel v. compeler
compelling adj. apremiante; urgente; preciso; obligatorio
compensate v. compensar
compensation n. compensación
compete v. competir
competence n. competencia; aptitud
competent adj. competente
competition n. competencia; con curso
competitive adj. competitivo
competitor n. competidor
compilation n. compilación
compile v. compilar
complain v. quejarse
complainant n. demandante; querellante
complaint n. queja; lamento; emfermedad
complaisant adj. complaciente
complement n. complemento
complementary adj. complementario
complete adj. completo
completion n. terminación
complex adj. complejo
compliant adj. complaciente
complicate v. complicar
complicated adj. complicado
complication n. complicacion
complicity n. complicidad
compliment n. honor; elogio
comply v. obedecer
component n. componente

compose v. componer
composed adj. tranquilo
composer n. compositor
composite adj. compuesto
composition n. composición
composure n. serenidad
compound adj. compuesto
comprehend v. comprender
comprehensible adj. comprensible
comprehension n. comprensión
comprehensive adj. comprensivo; general
compress n. compresa
compressed adj. comprimido
compression n. compresión
comprise v. constar de; comprender
compromise n. compromiso; v. componer
compromising adj. com prometedor
compulsive adj. compulsivo
compulsory adj. obligatorio
computation n. cálculo
compute v. computar
computer n. computadora
computerize v. computarizar
comrade n. camarada
con n. contra
concave adj. cóncavo
conceal v. ocultar; encubrir
concede v. conceder
conceited adj. vanidoso
conceivable adj. concebible
conceive v. concebir
concentrate v. concentrar(se)
concentration n. concentración
concentric adj. concéntrico
concept n. concepto
conception n. concepción
conceptual adj. conceptual
concern v. concernir; atañer
concerned adj. preocupado
concerning prep. acerca de
concert n. concierto
concerto n. concierto
concession n. concesión
conciliate v. conciliar
concise adj. conciso
conclude v. concluir
conclusion n. conclusión

conclusive *adj.* concluyente
concoction *n.* preparación
concord *n.* concordia
concrete *adj.* concreto
concur *v.* concurrir
concussion *n.* concusión
condemnable *adj.* condenable; censurable
condensation *n.* condensación
condense *v.* condensar(se)
condenser *n.* condensador
condescending *adj.* con descendiente
condiment *n.* condimento
condition *v.* condicionar
condone *v.* condonar; tolerar
conductor *n.* cobrador
confer *v.* conferenciar; consultar; otorgar
confess *v.* confesar
confide *v.* confiar; fiarse de
confidence *n.* confianza; confidencia
confidential *adj.* confidencial
confirm *v.* confirmar
conflict *v.* chocar
conformity *n.* conformidad
confrontation *n.* confrontación
confuse *v.* confundir
confusion *n.* confusión
congest *v.* acumular; congestionar
congestion *n.* congestión
conglomeration *n.* conglomeración
congratulation *n.* felicitación
congregate *v.* congregar(se)
conjunction *n.* conjunción
conjure *v.* conjurar
connect *v.* conectar
connotation *n.* connotación
connote *v.* connotar
consecutive *adj.* consecutivo
conservatory *n.* conservatorio
conserve *v.* conservar
consider *v.* considerar
consideration *n.* consideración
consist *v.* consistir
consolidate *v.* consolidar
consolidation *n.* consolidación
constancy *n.* constancia
constant *adj.* continuo; constante

consult *v.* consultar
consume *v.* consumir
consumption *n.* consunción; consumo
contain *v.* contener
contamination *n.* contaminación
contemplate *v.* proyectar; contemplar; reflexionar
contemporary *n.* contemporáneo; coetáneo
contend *v.* afirmar; contender
continental *adj.* continental
contingency *n.* contingencia
continue *v.* seguir; continuar
contraction *n.* contracción
contradict *v.* contradecir
contrast *v.* contrastar
contribution *n.* contribución
control *v.* dirigir; controlar
convention *n.* convención
converge *v.* converger
conversation *n.* conversación
converse *v.* conversar
conversion *n.* conversión
convey *v.* llevar
conviction *n.* convicción
convince *v.* convencer
convulsion *n.* convulsión
cook *n.* cocinero; *v.* cocinar
cookie *n.* galleta
cool *adj.* fresco
coordinate *v.* coordinar
coordination *n.* coordinación
copper *n.* cobre
copy *v.* copiar
cordiality *n.* cordialidad
corn *n.* maíz
corporal *adj.* corporal
corporation *n.* corporación
corpulent *adj.* corpulento
corral *v.* acorralar
correct *v.* corregir
correction *n.* corrección
correspond *v.* escribir (correspondencia); corresponder
correspondence *n.* correspondencia
corrode *v.* corroer
corrosion *n.* corrosión
corruption *n.* corrupción

cosmetic *n.* cosmético
cosmic *adj.* cósmico
cost *v.* costar; *n.* precio
couch *n.* sofá
count *n.* cuenta; conde; *v.* contar
country *n.* campo; país
couple *n.* pareja
courageous *adj.* valiente
course *n.* plato; dirección; curso
cousin *n.* prima; primo
cover *n.* cubierta; *v.* cubrir
cow *n.* vaca
cowboy *n.* vaquero
coyote *n.* coyote
crab *n.* cangrejo; jaiba; cascarrabias
cracker *n.* galleta
cradle *v.* mecer; acunar
crash *n.* choque; estallido
crate *n.* cajón
crater *n.* cráter
crave *v.* ansiar; suplicar
craving *n.* anhelo; antojo
crawl *v.* gatear; arrastrarse
crayon *n.* pastel; clarión
craze *v.* enloquecer
crazed *adj.* loco; enloquecido
crazy *adj.* loco
cream *n.* crema
creamy *adj.* cremoso
crease *v.* doblar; plegar
create *v.* producir; crear
creation *n.* creación
creative *adj.* creador
creativity *n.* originalidad
creator *n.* creador
creature *n.* criatura
credence *n.* crédito; creencia; fe
credential *n.* credencial
credible *adj.* creíble
credit *n.* crédito; reconocimiento
creditable *adj.* digno de crédito; estimable; loable
credulous *adj.* crédulo
creed *n.* credo
creepy *adj.* espeluznante; tétrico; rastrero
cremate *v.* cremar; incinerar

cremation *n.* cremación; incineración
crepe *n.* crespón
crescent *n.* luna creciente; media luna
crest *n.* cresta
cretin *n.* cretino
crew *n.* equipo; tripulación (barco, avión)
crib *n.* cuna; establo; pesebre
cricket *n.* grillo
crime *n.* crimen
criminal *n., adj.* criminal
crinkle *v.* arrugar(se)
cripple *v.* mutilar; lisiar
crisis *n.* crisis
crisp *adj.* crespo; quebradizo
crispy *adj.* crujiente; tostado; rágil
critic *n.* crítico
critical *adj.* crítico
criticism *n.* crítica
criticize *v.* criticar
critique *n.* crítica
crocodile *n.* cocodrilo
crocus *n.* azafrán
crook *n.* ángulo; báculo; recodo
crooked *adj.* corvo; torcido
crop *n.* fusta; cultivo; cosecha
cross *v.* cruzar; *n.* cruz
crossbeam *n.* traviesa
crosscurrent *n.* contracorriente
crossexamine *v.* interrogar; sobre lo preguntado
crossword puzzle *n.* crucigrama
crouch *v.* acuclillarse
crow *v.* cacarear; cantar (gallo)
crowd *n.* gentío; multitud
crowded *adj.* concurrido; abarrotado; atesrado
crown *n.* corona; copa (árbol, sombrero)
crowning *n.* coronación
crucible *n.* crisol
crude *adj.* tosco; ordinario; crudo
cruel *adj.* cruel
cruelty *n.* crueldad
cruise *v.* navegar; pasear; vagar; circular
crumb *n.* migaja
crumble *v.* desmigajar(se)

crumple v. estrujar(se)
crunchy adj. crujiente
crush v. aplastar; moler
crust n. costra; corteza
crustacean n. crustáceo
crusty adj. costroso; de corteza dura (pan)
cry v. llorar; exclmar; vocear
crypt n. cripta
crystal n. cristal
crystalline adj. cristalino
crystallize v. cristalizar(se)
cube n. cubo
cubic adj. cúbico
cubicle n. compartimiento
cucumber n. pepino
cuddle v. abrazar(se); acariciar
cue n. taco (billar); apunte (teatro); idea
culminate v. culminar
culpable adj. culpable
cult n. culto
cultivate v. cultivar
cultivation n. cultivo; cultura
cultivator n. cultivador
cultural adj. cultural
culture n. cultura
cultured adj. culto; de cultivo (perlas, bacterias)
cumbersome adj. embarazoso; engorroso; incómodo
cumulate v. acumular
cumulative adj. acumulativo
cunning adj. hábil; astuto
cup n. taza; jícara
cupful n. taza
curable adj. curable
curb n. bordillo de la acera; brocal (pozo); barbada (freno del caballo)
curd n. cuajada
cure n. cura
curiosity n. curiosidad
curious adj. curioso
curl v. enrollar(se); rizar(se); encrespar(se)
currency n. moneda; dinero en circulación

current n., adj. corriente; actual
currently adj. actualmente
curse n. desgracia; maldición
curtain n. telón; cortina
curvature n. curvatura
curve n. curva
curved adj. curvo
custodian n. custodio; guardián
custody n. custodia
custom n. costumbre
customarily adv. común- mente; habitualmente
cut adj. cortado; n. cortadura; v. cortar
cute adj. lindo; encantador; mono
cuticle n. cutícula
cutlery n. cubiertos; cuchillería
cyanide n. cianuro
cycle n. ciclo; órbita; bicicleta
cyclic adj. cíclico
cyclist n. ciclista
cyclone n. ciclón
cylinder n. cilindro
cylindrical adj. cilíndrico
cymbal n. címbalo; platillo
cynical adj. cínico
cynicism n. cinismo
cypress n. ciprés
cyst n. quiste
cystic adj. enquistado; cístico
cytoplasm n. citoplasma
czar n. zar
czarina n. zarina

D

dad n. papá
daily adj. diario
dainty adj. delicado
dairyman n. lechero
dam v. represar; n. presa
damage v. dañar; perjudicar
damp adj. húmedo
dance n. baile; v. bailar
dancer n. bailaín; bailarina
danger n. peligro
dangerous adj. peligroso
dare v. arriesgarse
daring n. audacia; osadía; arrojo
dark n. oscuridad; adj. oscuro

darken v. oscurecer

darkness n. oscuridad

dash v. precipitarse; chocar; salpicar

date n. cita; fecha

daughter n. hija

daughter-in-law n. nuera

day n. día

daytime n. día; luz del día

dazzle v. deslumbrar

dead adj. muerto

deaf adj. sordo

deafen v. ensordecer; aislar contra el ruido

deafness n. sordera

dealer n. negociante; distribuidor (autos); banquero (naipes)

death n. muerte

debate v. debatir

debilitate v. debilitar

debilitation n. debilitación

debt n. deuda

debtor n. deudor

decadence n. decadencia

decadent adj. decadente

decease v. morir; fallecer

deceased adj. muerto; difunto; finado

December n. diciembre

decent adj. decente

decide v. decidir

decided adj. decidido

decidedly adv. decididamente

decimal n. decimal

declaration n. declaración

declare v. declarar

decline v. rehusar

decorator n. decorador

decrease v. disminuir(se)

deduction n. descuento; rebaja; deducción

deep adj. profundo; hondo

deepen v. intensificar; ahondar

defect n. defecto

defection n. defección; deserción

defective adj. defectuoso

defend v. defender

defendant n. demandado; acusado

deficiency n. deficiencia

deflate v. desinflar

deflation n. desinflación

deform v. desfigurar; deformar

deformity n. deformidad

degenerate v. degenerar

degrade v. degradar

degree n. rango; grado

dehydrate v. deshidratar

dehydration n. deshidratacion

delete v. tachar; suprimir

deliberate v. deliberar

delicious adj. delicioso

delightful adj. encantador

deliver v. entregar

delivery n. entrega

demand v. demandar; exigir

democracy n. democracia

democrat n. demócrata;

democratic adj. democrático

demonstrate v. demostrar

demonstration n. demostración; manifestación

demoralize v. desmoralizar

denomination n. denominacion

denominator n. denominador; divisor

denote v. denotar

denounce n. denunciar

dense adj. denso; torpe

density n. densidad

dentist n. dentista

denunciation n. denuncia; denunciación; censura

departure n. salida; desviación

deport v. deportar

deportation n. deportación

deprave v. depravar

depraved adj. depravado

depression n. desaliento; depresión; hondonada

depth n. a fondo; profundidad; intensidad

derive v. derivar(se)

descend v. bajar; descender

describe v. describir

description n. descripción

deserve v. merecer

designation n. nombramiento; designación

desire v. desear

despair v. desesperarse

despite prep. a pesar de

dessert n. postre

destroy v. destruir
destructible adj. destructible
destruction n. destrucción
detain v. retener; detener; arrestar
deter v. detener
determination n. determinación
determine v. resolver; determinar
detestable adj. detestable
devastate v. devastar; asolar
devastation n. devastación
develop v. entrenar; desarrollar; urbanizar; contraer (enfermedad)
devil n. diablo
devote v. dedicar
devour v. devorar
diabetes n. diabetes
diabetic adj. diabético
diagnose v. diagnosticar
diagnosis n. diagnóstico
dial v. marcar (número telefónico)
dialogue n. diálogo
diary n. diario
dictator n. dictador
dictionary n. diccionario
die v. morir
difference n. diferencia
different adj. diferente; distinto
difficult adj. difícil
difficulty n. dificultad
diffusion n. difusión
dig n. excavación; codazo; v. extraer; investigar
digestion n. digestión
digit n. dedo; dígito
dignify v. dignificar
dilemma n. dilema
diligence n. diligencia; esmero
diligent adj. diligente
dilute v. diluir
dilution n. dilución
dim adj. oscuro; débil; difuso
diminish v. disminuir(se); rebajar(se)
dine v. cenar
dinner n. cena
diplomacy n. diplomacia
diplomat n. diplomático
direct v. dirigir; adj. directo
direction n. dirección

director n. director
disable v. incapacitar; lisiar
disappear v. desaparecer
disappearance n. desaparición
disastrous adj. desastroso
disavow v. desconocer; repudiar
discharge v. despedir; soltar
disciplinary adj. disciplinario
discipline v. disciplinar; n. castigo
disconnect v. desconectar
discontinuous adj. discontinuo; interrumpido
discover v. descubrir
discussion n. discusión
disease n. enfermedad
disguise n. disfraz, v. disfrazar
dish n. plato; manjar; vianda
dishonor v. deshonrar
dishonorable adj. deshonroso
disinfectant n. desinfectante
disinterest n. desinterés
disk n. disco
dislocate v. dislocar
dislocation n. dislocación
disobey v. desobedecer
disorder n. desorden
dispense v. dispensar
display n. demostrar
dispute n. disputa; v. disputar
disqualify v. descalificar
dissolve v. disolver(se)
dissuade v. disuadir
dissuasion n. disuasión
distance n. distancia
distant adj. distante
distill v. destilar
distillery n. destilería
distinction n. distinción
distinguish v. distinguir
distract v. distraer
distraction n. distracción
distribution n. distribución
disturb v. perturbar; inquietar
disturbance n. disturbio
diverge v. divergir
diversion n. diversión
diversity n. diversidad
divert v. divertir; apartar
divide v. dividir(se)
dizzy adj. mareado

do v. cumplir; hacer
doctor n. médico
document n. documento
dog n. perro
dogmatic adj. dogmático
doll n. muñeca
dollar n. dólar
domestic adj. doméstico
domesticate v. domesticar
domination n. dominación
don v. ponerse
donate v. donar
donor n. donante
door n. puerta
dormitory n. dormitorio
double v. doblar(se)
doubt n. duda; v. dudar
down prep., adv. abajo
dozen n. docena
dragon n. dragón
drama n. drama
dramatic adj. dramático
dramatist n. dramaturgo
draw v. sacar; dibujar;
  arrastrar
dream v. soñar, n. sueño
dreamer n. soñador
dredge v. dragar
dress n. vestido; traje; ropa; v.
  vestir(se)
drink n. bebida; v. beber
drive v. manejar; empujar;
  conducir; guiar
drowsy adj. soñoliento
drug n. droga
drunk adj. borracho; ebrio;
  embriagado
duality n. dualidad
duck n. pato
dull adj. estúpido; torpe;
  opaco; deslucido
duplicate adj. duplicado; v.
  duplicar
duplication n. duplicación
duration n. duración
during prep. durante
duty n. derechos de aduana;
  impuestos; deber; obligación
dwell v. habitar
dynamic adj. dinámico
dynamite n. dinamita
dysentery n. disentería

E

each adv. para cada uno; adj.
  cada
eager adj. anhelante; ansioso
eagerness n. ansia; afán
eagle n. águila
eaglet n. aguilucho
ear n. oído; oreja
eardrum n. tímpano del oído
earl n. conde
earliness n. precocidad
early adj. primitivo; prematuro;
  cercano; adv. temprano;
  pronto
earn v. merecer; ganar
earnestly adv. con seriedad;
  de veras
earnings n. ingresos; paga
earring n. pendiente; arete;
  zarcillo
earshot n. alcance del oído
earth n. mundo; tierra
earthy adj. terroso; grosero;
  sensual
ease v. facilitar; n. facilidad
easel n. caballete
easily adv. fácilmente
easiness n. facilidad; soltura
east n. este; oriente; levante
eastern adj. del este; oriental
eastward adv. hacia el este
easy adj. fácil; suave; cómodo;
  agradable
eat v. gastar; comer
eatable adj. comestible
eaves n. alero
eavesdrop v. escuchar a escondi-
  das; espiar
ebb v. menguar; decaer
ebony n. ébano
eccentric adj. excéntrico
eccentricity n. excentricidad
echo n. eco
eclipse v. eclipsar
ecliptic adj. eclíptico
ecological adj. ecológico
ecologist n. ecólogo
ecology n. ecología
economic adj. económico
economical adj. económico

economist *n.* economista
economize *v.* economizar
economy *n.* economía
ecstasy *n.* éxtasis
ecstatic *adj.* extático
eczema *n.* eczema; eccema
eddy *n.* remolino; contracorriente
edge *n.* filo; borde; orilla
edible *adj.* comestible
edict *n.* edicto
edification *n.* edificación
edifice *n.* edificio
edify *v.* edificar
edit *v.* editar
edition *n.* edición
editor *n.* editor; redactor
editorial *adj.* editorial
editorialist *n.* editorialista
educate *v.* educar
education *n.* educación
eel *n.* anguila
eerie *adj.* espantoso; fantástico
efface *v.* borrar; tachar
effect *v.* efectuar; *n.* resultado
effective *adj.* efectivo; eficaz
effectual *adj.* eficaz
effervesce *v.* estar en
efervescencia
effervescence *n.* efervescencia
effervescent *adj.* efervescente
efficiency *n.* eficiencia
efficient *adj.* eficiente
effigy *n.* efigie
effort *n.* esfuerzo
effortless *adj.* sin esfuerzo
effuse *n.* derramar; esparcir
effusion *n.* efusión
effusive *adj.* expansivo;
efusivo
egg *n.* huevo
egotist *n.* egotista; ególatra
eight *adj.* ocho
eighteen *adj.* dieciocho
eighth *adj.* octavo
eighty *adj.* ochenta
either *adv.* tampoco; *adj.*
cualquier
elate *v.* alegrar
elbow *n.* codo
elect *v.* elegir
election *n.* elección

elective *adj.* electivo
electrician *n.* electricista
electricity *n.* electricidad
elegant *adj.* elegante
elementary *adj.* elemental
elephant *n.* elefante
elevate *v.* elevar
elevation *n.* elevación
eleven *adj.* once
eligibility *n.* elegibilidad
eliminate *v.* eliminar
elimination *n.* eliminación
emancipate *v.* emancipar
emerald *n.* esmeralda
emerge *v.* salir; brotar
emergence *n.* salida;
surgimiento
emigrate *v.* emigrar
emigration *n.* emigración
eminent *adj.* eminente
emit *v.* emitir
emotion *n.* emoción
empire *n.* imperio
employ *v.* emplear
employee *n.* empleado
empty *v.* vaciar; *adj.* desocupado;
vacío
emulsion *n.* emulsión
enchant *v.* encantar
enchanting *adj.* encantador
encyclopedia *n.* enciclopedia
end *n* final; fin
ending *n.* fin
endorse *v.* endosar
endorsement *n.* endoso; respaldo
endure *v.* durar; aguantar;
resistir
enemy *n.* enemigo
energetic *adj.* enérgico
energy *n.* energía
engage *v.* engranar; apalabrar;
comprometer
engagement *n.* obligación; com
promiso
engineer *n.* ingeniero
engineering *n.* ingeniería
English *n.* inglés
enjoy *v.* disfrutar
enjoyment *n.* disfrute; goce;
placer
enormous *adj.* enorme
enough *adv.* bastante;

suficiente
enslave v. esclavizar
entertainment n. espectáculo
enthusiasm n. entusiasmo
enthusiast n. entusiasta
entire adj. entero; completo
entirely adv. totalmente
entrance n. entrada; admisión
entrust v. encargar; encomendar
entry n. partida; entrada; acceso; artículo (diccionario); concursante
envelop v. envolver
enzyme n. enzima
epidemic n. epidemia
episode n. episodio
epoch n. época
equal v. igualar; n. igual
equality adj. igualdad
equally adv. igualmente
equipment n. equipo
era n. era
erase v. borrar
eraser n. borrador
erect v. erigir
erosion n. erosión
erudition n. erudición
eruption n. erupción
escort v. acompañar; n. acompañante
especial adj. especial
especially adv. especialmente
essential adj. esencial
esthetic adj. estético
estimate v. estimar
eternal adj. eterno
eternally adv. eternamente
eternity n. eternidad
ethical adj. ético
eulogize v. elogiar
eulogy n. elogio; panegírico
euphoria n. euforia
euphoric adj. eufórico
evacuation n. evacuación
evade v. evadir
evaluate v. evaluar
evaluation n. evaluación
evaporate v. evaporar(se)
evaporation n. evaporación
evasion n. evasión
even adj. llano; liso; parejo;

apacible; par (número); v. igualar
eventuality n. eventualidad
ever adv. Siempre; nunca; jamás
every adj. todos; cada
evidence n. evidencia
evil n. mal; maldad; perversidad
evolution n. evolución
exact adj. exacto
exaggeration n. exageración
exaltation n. exaltación
examine v. examinar
example n. ejemplo
excavation n. excavación
exceed v. superar; exceder
excellence n. excelencia
excellent adj. excelente
exception n. excepción
excessive adj. excesivo
excite v. excitar
exclaim v. exclamar
exclamation n. exclamación
excuse v. excusar; perdonar
exercise n. ejercicio
exhibition n. exposición
exhort v. exhortar
exile n. exilado; destierro
exist v. existir
existence n. existencia
exit n. salida
exotic adj. exótico
expansion n. expansión
expectancy n. expectación
expectation n. expectación
expedition n. expedición
expel v. expulsar
experience v. experimentar
experiment n. experimento
expire v. terminar
explanation n. explicación
exploration n. exploración
explorer n. explorador
explosion n. explosión
exportation n. exportación
express v. expresar

expression n. expresión
expressive adj. expresión
extend v. extender
extension n. extensión
exterior adj. exterior
extinct adj. extinto
extinction n. extinción
extra n. extra
extraordinary adj. extraordinario
extreme adj. extremo
exultation n. exultación
eye n. ojo

F

fable n. fábula
fabric n. tela
fabricate v. inventar
fabulous adj. fabuloso
face n. cara; rostro
facial adj. facial
facilitate v. facilitar
facility n. facilidad
fact n. hecho
faction n. facción
factor n. factor
factory n. fábrica
faculty n. facultad
fail v. acabar; faltar; fallar
failure n. fracaso
faintness n. debilidad
fair adj. justo; rubio
faith n. fe
faithful adj. fiel
fake n. impostor
falcon n. halcón
fall v. caer(se)
false adj. falso
falsehood n. mentira
falsely adv. falsamente
falsify v. falsificar
falsity n. falsedad
fame n. fama
familiar adj. familiar
family n. familia
famous adj. famoso
fan n. aficionado
fancy n. fantasía
fantastic adj. fantástico
fantasy n. fantasía
far adv. lejos

farewell n. adiós
farm n. granja
fascinate v. fascinar
fast adj. rápidamente; rápido
fat adj. gordo
fatal adj. fatal
fatality n. fatalidad
fate n. suerte
father n. padre
father-in-law n. suegro
fatigue n. fatiga
fault n. culpa; falta
favor n. favor
favorable adj. favorable
fear n. miedo
fearful adj. temeroso
fearsome adj. temible
feather n. pluma
feathery adj. plumoso
February n. febrero
federal adj. federal
federation n. federación
feed v. alimentar
feel v. sentir(se)
feeling n. emoción
felicity n. felicidad
feline adj. felino
fell v. talar
female n. hembra
feminine adj. femenino
femur n. fémur
fence v. esgrimir
fencing n. esgrima
fermentation n. fermentación
ferocity n. ferocidad
fertile adj. fecundo; fértil
fertility n. fecundidad
fertilize v. fertilizar
festival n. fiesta
festive adj. festivo
feudalism n. feudalismo
fever n. fiebre
few adj. pocos
fib v. mentir
fiction n. ficción
fictitious adj. ficticio
fidelity n. fidelidad
field n. prado; campo
fifteen adj. quince
fifth adj. quinto
fifty adj. cincuenta
fight v. pelear; luchar; n.

figure 113 front

pelea; lucha
figure *n.* tipo; figura
fill *v.* llenar
film *n.* película
final *adj.* final
finalist *n.* finalista
finality *n.* finalidad
finally *adv.* finalmente
financial *adj.* financiero
find *v.* hallar; encontrar
fingernail *n.* uña
fire *n.* fuego
firecracker *n.* petardo
fireman *n.* bombero
fireplace *n.* hogar
firm *adj.* firme
firmly *adv.* firmemente
first *adj.* primero
fish *n.* pez
fisherman *n.* pescador
fission *n.* fisión
fit *v.* venir bien; acomodar;
 adj. adecuado
five *adj.* cinco
fix *v.* arreglar
flag *n.* bandera
flame *n.* llama; *v.* llamear
flap *v.* batir
flat *adj.* plano; llano
flavor *n.* sabor
flea *n.* pulga
flee *v.* fugarse; huir
flexible *adj.* flexible
flight *n.* vuelo
flood *n.* diluvio
floral *adj.* floral
florist *n.* florista
flour *n.* harina
flower *n.* flor
fluid *adj.* flúido
fluorescent *adj.* fluorescente
flute *n.* flauta
fly *v.* volar; *n.* mosca
focus *v.* enfocar
fog *n.* niebla
fold *v.* plegar; doblar
folk *n.* gente
follow *v.* perseguir; seguir
follower *n.* seguidor
food *n.* alimento
foot *n.* pata; pie
football *n.* futbol

footstep *n.* paso
for *conj.* pues; *prep.* para; por
forbid *v.* prohibir
force *v.* forzar; *n.* fuerza
forehead *n.* frente
foreign *adj.* extranjero
foreigner *n.* extranjero
forest *n.* bosque
foretell *v.* predecir
forfeit *v.* perder
forget *v.* olvidar(se)
forgetful *adj.* olvidadizo
forgive *v.* perdonar
fork *n.* tenedor
formality *n.* formalidad
formation *n.* formación
formula *n.* fórmula
fort *n.* fuerte
fortification *n.* fortificación
fortune *n.* fortuna
forty *adj.* cuarenta
forward *adv.* adelante
fossil *n.* fósil
foul *adj.* sucio
foundation *n.* fundación
fountain *n.* fuente
four *adj.* cuatro
fourteen *adj.* catorce
fourth *adj.* cuarto
fox *n.* zorra; zorro
fraction *n.* fracción
fracture *v.* quebrar; *n.* fractura
fragile *adj.* frágil
fragment *n.* fragmento
fragrant *adj.* oloroso
frankly *adv.* francamente
frankness *n.* franqueza
frantic *adj.* frenético
fraternity *n.* fraternidad
free *v.* libertar; *adj.* libre
freedom *n.* libertad
French *n., adj.* francés
frequency *n.* frecuencia
frequent *adj.* frecuente
fresh *adj.* fresco
freshen *v.* refrescar
Friday *n.* viernes
friend *n.* amigo, amiga
friendly *adj.* amistoso
frigid *adj.* frío
from *prep.* desde; de
front *n.* frente

frown n. ceño
fruit n. fruta
frustrate v. frustrar
fry v. freír
fugitive n., adj. fugitivo
full adj. completo; lleno
fully adv. completamente
function v. funcionar
functional adj. funcional
fundamental adj. fundamental
funny adj. cómico
fur n. piel
furniture n. mueblaje
further adj. & adv. más lejos
fuzz n. pelusa

G

gabardine n. gabardina
gad v. vagar
gadfly n. tábano
gadget n. aparato
gag v. amordazar
gain v. ganar
gainsay v. contradecir
gala n. fiesta
galaxy n. galaxia
gallantry n. galantería
gallery n. galería
gallon n. galón
game n. partido; juego
gap n. hueco
garage n. garaje
garbage n. basura
garden n. jardín
garnish v. adornar
gas n. gasolina
gaseous adj. gaseoso
gasoline n. gasolina
gastric adj. gástrico
gate n. puerta
gather v. fruncir; reunir
gaze v. mirar
gazette n. gaceta
gear v. engranar
gene n. gen
genealogy n. genealogía
general n. general
generality n. generalidad
generalize v. generalizar
generation n. generación
generosity n. generosidad

generous adj. generoso
genital adj. genital
genius n. genio
gentleman n. caballero
gently adv. suavemente
geographer n. geógrafo
geography n. geografía
geology n. geología
geometric adj. geométrico
germinate v. germinar
germination n. germinación
gesture n. gesto
get v. lograr; obtener
ghost n. fantasma
giant adj. gigantesco
gigantic adj. gigantesco
giraffe n. jirafa
girl n. chica; niña
give v. entregar; dar
glacial adj. glacial
glacier n. glaciar
glad adj. alegre
gladness n. alegría
glance v. rebotar; mirar
glide v. deslizarse
globule n. glóbulo
gloom n. tristeza
gloomy adj. melancólico;
   lóbrego
glorify v. glorificar
glorious adj. glorioso
glove n. guante
glue v. encolar
gnaw v. roer
go v. ir
goat n. cabra
God n. Dios
gold n. oro
golf n. golf
good adj. bien; bueno
goose n. ganso
govern v. gobernar
governor n. gobernador
grace n. gracia
gracious adj. agradable; gentil
gradation n. gradación
gradual adj. gradual
gram n. gramo
grammatical adj. gramatical
grand adj. magnífico; grandioso
granddaughter n. nieta
grandfather n. abuelo

grandmother n. abuela
grandson n. nieto
grant v. conceder; otorgar
grape n. uva
graphic adj. gráfico
grass n. hierba; pasto; césped; grama
grasshopper n. saltamontes
gusto n. gusto; placer; deleite
gym n. gimnasio
gymnast n. gimnasta
gymnastic adj. gimnástico
gynecology n. ginecología

H

habit n. costumbre; hábito
habitat n. hábitat; habitación
habitation n. habitación
hail n. granizo; v. llover (balas, piedras) granizar
hall n. sala; salón; pasillo; corredor
halt v. parar; detener; interrumpir
ham n. jamón
hamburger n. hamburguesa
hammer v. martillar, n. martillo
hand n. mano; manecilla (reloj)
handsome adj. hermoso
hang v. caer; colgar
happen v. pasar; suceder
happening n. acontecimiento; suceso
happily adv. alegremente; felizmente
happiness n. algría; felicidad
happy adj. feliz
harbor n. puerto
hard adj. firme; duro
hardy adj. robusto; fuerte; resistente
harm v. dañar; perjudicar; estropear
harmful adj. dañino; perjudicial; peligroso; nocivo
harmony n. armonía
harsh adj. severo; áspero; crudo
harshness n. severidad; cruel-dad; aspereza
harvest v. cosechar
hat n. sombrero
hatch v. empollar; n. por tezuela
hatchet n. machado
hate n. odio, v. odiar
hateful adj. odioso
have v. tener; haber
hawk n. halcón
hazard v. arriesgar; n. azar; peligro; riesgo
he pron. él
head n. cabeza; cara (moneda); director
health n. salud
hear v. oír
hearing n. oído
heart n. corazón
heat v. calentar; n. calor
heater n. calentador
heaven n. cielo
heavy adj. fuerte; pesado
heel n. talón
height n. altura
heighten v. elevar
heir n. heredero
heiress n. heredera
helicopter n. helicóptero
hell n. infierno
hello int. hola
help n. ayuda; v. ayudar
helpful adj. útil
hemisphere n. hemisferio
hemispheric adj. hemisférico
hemp n. cáñamo
hen n. gallina; hembra de ave
heraldry n. heráldica
herb n. hierba; (esp. medicinal o aromática)
here adv. aquí
hereditary adj. hereditario
heredity n. herencia
hero n. héroe
heroic adj. heroico
heroine n. heroína
hesitant adj. vacilante
hesitate v. vacilar
hexagonal adj. hexagonal
hide v. ocultar(se); esconder(se)
high adj. alto
hike n. caminata
hill n. colina; cerro

himself *pron.* él mismo
hinder *v.* impedir; obstaculizar
hip *n.* cadera
his *pron.* suyo; de él
historian *n.* historiador
historic *adj.* histórico
hit *n.* golpe; acierto; éxito; *v.* golpear
hoax *n.* engaño; fraude
hold *v.* contener; tener; detener; sujetar; aguantar pustentar
hollow *adj.* vacío; hueco
home *n.* casa; hogar
homicide *adj.* homicidio
homily *n.* homilía
honest *adj.* honrado; íntegro; recto
honey *n.* miel
honor *v.* honrar; *n.* honor
honorable *adj.* honorable
hop *n.* salto, *v.* saltar
hope *v.* desear; *n.* esperanza
horizontal *adj.* horizontal
hormone *n.* hormona
horrible *adj.* horrible
horror *n.* horror
horse *n.* caballo; potro (gimnasia); caballete (carpintería)
hospital *n.* hospital
hospitality *n.* hospitalidad
hostess *n.* huéspeda; anfitriona
hostile *adj.* hostil
hostility *n.* hostilidad
hot *adj.* caliente
hotel *n.* hotel
hour *n.* hora
house *n.* casa
how *adv.* cómo
hug *v.* abrazar
huge *adj.* enorme
human *n.* humano
humanity *n.* humanidad
humanize *v.* humanizar
humid *adj.* húmedo
humidity *n.* humedad
humiliate *v.* humillar
humiliation *n.* humillación
humor *v.* complacer; *n.* humorismo
hundred *adj.* ciento; cien

hunger *n.* hambre
hunt *v.* cazar
hunter *n.* cazador
husband *n.* esposo
hydrogen *n.* hidrógeno
hygiene *n.* higiene
hymn *n.* himno
hypnotize *v.* hipnotizar
hypocrite *n.* hipócrita
hypothesis *n.* hipótesis
hysteric *adj.* histérico

I

I *pron.* yo
ice *n.* hielo
ice cream *n.* helado
icy *adj.* helado; glacial
idea *n.* idea
ideal *n. & adj.* ideal
idealize *v.* idealizar
identification *n.* identificación
identify *v.* identificar
identity *n.* identidad
idolize *v.* idolatrar
if *conj.* si
ignorance *n.* ignorancia
ignorant *adj.* ignorante
ill *adj.* enfermo
illegible *adj.* ilegible
illness *n.* enfermedad
illusion *n.* ilusión
illustrate *v.* ilustrar
imaginary *adj.* imaginario
imagination *n.* imaginación
imagine *v.* imaginar
imitate *v.* imitar
immature *adj.* inmaduro
immense *adj.* inmenso
immersion *n.* inmersión
immigrate *v.* inmigrar
immigration *n.* inmigración
immoral *adj.* inmoral
immunity *n.* inmunidad
impeach *v.* acusar
impel *v.* impulsar; impeler
imperious *adj.* imperioso
impersonal *adj.* impersonal
implore *v.* implorar
impolite *adj.* descortés
importance *n.* importancia
important *adj.* importante

impose v. imponer
impostor n. impostor
impractical adj. que no es práctico
impress v. imprimir
impression n. impresión
imprint v. imprimir; fijar; grabar (en la memoria)
improve v. mejorar
improvement n. mejora
improvise v. improvisar
impulse n. impulso
in adv. dentro; prep. durante; en
inability n. inhabilidad; ineptitud; incapacidad
incapacitate v. incapacitar
inch n. pulgada
incidental adj. incidental
incinerate v. incinerar
incision n. incisión
incite v. incitar
inclination n. inclinación
inclusion n. inclusión
incomparable adj. incomparable
incompetent adj. incompetente
incomplete adj. incompleto
incorrect adj. incorrecto
increase v. aumentar; acrecentar
incriminate v. incriminar
indecency n. indecencia
indecent adj. indecente
indefinite adj. indefinido
indent v. mellar; endentar; sangrar (escrito)
indentation n. mella; abolladura; sangría
indicate v. indicar
indication n. indicación
indifferent adj. indiferente
indigestion n. indigestión
indirect adj. indirecto
indiscretion n. indiscreción
individual n. individuo
indoors adv. dentro
industrial adj. industrial
inertia n. inercia
inevitable adj. inevitable
infamy n. infamia
infancy n. infancia
infect v. infectar
infection n. infección
inferior adj. inferior

infinity n. infinidad
inflammable adj. inflamable
inflate v. inflar
inflation n. inflación
inform v. informar
information n. información
informative adj. informativo
infuse v. infundir
infusion n. infusión
ingredient n. ingrediente
inhabit v. habitar
inheritance n. herencia
inhibition n. inhibición
initiate v. iniciar
initiation n. iniciación
inject v. inyectar
injection n. inyección
ink n. tinta
inn n. posada
inner adj. interior
innocent adj. inocente
inoculate v. inocular
inoculation n. inoculación
inscribe v. inscribir
inscription n. inscripción
insect n. insecto
insertion n. inserción
inside n. interior
insipid adj. insípido
insist v. insistir
insolence n. insolencia
insolent adj. insolente
inspection n. inspección
inspiration n. inspiración
instant n. instante
instigate v. instigar
institution n. institución
instruction n. instrucción
insulin n. insulina
integrate v. integrar
integration n. integración
intellect n. intelecto
intellectual adj. intelectual
intelligence n. inteligencia
intelligent adj. inteligente
intense adj. intenso; fuerte; vivo
intensity n. intensidad
intention n. intención
intercede v. interceder
intercept v. interceptar
interest n. interés
interior adj. interior

intermission n. pausa; intermdio; intermisión;

internal adj. interno; doméstico interior

international adj. internacional

interrogate v. interrogar

interrogation n. interrogación; bocacalle

intervene v. intervenir

intimate v. intimar

intimidate v. intimidar

into prep. en; a

intolerant adj. intolerante

intonation n. entonación

intrepid adj. intrépido

intricate adj. intrincado

introduce v. introducir

introduction n. introducción

invade v. invadir

invalid adj. inválido

invasion n. invasión

invention n. invención

invert v. invertir

invest v. investir

investigate v. investigar

investigation n. investigación

invisible adj. invisible

invitation n. invitación

invite v. invitar

ion n. ion

iron v. planchar (ropa); herrar n. plancha; adj. férreo

irony n. ironía

irrational adj. irracional

irregular adj. irregular

irresponsible adj. irresponsable

island n. isla

isle n. isla; isleta

isolate v. aislar

issue v. publicar; salir; n. resultado; emisión

it pron. le; la; lo; ello; ella; éll

itinerary n. itinerario

ivy n. hiedra

J

jab v. golpear; herir con arma blanca

jackal n. chacal

jackass n. burro; asno

jacket n. chaqueta; envoltura; forro

jackknife n. navaja; de bolsillo

jackpot n. premio gordo

jade n. jade

jaguar n. jaguar

jail v. encarcelar, n. cárcel

jam v. apiñar; atascar

jamboree n. francachela; reunión de muchachos exploradores

jangle n. sonido discordante

janitor n. portero

January n. enero

jar n. jarra; tarro; cántaro

jargon n. jerga; jerigonza

jasmine n. jazmín

jaundice n. icterica

jaunt n. excursión; paseo

javelin n. jabalina

jaw n. quijada; mandíbula

jay n. arrendajo; grajo (ave)

jazz n. jazz

jealous adj. celoso

jeer v. mofarse; befar

jell v. cuajar(se); coagular; formarse (opinión, proyecto)

jelly n. jalea

jellyfish n. medusa; aguamala; aguamar

jeopardize v. arriesgar; poner en peligro

jerk v. arrojar; sacudir; tasajear

jersey n. jersey; raza de ganado lechero

jest n. chanza; broma

jet n. chorro; surtidor; avión a reacción; azabache

jetsam n. echazón; cosa deschada

jettison n. echazón

jetty n. malecón; muelle; rompeolas

jewel n. joya

jeweler n. joyero

jewelry n. joyas

job n. trabajo

join v. unir(se); juntar(se)

journal n. periódico; diario personal

journalism n. periodismo

journalist n. periodista

journey v. viajar; n. viaje

joyous adj. alegre

judge *n.* juez; *v.* juzgar
judicial *adj.* judicial
juice *n.* jugo
July *n.* julio
jump *n.* salto, *v.* saltar
jumper *n.* saltador; alambre de cierre
June *n.* junio
jungle *n.* selva
junior *adj.* más joven; menor
jurist *n.* jurista
jury *n.* jurado
justify *v.* justificar

K

kaleidoscope *n.* calidoscopio
kangaroo *n.* canguro
keep *v.* detener; tener; cumplir; conservar; cuidar; mantener
keg *n.* barrilito
kennel *n.* perrera
kerchief *n.* pañuelo; pañoleta
kettle *n.* tetera
key *n.* llave; clave; persona o cosa principal
kidney *n.* riñón
kilogram *n.* kilogramo
kilometer *n.* kilómetro
kind *adj.* bueno; *n.* género
kindly *adj.* bondadoso
kindness *n.* benevolencia; bondad
king *n.* rey
kingdom *n.* reino
kiss *n.* beso; *v.* besar
kitchen *n.* cocina
kitten *n.* gatito
knee *n.* rodilla
knife *v.* acuchillar, *n.* cuchillo
knight *n.* caballero; caballo (ajedrez)
knock *v.* golpear
knot *v.* anudar
knowledge *n.* saber

L

labor *v.* trabajar, *n.* trabajo
laboratory *n.* laboratorio
laborious *adj.* laborioso
lacerate *v.* lacerar

laceration *n.* laceración
lacquer *n.* laca
lactic *adj.* láctico
lad *n.* chico; niño; muchacho
ladder *n.* escalera
lady *n.* dama
lagoon *n.* laguna
lake *n.* lago
lamb *n.* cordero; borrego; carnero
laminate *v.* laminar
lamp *n.* lámpara
land *v.* país; tierra; suelo; terruño
language *n.* lenguaje
lantern *n.* linterna
large *adj.* grande
lass *n.* muchacha
last *adv.* finalmente; *adj.* final
late *adv.* tarde
latitude *n.* latitud
laugh *n.* risa, *v.* reír(se)
laughing *adj.* risueño; sonriente
laughter *n.* risa
lava *n.* lava
law *n.* derecho; ley
layer *n.* estrato
lazy *adj.* perezoso
lead *v.* mandar; conducir; dirigir
leader *n.* líder
leaf *n.* hoja; folio; fronda
league *n.* liga; legua
lean *adj.* magro; flaco; delgado
learn *v.* aprender
least *adv.* menos, *adj.* menor
leave *v.* salir; dejar; irse
left *adj.* izquierdo
leg *n.* pierna; pata; pernil
legal *adj.* legal
legality *n.* legalidad
legend *n.* leyenda
legendary *adj.* legendario
legislate *v.* legislar
legislation *n.* legislación
legitimate *adj.* legítimo
lemon *n.* limón; algo en malas condiciones (auto)
lemonade *n.* limonada
leopard *n.* leopardo
less *adv.,* menos *adj.* menor
lesson *n.* lección
let *v.* dejar; permitir
letter *n.* carta; letra (alfabeto)
lettuce *n.* lechuga

liability n. obligación
liberal adj. liberal
liberate v. libertar; liberar
liberty n. libertad
library n. biblioteca
lie v. mentir; acostarse
life n. vida
lift v. levantar(se); elevar
light n. lámpara; luz
lightly adv. ligeramente; leve-
mente; superficialmente
like n. gusto; semejante; igual;
v. gustar
lilac n. lila
lily n. lirio
limbo n. limbo
lime n. lima; limón verde; cal
limit v. limitar
limousine n. limosina
line v. alinear; rayar, n. raya;
línea
lion n. león
lip n. labio
liquid n. líquido
liquidate v. liquidar
liquor n. licor
list n. lista; nómina; raya de color
literal adj. literal
literary adj. literario
literature n. literatura
little n. &, adv. poco; adj. pequeño
live v. vivir
lizard n. lagarto; lagartija
lobster n. langosta
local adj. local
locality n. localidad
locate v. encontrar; situar; ubicar
lone adj. solitario; solo; único
lonely adj. solo; triste
long adj. largo
look n. mirada, v. buscar; mirar
loose v. soltar, adj. disoluto;
suelto; holgado
lost adj. perdido
lotion n. loción
lottery n. lotería
loud adj. alto (voz);
fuerte (sonido)
love v. amar;
querer, n. amor
lovely adj. hermoso;
exquisito

low adv., adj. bajo, adv. abajo
lower v. bajar; rebajar;   reducir
loyal adj. fiel; leal
loyalty n. fidelidad; lealtad
lubricant n. lubricante
lubricate v. lubricar
luck n. suerte
luggage n. equipaje
lumber n. leño; maderos; madera
(aserrada)
lunar adj. lunar
lunch v. almorzar, n. almuerzo
luster n. lustre
luxury n. lujo
lyric adj. lírico

M

macaroni n. macarrones
macaroon n. mostachón; almen-
drado
macaw n. guacamayo; guaca-
maya
machete n. machete
machinate v. maquinar
machination n. maquinación;
intriga
machine n. máquina
machinery n. maquinaria
machinist n. maquinista
mackerel n. caballa
macrame n. macramé
macrobiotics n. macrobiótica
macrocosm n. macrocosmo
macroscopic adj. macro scópico
mad adj. furioso; descabellado;
loco
madcap adj. alocado
madden v. enloquecer; enfurecer
maddening adj. enloquecedor;
irritante
madeup adj. inventado
madness n. locura; furia
magazine n. revista; cargador
(cartuchos, balas)
maggot n. gusano
magic n. magia
magical adj. mágico
magician n. mago
magisterial adj.
magistral
magistrate n. magistrado

magnesium n. magnesio
magnetic adj. magnético
magnetize v. magnetizar
magnificence n. magnificencia
magnificent adj. magnífico
magnifier n. amplificador; lupa
magnify v. aumentar
magnitude n. magnitud
mahogany n. caoba
maid n. soltera;criada; sirvienta
mail n. correo
mailbox n. buzón
maintain v. mantener
maintenance n. mantenimiento
majestic adj. majestuoso
majesty n. majestad
major adj. mayor
majority n. mayoría
make v. ganar; crear; hacer
maker n. fabricante
making n. fabricación
malady n. dolencia
malaria n. malaria
malcontent adj. malcontento; descontento
male adj. masculino; macho
malediction n. maldición; calumnia
malevolence n. malevolencia; malavoluntad
malevolent adj. malévolo; maligno
malfunction v. funcionar mal
malice n. malicia; mala voluntad
malignancy n. malignidad; malevolencia
malignant adj. maligno
mall n. alameda; paseo; galería comercial
malleable adj. maleable
malnourished adj. desnutrido
malnutrition n. desnutrición
malt n. malta; leche malteada
maltreat v. maltratar
maltreatment n. maltrato
mammal n. mamífero
mammary adj. mamario
man n. hombre; varón
manage v. manejar; administrar; lograr (objetivo)
management n. gerencia

mandarin n. mandarín
mandate n. mandato; orden; decreto
mandatory adj. forzoso; obligatorio
mandolin n. mandolina
maneuver v. maniobrar
maneunerable adj. maniobrable
mangle v. mutilar; desfigurar
mango n. mango; mangó
manhood n. estado adulto; hombría
mania n. manía
maniac adj. maniaco
manicure n. manicura
manicurist n. manicuro; manicutista
manifest adj. manifiesto
manifestation n. manifestación; demostración (pública)
manifesto n. manifiesto; proclama
manipulate v. manipular
manipulative adj. de manipuleo
manliness n. hombría
manly adj. masculino
mannequin n. maniquí; modelo
manner n. manera
mannered adj. de maneras o modales; amanerado
mannerism n. amaneramiento; manerismo; pose; afectación
mannish adj. hombruna
mantel n. manto o repisa de la chimenea
mantle n. manto; capa
manual adj. manual
manufacture n. manufactura
manufactured adj. manufacturado
manuscript n. manuscrito
many adj. muchos
map n. mapa
maple n. arce
mapmaking n. cartografía
mar v. desfigurar; echar a perder
marathon n. maratón
marauder n. merodeador; saqueador
marble n. mármol

marbled *adj.* jaspeado
march *v.* marchar; avanzar
March *n.* marzo
margarine *n.* margarina
margin *n.* margen
marginal *adj.* marginal
marigold *n.* maravilla; caléndula;
  cempasúchil
marina *n.* marina
marine *n.* marino
mariner *n.* marinero
marital *adj.* marital
maritime *adj.* marítimo
mark *n.* marca; señal; huella; nota
marked *adj.* marcado
marker *n.* marcador
market *v.* vender; *n.* mercado
marketable *adj.* vendible; comer-
  ciable
marketer *n.* vendedor
marking *n.* marca
marmalade *n.* mermelada
maroon *v.* abandonar; a la suerte;
  desamparar
marquis *n.* marqués
marriage *n.* matrimonio; boda;
  nupcias
married *adj.* casado
marrow *n.* médula
marry *v.* casar(se)
marsh *n.* pantano; ciénaga
marshal *n.* mariscal
marshy *adj.* pantanoso
marsupial *adj.* marsupial
mart *n.* mercado; centro
  comercial
martial *adj.* marcial
martyr *n.* mártir
martyrdom *n.* martirio
marvel *s.* maravilla
marvellous *adj.* maravilloso
mascot *n.* mascota
masculine *adj.* masculino
masquerade *n.* mascarada
master *n.* maestro; amo; señor
masticate *v.* masticar
material *adj.*, *n.* material
maternal *adj.* maternal
maternity *n.* maternidad
math *n.* matemáticas
mathematics *n.* matemáticas
mature *v.* madurar; *adj.* maduro

May *n.* mayo
may *v.* poder
me *pron.* me; mí
meal *n.* comida
mean *v.* intentar; proponerse;
  significar
measure *v.* medir
measurement *n.* medida; dimensión
mechanic *n.* mecánico
mechanical *adj.* mecánico
medal *n.* medalla
mediate *v.* mediar
medical *adj.* médico; de medicina
  (estudiante)
medication *n.* medicamento;
  medicina; remedio; medicación
medicine *n.* medicina
meditate *v.* meditar
meditation *n.* meditación
meet *v.* reunirse; encontrar(se)
melody *n.* melodía
melon *n.* melón
member *n.* miembro
memorable *adj.* memorable
mental *adj.* mental
mention *v.* mencionar, *n.* mención
mercury *n.* mercurio
merit *v.* merecer
merry *adj.* festivo
message *n.* comunicación
messenger *n.* mensajero
metal *n.* metal
meteorology *n.* meteorología
method *n.* método
microbe *n.* microbio
microphone *n.* micrófono
microscope *n.* microscopio
middle *n.*, *adj.* medio
midnight *n.* medianoche
migrate *v.* emigrar
military *adj.* militar
militia *n.* milicia
milk *n.* leche
million *n.* millón
millionaire *n.* millonario
mind *v.* obedecer; *n.* mente
mineral *n.* mineral
minister *n.* ministro
minor *adj.* menor
minority *n.* minoría
minus *prep.* menos

miracle *n.* milagro
miraculous *adj.* milagroso
mirror *n.* espejo
mischievous *adj.* malicioso; dañino; travieso
miss *v.* perder
mission *n.* misión
missionary *n.* misionero
mistake *v.* equivocar(se); confundir
mister *n.* señor
mistreat *v.* maltratar
mitten *n.* mitón; guante deportivo
mix *v.* mezcla; *v.* mezclar(se); combinar(se)
mixture *n.* mezcla; mezcolanza
model *v.* modelar, *n.* modelo
moderate *v.* moderar, *adj.* moderado
modern *n.* moderno
modest *adj.* modesto
modify *v.* modificar
modulate *v.* modular
moist *adj.* húmedo
mold *v.* moldear; *n.* molde
molecule *n.* molécula
mollusk *n.* molusco
mom *n.* mamá
moment *n.* momento
monastery *n.* monasterio
Monday *n.* lunes
money *n.* dinero
monitor *n.* monitor
monkey *n.* mono; mico; chango
monogram *n.* monograma
monotone *n.* monotonía
monotonous *adj.* monótono
monster *n.* monstruo
month *n.* mes
moon *n.* luna
mop *n.* estropajo; trapeador
moral *adj.* moral
more *n., adv., & adj.* más
moreover *adv.* además
morning *n.* mañana
mortal *n. adj.* mortal
mortality *n.* mortalidad
mortuary *n.* mortuorio
mosquito *n.* mosquito
most *adj.* muy; más
mother *n.* madre
motherhood *n.* maternidad

mother-in-law *n.* suegra
motorcycle *n.* motocicleta
mountain *n.* montaña
mouse *n.* ratón
mouth *n.* boca
move *v.* mudar; mover; conmover; recomendar
movie *n.* película
Mr. *n.* señor
Mrs. *n.* señora
Ms. *n.* señora; señorita
much *adj.* muy; *n., adv., & adj.* mucho
multiple *adj.* múltiple
multiplication *n.* multiplicación
multiply *v.* multiplicar
municipal *adj.* municipal
muscle *n.* músculo
muscular *adj.* musculoso
music *n.* música
musical *adj.* musical
musician *n.* músico
must *v.* deber
mustache *n.* bigote
mutilate *v.* mutilar
my *adj.* mi
myself *pron.* yo mismo
mystery *n.* misterio
myth *n.* mito
mythology *n.* mitología

N

nab *v.* prender; atrapar; arrestar
nag *n.* jaca; rocín
nail *v.* clavar; *n.* clavo
name *v.* apellido; nombre; reputación; fama
napkin *n.* servilleta; almohadilla (sanitaria)
narcotic *adj.* narcótico
narrate *v.* narrar
narration *n.* narración
narrative *adj.* narrativo
nasal *adj.* nasal
natal *adj.* natal
nation *n.* nación
national *n., adj.* nacional
native *adj.* nativo
nativity *n.* natividad
natural *adj.* natural
nature *n.* natura; naturaleza

nausea n. náusea
nautical adj. náutico
naval adj. naval
navigable adj. navegable
navigate v. navegar
navigation n. navegación
near prep. cerca de, adv. cerca; adj. próximo
necessary adj. necesario
necessitate v. necesitar
necessity n. necesidad
neck n. cuello
necklace n. collar
neckline n. escote
nectar n. néctar
need v. necesitar
negative n. negativa
negotiation n. negociación
neighbor n. prójimo; vecino
neighborhood n. barrio; vecindario
neither pron. ninguno, conj. tampoco; ni
neologist n. neólogo
nephew n. sobrino
nervous adj. nervioso
neutral n., adj. neutral
neutrality n. neutralidad
neutralize v. neutralizar
neutron n. neutrón
never adv. jamás; nunca
new adj. nuevo
newly adv. nuevamente; recién
news n. nuevas; noticias
next adj. próximo
nice adj. agradable; amable
nick n. muesca
nickel n. níquel
niece n. sobrina
night n. noche
nightgown n. camisón
nighttime n. noche; de noche
nine adj. nueve
nineteen adj. diecinueve
ninety adj. noventa
ninth adj. noveno
no n., adv. no
nobody n., pron. nadie
noise n. ruido
noisy adj. ruidoso
none pron. nadie; nada
noon n. mediodía

nor conj. ni
normal adj. normal
normally adv. normalmente
north n. norte
northeast n. nordeste; noreste
northwest n. noroeste
nose n. nariz
not adv. no
notable adj. notable
notation n. notación
note v. notar; anotar; n. nota; fama; apunte
notify v. notificar
notion n. noción
notorious adj. notorio
November n. noviembre
now adv. ahora
nuclear adj. nuclear
number v. contar; numerar; n. número
numerical adj. numérico
numerous adj. numeroso
nut n. nuez
nutrition n. nutrición
nylon n. nilón

O

oak n. roble
oar n. remo
oasis n. oasis
obedience n. obediencia
obese adj. obeso
obey v. obedecer
objection n. objeción
objective n. adj. objetivo
obligate v. obligar; comprometer
obligation n. obligación
oblige v. obligar; complacer
oblong adj. oblongo
obscurity n. oscuridad
observance n. observación
observation n. observación
obstinate adj. obstinado
obstruct v. obstruir
obtain v. obtener
occasion n. casión
occasional adj. ocasional
occupation n. ocpación
occur v. ocurrir

ocean *v.* océano
octagon *n.* octagono
October *n.* octubre
odd *adj.* raro; suelto; impar
oddity *n.* rareza; singularidad
odious *adj.* odioso
odor *n.* olor
odorless *adj.* inoloro
of *prep.* de
off *adv.* fuera; lejos; a gran distancia
offense *n.* ofensa
offer *n.* ofrecimiento, *v.* ofrecer
office *n.* oficina; despacho
officer *n.* oficial; funcionario
official *n., adj.* oficial
oil *n.* aceite; petróleo; óleo
oily *adj.* aceitoso; grasiento
ointment *n.* pomada
old *adj.* anciano; viejo
omission *n.* omisión
omit *v.* omitir
omnibus *n.* ómnibus
on *prep.* sobre
once *n., adv.* una vez
oncology *n.* oncología
onion *n.* cebolla
only *adj., adv.* sólo
onto *prep.* sobre; en
opacity *n.* opacidad
opal *n.* ópalo
open *v.* abrir; descubrir; revelar; *adj.* abierto; libre; despejado
opening *n.* abertura; apertura; inauguración
opera *n.* ópera
operation *n.* operación
opinion *n.* opinión
opportune *adj.* oportuno
opportunity *n.* oportunidad
opposite *adj.* opuesto
optical *adj.* óptico
option *n.* opción
optional *adj.* opiónal
or *conj.* o; o sea
oral *adj.* oral
orange *adj.* anaranjado;*n.* naranja
oration *n.* oración
orchestra *n.* orquesta
order *n.* orden
ordinary *adj.* ordinario

organism *n.* organismo
organization *n.* organización
organize *v.* organizar
original *adj.* original
originate *v.* originar
ostentation *n.* ostentación
other *prep.* el otro; *adj.* otro
ounce *n.* onza
our *adj.* nuestro
ourselves *pron.* nosotros; mismos
out *prep.* fuera de; *adv.* fuera
outer *adj.* externo; exterior
outfit *n.* traje; equipo; avíos
outline *v.* trazar; resumir bosquejar; *n.* bosquejo; resumen; boceto; esbozo
outside *adv.* afuera; fuera; *n.* exterior
outward *adj.* exterior; de fuera
ovation *n.* ovación
oven *n.* horno
over *adj.* sobrante; *prep.* sobre; encima de; *adv.* al otro lado; encima; otra vez; de más
overlap *v.* solapar; traslapar; sobreponer
overnight *adj.* de noche
oversight *n.* olvido; inadvertencia; descuido
overturn *v.* volcar; derrocar
overweight *adj.* gordo; pesado
owe *v.* tener deudas
owl *n.* búho; lechuza; tecolote; mucaro; trasnochador
own *v.* reconocer; confesar
oxide *n.* óxido
oxygen *n.* oxígeno
oyster *n.* ostra
ozone *n.* ozono

P

pace *n.* paso; manera de caminar o andar
pacific *adj.* pacífico
pacifism *n.* pacifismo
pacify *v.* pacificar
pack *n.* fardo; paquete; mochila; morral
package *n.* paquete
pact *n* pacto; compromiso; con-

venio

pad n. almohadilla; hoja de ciertas plantas acuáticas

paddle n. canalete; remo

padlock n. candado

pagan n. pagano

page n. página; paje; botones (hotel); acomodador (teatro)

pageant n. espectáculo; público

pail n. cubo; balde

pain v. doler; n. dolor

painful adj. doloroso

paint n. pintura; colorante; v. pintar; teñir

painting n. pintura; cuadro

pair n. pareja; par

pajamas n. pijama

palace n. palacio

palatble adj. sabroso

palate n. paladar

pale adj. pálido; claro

paleontology n. paleontología

palette n. paleta

palisade n. palizada

pall v. perder su sabor

pallid pálido

pallor n. palidez

palm n. palma; palmera

palmistry n. quiromancia

palpable adj. palpable

palpitation n. palpitación

paltry adj. miserable; despreciable

pamper v. mimar

pamphlet n. folleto

pan n. cazuela; cacerola; perol; sartén

panacea n. panacea

pancake n. panqueque

pancreas n. páncreas

pandemonium n. pande monio

pane n. hoja de vidrio; cristal de ventana

panel n. panel

pang n. punzada; dolor

panhandle v. mendigar

panic n. terror; pánico

panorama n. panorama

pansy n. pensamiento; trinitaria

pants n., pl. pantalones

pantheism n. panteismo

panther n. pantera

pantomime n. pantomima

pantry n. despensa

papa n. papá

papacy n. papado; pontificado

paper n. papel

papiermâché n. cartón piedra

papoose n. crío; niño indio norteamericano

papyrus n. papiro

par n. par; paridad; equivalencia

parable n. parábola

parachute n. paracaídas

parade n. parada; desfile

paradise n. paraíso

paradox n. paradoja

paraffin n. parafina

paragraph n. párrafo

parallel adj. paralelo

paralysis n. parálisis

paralyze v. paralizar

parameter n. parámetro; límite

paranoia n. paranoia

paraphernalia n. arreos; objetos de uso personal

paraphrase n. paráfrasis

parasite n. parásito

paratrooper n. paracaidista

parcel n. paquete; bulto

parch v. resecar; (al fuego, sol, frío)

parchment n. pergamino

pardon n. perdón; indulto; v. perdonar; indultar

pare v. pelar (fritas); descortezar

parent n. madre; padre

parrenthesis n. paréntesis

pariah n. paria

parish n. parroquia; condado (Luisiana)

park v. aparcar; estacionar; n. parque

parley v. parlamentar; conferenciar

parliament n. parlamento

parlor n. sala de recibo

parochial adj. parroquial; estrecho; de miras

parody n. parodia

parole n. libertad vigilada o bajo palabra

parrot n. loro; cotorra; papa

gayo

parry v. parar; evitar (golpe)

parsley n. perejil

parson n. clérigo (especialmente protestante)

part v. separar(se); partir(se); n. parte

partial adj. parcial

partiality n. parcialidad

participant adj. partícipe

participate v. participar

participation n. participación

participle n. participio

particle n. partícula

particular adj. particular

particularity n. minuciosidad; singularidad tabique

parting adj. despedida; division; separación

partisan n. partidario; guerrillero

partition n. partición; tabique

partner n. socio; compañero; pareja

partridge n. perdiz

party n. fiesta; bando; facción; partido (político)

pass v. aprobar; pasar

passage n. pasaje; travesía; pasadizo

passenger n. pasajero; viajero

passion n. pasión

passionate adj. apasionado

passive adj. pasivo

passport n. pasaporte

password n. santo y seña

past n., adj. pasado

paste n. engrudo; pasta

pasteurize v. pasteurizar

pastime n. pasatiempo

pastor n. pastor; clérigo (especialmente protestante)

pastry n. pasteles; pastelería

pasture n. pasto; apacentadero

pat n. palmadita; golpecito; trocito (mantequilla)

patch n. pedazo; parche;remiendo

patent n. patente

paternal adj. paterno

paternity n. paternidad

path n. senda; sendero; trayectoria

pathetic adj. patético

pathology n. patología

patience n. paciencia

patient adj. paciente

patio n. patio

patriarchy n. patriarcado

patrimony n. patrimonio

patriot n. patriota

patrol v. patrullar

patron n. cliente; patrocinador; patrón (santo)

pattern n. patrón; molde; modelo; ejemplo

pauper n. pobre; indigente; mendigo

pause n. pausa

pave v. empedrar; pavimentar

pavement n. pavimento

pavilion n. pabellón; ala de un edificio

pay v. pagar; ser provechoso

payroll n. nómina de pago

pea n. guisante; arveja

peace n. paz; calma; tranquilidad

peaceful adj. tranquilo; sosegado

peach n. melocotón

peacock n. pavo real; pavón

peak n. pico; cumbre

peal v. repicar

peanut n. cacahuate; maní

pear n. pera

pearl n. perla

peasant n. campesino

pebble n. guijarro

peccadillo n. pecadillo

peculiar adj. peculiar

peculiarity n. peculiaridad; rasgo característico

pedal n. pedal

peddle v. vender por las calles como buhonero

peddler n. buhonero; mercachifle

pedestal n. pedestal

pedestrian n. peatón

pedigree n. raza pura (animales) genealogía

peel v. pelar; descascarar

peer n. par; igual; semejante

peg n. clavija; estaca
pellet n. bolita; pella; perdigón
pelt n. piel; pellejo
pelvis n. pelvis
pen n. pluma de escribir; corral; prisión
penalty n. pena; castigo; sanción
pencil n. lápiz; estilo de pintar
pendant n. pendiente; medallón
pending adj. pendiente
pendulum n. péndulo
penetrate v. penetrar
penicillin n. penicilina
peninsula n. península
penitent n. penitente
penitentiary n. presidio; penteciaria
penny n. centavo; penique
pension n. pensión
pensive adj. pensativo
pentagon n. pentágono
peon n. peón
peony n. peonía
people n. gente; pueblo
pepper n. pimienta; pimiento
peppermint n. menta
per prep. por; según
perceive v. percibir
percent n. por ciento
percentage n. porcentaje
perception n. percepción
perdition n. perdición
perennial adj. perenne
perfect adj. perfecto
perfection n. perfección
perforate v. perforar
perform v. efectuar; hacer; representar; ejercer
performance n. representación; función; desempeño
perfume n. perfume
peril n. peligro; riesgo
perimeter n. perímetro
period n. período; época; frase musical completa; punto (gramatical)
periodical adj. publicación; periódica
periphery n. periferia
periscope n. periscopio
perish v. perecer

perjure v. perjurar(se)
perjury n. perjurio
permanent adj. permanente
permission n. permiso
permit v. permitir; tolerar
perpendicular adj. perpendicular
perpetual adj. perpetuo; continuo
perplex v. confundir; des concertar
persecute v. perseguir; hostigar
persecution n. persecución
persist v. persistir
person n. persona
personality n. personalidad; características ndividuales; personaje conocido
personnel n. personal
perspective n. perspectiva
perspire v. sudar
persuade v. persuadir
perversion n. perversión
petition n. petición
pharmacy n. farmacia
philosophy n. filosofía
phobia n. fobia
photocopy n. fotocopia
photograph n. foto; fotografía
photography n. fotografía
phrase n. frase; locución
physical adj. físico
physician n. médico
piano n. piano
pick v. picar; elegir
picture n. foto; cuadro; película
pie n. pastel; empanada
piece n. pedazo
pig n. cerdo; puerco; cochino; marrano; chancho
pigeon n. paloma
pillar n. pilar; columna; poste
pine n. pino
pink adj. rosado
pipe n. pipa; tubo; tubería
pity n. lástima
place v. poner; n. posición; sitio
placid adj. plácido
plague n. plaga; epidemia; calamidad
plain adj. llano; sencillo; fácil; n. llano; llanura; planicie
plan v. planear, n. plano; plan

plane *n.* avión; plano; cepillo
planet *n.* planeta
plant *v.* plantar; sembrar; *n.* planta; fábrica
plasma *n.* plasma
plastic *n., adj.* plástico
plate *n.* plato; placa; chapa
play *v.* tocar instrumento musical; jugar; *n.* juego
plea *n.* defensa; peticion; argumento
plead *v.* suplicar; defender; argüir
pleasure *n.* placer
plentiful *adj.* abundante
plenty *n.* abundancia
plum *n.* ciruela
plumage *n.* plumaje
plural *n., adj.* plural
pocket *n.* bolsillo; área o grupo aislado
poem *n.* poema
poet *n.* poeta
poetic *adj.* poético
point *n.* punto; sitio; lugar; punta (herramienta, arma, pluma)
police *n.* policía
political *adj.* político
politician *n.* político
politics *n.* políticia
pollution *n.* polución
pompous *adj.* pomposo
pond *n.* estanque; charca
pony *n.* jaca
pool *n.* piscina; alberca; pileta; estanque
poor *adj.* pobre
Pope *n.* Pope
popular *adj.* popular
populate *v.* poblar
population *n.* población
port *n.* puerto; babor; tipo de vino
portion *n.* parte; porción
pose *v.* plantear; posar; hacerse pasar por
position *n.* posición
positive *adj.* positivo
possess *v.* poseer
possession *n.* posesión
possibility *n.* posibilidad
possible *adj.* posible

post *n.* poste; puesto; correo
postage *n.* porte; franqueo
postcard *n.* tarjeta
poster *n.* cartel
posterior *adj.* posterior
postman *n.* cartero
postmark *n.* matasellos
post-mortem *n.* que ocurre después de la muerte; autopsia
postpone *v.* aplazar
postscript *v.* posdata
posture *n.* postura
pot *n.* olla; tiesto; puchero; montón
potassium *n.* potasio
potato *n.* papa; patata
potent *adj.* potente; fuerte
potential *adj.* potencial
potion *n.* poción; brebaje
pottery *n.* alfarería; cerámica
pouch *n.* bolsa; zurrón; morral; valija (diplomática)
poultry *n.* aves de corral
pound *n.* libra
pour *v.* diluviar; vaciar; derramar; escanciar (vino)
pout *v.* hacer pucheros
poverty *n.* pobreza
powder *n.* polvo
power *n.* fuerza; poder
powerful *adj.* potente; poderoso
practical *adj.* práctico
practice *v.* practicar; ejercer
pragmatic *adj.* pragmático
prairie *n.* pradera; llanura; planicie
praise *v.* alabar
pray *v.* rezar; orar; suplicar
prayer *n.* oración; plegaria
preamble *n.* preámbulo
precaution *n.* precaución
precede *v.* preceder
precedent *n.* precedente
precinct *n.* recinto; distrito electoral
precious *adj.* precioso
precipice *n.* precipicio
precipitation *n.* precipitación
precise *adj.* preciso; exacto
precocious *adj.* precoz
precursor *n.* precursor
predecessor *n.* predecesor;

antecesor

predicament *n.* apuro; situación difícil; predicamento

predict *v.* pronosticar

prediction *n.* pronóstico; predicción

predominant *adj.* predominante

preface *n.* prólogo; prefacio

prefer *v.* preferir

preference *n.* preferencia

prefix *n.* prefijo

prehistoric *adj.* prehistórico

prejudice *n.* prejuicio

preliminary *n.* preliminar

prelude *n.* preludio

premeditate *v.* premeditar

premiere *n.* estreno

premium *n.* prima; gratificación

premonition *n.* presentimiento; premonición; corazonada

preoccupied *adj.* preocupado

preparation *n.* preparación

prepare *v.* preparar(se)

preposition *n.* preposición

preposterous *adj.* absurdo

prerequisite *adj.* requisito previo

prescribe *v.* prescribir; recetar

prescription *n.* receta

presence *n.* presencia

present *adj.* presente, *v.* presentar, *n.* regalo

presentation *n.* presentación

preserve *v.* preservar; conservar

preside *v.* presidir

president *n.* presidente

press *n.* prensa; imprenta

pressure *n.* presión; urgencia

prestige *n.* prestigio

presume *v.* presumir; suponer

pretend *v.* pretender

pretense *n.* pretexto; pretensión; jactancia

pretty *adj.* guapo; bonito; mono

prevail *v.* prevalecer; predominar; prevenir; precaver

prevent *v.* impedir

previous *adj.* previo

prey *n.* presa; víctima

price *n.* precio; costo

priceless *adj.* inapreciable; divertido

prick *v.* punzar; espolear

pride *n.* orgullo; dignidad; amor propio

priest *n.* sacerdote

prim *adj.* estirado; formal; decoroso

primary *adj.* primario

prime *adj.* primero; original; pristino; principal

primitive *adj.* primitivo

primogeniture *n.* primogenitura

prince *n.* príncipe

princess *n.* princesa

principal *n., adj.* principal; director; rector

principality *n.* principado

principle *n.* principio; norma; raíz; causa

print *v.* imprimir

printing *n.* imprenta; tirada

prior *adj.* anterior; previo

priority *n.* prioridad; precedencia

priory *n.* priorato

prism *n.* prisma

prison *n.* cárcel; prisión

privacy *n.* soledad; retiro; intimidad

private *adj.* privado

privilege *n.* privilegio

prize *n.* premio; presa; botín

probable *adj.* probable

probe *n.* sonda; investigación

problem *n.* problema

procedure *n.* procedimiento

proceed *v.* proceder

process *n.* proceso

proclaim *v.* proclamar

proclivity *n.* proclividad; inclinación

procrastinate *v.* dilatar; aplazar

procure *v.* obtener; al cahuetear

prod *v.* punzar; aguijar; estimular

prodigal *adj.* pródigo

prodigy *n.* prodigio

produce *v.* producir

product *n.* producto

profane *adj.* profano

profanity *n.* profanidad; falta de respeto; blasfemia

profession *n.* profesión

professor *n.* profesora; profesor

proficiency *n.* pericia; aprovechamiento

profile n. perfil
profit n. ganancia; beneficio
profound adj. profundo
profuse adj. profuso
profusion n. profusión
progeny n. progenie; prole
prognosis n. pronóstico; prognosis
program n. programa
progress n. progreso; desarrollo
progressive adj. progresivo
prohibit v. prohibir
prohibition n. prohibición
project n. proyecto; plan; v. proyectar; dirigir sobre; planear
projectile n. proyectil
prolific adj. prolífico
prologue n. prólogo
prolong v. prolongar
prominent adj. prominente
promiscuous adj. promiscuo; libertino
promise v. prometer; n. promesa
promote v. promover; fomentar; ascender
promotion n. promoción; scenso
prompt adj. puntual; pronto
pronoun n. pronombre
pronounce v. pronunciar(se)
pronounced adj. marcado; pronunciado
pronunciation n. pronunciación
proof n. prueba
prop n. apoyo; puntal; soporte; pl. utilería decorados
propaganda n. propaganda
propel v. propulsar; impulsar
propeller n. hélice; propulsor
propensity n. propensión; inclinación
proper adj. propio; apropiado; decente
property n. propiedad
prophecy n. profecía
prophesy v. profetizar
prophet n. profeta
propitious adj. propicio
proportion n. proporción
propose v. proponer(se); declararse
proposition n. proposición; prop-

uesta
proprietor n. propietario
propriety n. corrección; decoro
proscribe v. proscribir
prose n. prosa
prosecute v. proseguir; enjuiciar; encausar; procesar
prospect n. perspectiva; esperanza; clientre en perspectiva
prosper v. prosperar
prosperity n. prosperidad
prostrate v. postrar(se); derribar; humillar
protagonist n. protagonista
protect v. proteger
protein n. proteína
protest n. protesta; v. protestar
protocol n. protocolo
proton n. protón
protoplasm n. protoplasma
protrude v. salir fuera; sobresalir; resaltar
proud adj. orgulloso; imponente; arrogante
prove v. probar
proverb n. proverbio
provide v. proveer
province n. provincia
provision n. provisión
provocative adj. provocativo; provocador; estimulante
provoke v. provocar; irritar; estimular
proxy n. poder; apoderado; representante
prude n. gasmoño
prune n. ciruela pasa
pry v. meterse; fisgonear; forzar
psalm n. salmo
pseudonym n. seudónimo
psychedelic adj. psicodélico; sicodélico
psychiatrist n. psiquiatra; siquiatra
psychiatry n. psiquiatría; siquiatría
psychoanalysis n. psicoanálisis
psychological adj. psicológico; sicológico; sicologia
psychology n. psicología
psychosis n. psicosis; sicosis
ptomaine n. ptomaína

puberty *n.* pubertad
public *n., adj.* público
publication *n.* publicación
publish *v.* publicar
publisher *n.* editor; publicador
pucker *v.* arrugar; fruncir
pudding *n.* pudín; budín
puddle *n.* charco
puff *v.* soplar; inflar
pugnacious *adj.* pugnaz
puke *v.* vomitar
pull *v.* tirar; arrastrar
pulley *n.* polea
pulmonary *adj.* pulmonar
pulp *n.* pulpa; pasta de madera
pulpit *n.* púlpito
pulse *n.* pulso
pulverize *v.* pulverizar
pumice *n.* piedra pómez
pump *n.* bomba; inflador;
    zapatilla fina
pumpkin *n.* calabaza
pun *n.* juego de palabras o voca-
    blos
punch *v.* punzar perforar;
    golpear; marcar (hora)
punctual *adj.* puntual
punctuation *n.* puntuación
puncture *n.* pinchazo; puntura
punish *v.* castigar; golpear seve-
    vamente (boxeo)
puny *adj.* encanijado;
    insignificante
pupa *n.* crisálida
pupil *n.* estudiante; pupila
puppet *n.* títere
purchase *v.* comprar
pure *adj.* puro
purgatory *n.* purgatorio
purify *v.* purificar
purple *adj.* purpúreo
purpose *n.* fin; propósito;
    resolución
purr *n.* ronroneo
purse *n.* bolsa; cartera; premio;
    bolsa (competencia)
pursue *v.* perseguir;
    darcaza; acosar
pursuit *n.*
    perseguimiento;
    busca; ocpación
pus *n.* pus

push *v.* empujar;
    apretar; promover (ventas)
put *v.* meter; poner(se); colocar
    (se)
putrefy *v.* pudrir; descomponer
putrid *adj.* podrido; pútrido
putty *n.* masilla
pyramid *n.* pirámide
pyre *n.* pira
python *n.* pitón

Q

quack *v.* graznar; *n.* graznido;
    charlatán; farsante
quadrangle *n.* cuadrángulo
quadrant *n.* cuadrante
quadratic *adj.* cuadrático
quadriceps *n.* cuadríceps
quadrilateral *n., adj.* cuadrilátero
quadriplegia *n.* cuadriplejía
quadruple *v.* cuadruplicar(se)
quagmire *n.* pantano
quail *n.* codorniz
quake *v.* temblar
qualification *n.* calificación;
    idoneidad
qualified *adj.* acreditado; capaci-
    tado
qualifier *n.* calificativo
qualify *v.* habilitar; templar;
    suavizar
qualifying *adj.* eliminatoria
qualitative *adj.* cualitativo
quality *n.* calidad
qualm *n.* duda; escrúpulo;
    remordimiento de conciencia
quantitative *adj.* cuantitativo
quantity *n.* cantidad
quarantine *n.* cuarentena
quarrel *n.* riña; querella
quarreler *n.* pendenciero;
    eleador
quarrelsome *adj.* pendeciero;
    pleitista
quarry *n.* cantera
quart *n.* cuarto; (galón, esgrima,
    naipes)
quarter *n.* cuarto; cuarta parte;
    trimestre; moneda de veinticinco
    centavos
quarterdeck *n.* alcázar

quarterly *adj.* trimestral
quartet *n.* cuarteto
quartz *n.* cuarzo
quaver *v.* temblar; estremecerse
queen *n.* reina
quench *v.* matar; apagar; refrescar
quenchable *adj.* apagable; extinguible
question *n.* pregunta; objeción; tema
quick *adj.* listo; rápido
quiet *adj.* silencioso; discreto; apartado; sencillo
quit *v.* dejar; irse; descontinuar
quotation *n.* cita
quote *v.* citar

R

rabbi *n.* rabino; rabí
rabbit *n.* conejo
rabble *n.* chusma; plebe
rabid *adj.* rabioso
rabies *n.* rabia; hidrofobia
raccoon *n.* mapache; osito lavador
race *v.* correr de prisa; competir con alguien; *n.* raza; carrera
racer *n.* corredor; caballo de carrera
racetrack *n.* pista
racial *adj.* racial
racism *n.* racismo
racist *n.* racista
rack *n.* potro; de tormento; costillar (cordero, res)
racket *n.* raqueta; bullicio; gritería
racy *adj.* picante; vivo
radar *n.* radar
radial *adj.* radial
radiance *n.* resplandor; brillo
radiant *adj.* radiante
radiate *v.* radiar; emitir; brillar
radiation *n.* radiación
radiator *n.* radiador
radical *n., adj.* radical
radicle *n.* radícula
radio *n.* radio
radioactive *adj.* radiactivo
radioactivity *n.* radiactividad

radiobroadcast *v.* radiar; radiodifundir
radiologist *n.* radiólogo
radiology *n.* radiología
radish *n.* rábano
radius *n.* radio
radon *n.* radón
raffish *adj.* pícaro; ruin; vulgar
raffle *n.* rifa
raft *n.* balsa; masa flotante (hielo)
rag *n.* trapo; *pl.* harapos
rage *v.* enfurecerse
ragged *adj.* desigual; andrajoso
raid *v.* atacar por sorpresa
rail *n.* carril; riel
railing *n.* baranda
railroad *n.* ferrocarril
railway *n.* ferrocarril
rain *v.* llover, *n.* lluvia
rainbow *n.* arco iris
raincoat *n.* impermeable; capote
raindrop *n.* gota de lluvia
rainfall *n.* precipitación; lluvia
rainwear *n.* ropa impermeable
rainy *adj.* lluvioso
raise *v.* criar; levantar
raised *adj.* repujado; en relieve
raisin *n.* pasa; pasita
rake *v.* rastrillar; ganar en abundancia; censurar *n.* rastro
rally *n.* reunión, *v.* reunir(se)
ram *n.* carnero
ramble *v.* divagar; callejear
rambler *n.* vagabundo; callejero
rambunctious *adj.* alborotador; travieso; enredador
ramification *n.* ramificación
ramp *n.* rampa
rampage *n.* alboroto; comportamiento violento
rampant *adj.* desenfrenado; exuberante
ranch *n.* hacienda; finca de ganado; rancho; estancia
rancher *n.* hacendado; ganadero; ranchero; estanciero

rancid *adj.* rancio; desagradable

rancor *n.* rencor

random *adj.* fortuito; al azar

range *v.* colocar; alinear; fluctuar; extenderse

ranger *n.* guardabosques

rank *n.* rango; fila; orden

ranking *adj.* superior; má alto rango

rankle *v.* encocorar

ransack *v.* saquear; robar; escudriñar

ransom *v.* rescatar, *n.* rescate

rant *v.* vociferar; despotricar

rap *v.* golpear; reprender severamente; charlar

rapacious *adj.* rapaz

rapacity *n.* rapacidad

rape *v.* violar, *n.* violación

rapid *adj.* rápido

rapidity *n.* rapidez

rapine *n.* rapiña

rapport *n.* relación; afinidad; simpatía

rapt *adj.* absorto; extasiado

rapture *n.* rapto; éxtasis

rapturous *adj.* extasiado

rare *adj.* poco asado; raro; enrarecido; extraordinario

rarefied *adj.* refinado; delicado

rarefy *v.* enrarecer(se); refinar(se)

raring *adj.* impaciente; ansioso

rarity *n.* rareza

rascal *n.* bribón; pillo

rash *n.* erupción; proliferación

raspberry *n.* frambuesa

raspy *adj.* áspero; irritable; chillón

rat *n.* rata; canalla

rate *v.* tasar; considerar; valuar; *n.* razón; valor; costo; tasa

rather *adv.* un poco;preferentemente

ratify *v.* ratificar

rating *n.* popularidad;clasificación

ratio *n.* proporción

ratiocinate *v.* raciocinar

ration *n.* ración

rational *adj.* racional

rationale *n.* explicación; razón fundamental

rationality *n.* racionalidad

rationalization *n.* racionalización

rationalize *v.* racionalizar

rationing *n.* racionamiento

rattle *n.* ruido; cascabeleo

rattrap *n.* ratonera

raunchy *adj.* sucio; destartalado

ravage *v.* destruir; *n.* estrago

rave *v.* delirar; rabiar; hablar con sumo entusiasmo

raven *n.* cuervo

ravenous *adj.* voraz; famélico

ravine *n.* barranco; hondonada

raving *adj.* extraordinario; desvariado

ravish *v.* raptar; violar; atraer; cautivar

ravishing *adj.* encantador

raw *adj.* novato; crudo; frío

ray *n.* rayo

rayon *n.* rayón

reach *n.* alcance, *v.* extenderse; alargar

react *v.* reaccionar

reaction *n.* reacción

reactionary *n.* reaccionario

reactor *n.* reactor

read *v.* decir; leer; interpretar

reading *n.* lección; lectura; interpretación

readjust *v.* reajustar

ready *adj.* listo; fácil (respuesta)

real *adj.* real

reality *n.* realidad

realize *v.* realizar

really *adv.* realmente

realm *n.* reino

reason *v.* razonar; *n.* razón

reasonable *adj.* razonable

rebel *adj.*, *n.* rebelde

rebellion *n.* rebelión

rebuke *n.* reprimenda; repulsa

recall *v.* retirar; hacer; volver

recant *v.* retractar(se); desdecirse

recede *v.* retroceder; contraerse; alejarse

receipt *n.* recibo; *pl.* ingresos

receive *v.* acoger; recibir

recent *adj.* reciente

receptacle *n.* receptáculo

reception *n.* recepción
recess *n.* nicho; cavidad; recreo
recession *n.* retroceso; recesión; depresión económica
recipe *n.* receta
reciprocal *adj.* recíproco
recital *n.* recital
recitation *n.* recitación
recite *v.* recitar
reckon *v.* considerar; calcular; estimar
reclaim *v.* reclamar; hacer utilizable; ganar terreno (al mar)
recline *v.* recostar(se); reclinar(se)
recluse *n.* recluso
recognition *n.* reconocimiento; agradecimiento
recompense *n.* recompensa; compensación
reconcile *v.* reconciliar
reconstruct *v.* reconstruir
record *n.* disco; registro; inscripción; crónica; expediente académico; *v.* registrar
recover *v.* recobrar
recruit *n.* recluta
rectangle *n.* rectángulo
rectify *v.* rectificar
recuperate *v.* recuperar
red *adj.* rojo
reddish *adj.* rojizo
redeem *v.* redimir
redemption *n.* redención
redo *v.* rehacer
reduce *v* disminuir; reducir
reduction *n.* reducción
reef *n.* escollo; arrecife
reek *n.* olor; tufo; aire fétido
refer *v.* referir(se)
referee *n.* árbitro
reference *n.* referencia
refill *v.* rellenar; reenvasar
refine *v.* reflnar
refinery *n.* refinería
reflect *v.* reflejar
reflection *n.* reflejo
reflex *adj.* reflejo
reflexive *adj.* reflexivo
reform *n.* reforma; *v.* reformarse; reformar

refract *v.* refractar
refrain *v.* refrenarse de; abstenerse de
refresh *v.* refrescar; enfriar
refreshment *n.* refresco
refrigerate *v.* refrigerar
refuge *n.* refugio
refugee *n.* refugiado
refund *n.* reembolso
refuse *v.* rehusar
regain *v.* recobrar; recuperar
regard *v.* considerar; contemplar; referirse a
regenerate *v.* regenerar
regent *n.* regente
regime *n.* régimen; sistema (social, gobierno)
regiment *n.* regimiento
region *n.* región
register *v.* registrar; matricular; empadronar; inscribir; *n.* registro; lista; matrícula
regret *n.* sentimiento; arrepentimiento
regular *adj.* regular
regulation *n.* regulación
rehabilitate *v.* rehabilitar
rehabilitation *n.* rehabilitación
rehearse *v.* ensayar
reign *v.* reinar; *n.* reinado
reimburse *v.* reembolsar
rein *n.* rienda
reincarnation *n.* reencarnación
reinforce *v.* reforzar
reiterate *v.* reiterar
reject *v.* rechazar
relapse *n.* recaída, *v.* recaer; reincidir
relate *v.* relatar
related *adj.* afín
relation *n.* relación; relato; pariente; familiar
relax *v.* relajar; aflojar; suavizar; mitigar
release *n.* descargo; exoneración; divulgación; comunicado (prensa)
relent *v.* ceder; aplacarse
reliable *adj.* confiable
relic *n.* reliquia
relief *n.* alivio; auxilio; socorro
relieve *v.* aliviar; relervar; destituir;

exonerar

religion *n.* religión

relish *n.* gusto; placer; apetito; apetencia, *v.* gustar; aderezar; saborear

rely *v.* contar (con); confiar (en)

remain *v.* quedar(se); permanecer; demorarse

remedy *n.* remedio

remember *v.* acordarse de; recordar

remembrance *n.* recuerdo; reminiscencia

remind *v.* recordar; traer a la memoria

reminiscence *n.* reminiscencia; remembranza

remiss *adj.* descuidado; desidioso; flojo

remit *v.* remitir

remittance *n.* remesa

remorse *n.* remordimiento

remote *adj.* remoto

remove *v.* apartar(se); quitar(se)

rend *v.* hender; arrancar; rasgar; desgarrar

render *v.* volver; rendir (honores); dar (gracias); emitir (sentencia)

rendezvous *v.* reunirse

renew *v.* renovar(se)

renounce *v.* renunciar

renown *n.* renombre

rent *v.* alquilar, *n.* alquiler

repair *v.* remendar; reparar

repay *v.* pagar; recompensar; reciprocar

repeat *v.* repetir(se)

repel *v.* repeler; rechazar

repercussion *n.* repercusión

replace *v.* reponer; sustituir

reply *n.* respuesta

report *v.* informar; narrar; referir

reprehensible *adj.* reprensible; censurable

representation *n.* representación

repress *v.* reprimir; oprimir; represar

reproach *n.* reproche

reproduce *v.* reproducir; copiar

reptile *n.* reptil

republic *n.* república

repulse *n.* repulsa; repulsión; rechazo; desaire

reputation *n.* reputación

request *v.* rogar; solicitar; demandar

require *v.* necesitar; exigir; obligar

rescue *n.* rescate

research *v.* investigar

resent *v.* resentirse por; tomar a mal

reservation *n.* reservación; cautela

reserve *v.* reservar

reside *v.* vivir; residir

resident *n., adj.* residente

resign *v.* resignarse; renunciar

resignation *n.* resignación; renuncia

resin *n.* resina

resist *v.* resistir

resistance *n.* resistencia

resolution *n.* resolución

resolve *v.* resolver(se)

resort *n.* recurso; lugar de recreo

resource *n.* recurso; medio

respect *n.* respeto; consideración; honra; punto de vista

respectable *adj.* respetable

respective *adj.* respectivo

respiration *n.* respiración

respirator *n.* respirador

respiratory *adj.* respiratorio

respite *n.* respiro; alivio

resplendent *adj.* resplandeciente

respondent *adj.* respondedor; demandado (divorcio)

response *n.* respuesta

responsible *adj.* responsable

rest *v.* descansar; reposar

restaurant *n.* restaurante

restful *adj.* sosegado; descansado

restitute *v.* restituir

restitution *n.* restitución

restless *adj.* inquieto; intranquilo

restoration *n.* restauración

restore *v.* restaurar; reparar; reconstruir

restrain *v.* refrenar; represar;

sujetar

restrict v. restringir; limitar; prohibir

restriction n. restricción

result n. resultado, v. resultar

resuscitate v. resucitar

retain v. retener; quedarse con

retard v. retardar; retrasar; demorar

retina n. retina

retire v. retirarse; irse a dormir

retract v. retractar(se); retirar (palabras); contraer (garras)

retrieve v. recobrar

retroactive adj. retroactivo

return v. volver; regresar; revertir

reunion n. reunión

reveal v. revelar; dar a conocer

revelation n. revelación

revenge v. engar(se)

reverse adj. inverso; opuesto

review n. reseña

revise v. repasar; revisar

revision n. revisión

revive v. revivir; resucitar; reactivar; reavivar

revoke v. revocar; derogar; cancelar

revolution n. revolución

revolve v. revolverse; dar vueltas (ideas en la cabeza)

reward n. recompensa; remuneración; premio

rhapsody n. rapsodia

rhetorical adj. retórico

rheumatic adj. reumático

rheumatism n. reumatismo

rhyme v. rimar; n. rima

rhythm n. ritmo

rib n. costilla

ribbon n. cinta; banda; listón

rice n. arroz

rich adj. fértil; rico; condimentado; grasoso

rid v. librar(se); quitar de encima

riddle n. acertijo; adivinanza; misterio

ride v. montar; viajar (en vehículo)

ridicule v. ridiculizar

ridiculous adj. ridículo

rifle n. rifle; fusil

right adj. exacto; derecho; legitimo; derecha (tela, mano)

rigid adj. rígido; tieso; inflexible

rigorous adj. riguroso; severo; duro; estricto

rind n. corteza (gueso, naranja); pellejo (tocino); superficie

ring v. sonar; teléfono; timbre; circundar; zumbar (oídos); n. anillo; sortija; rizo (cabello); cuadrilátero (boxeo); redondel (toros); circulo (gente)

rink n. pista

rip v. arrancar; rasgar

ripe adj. maduro

rise v. subir; levantarse; ascender

risk n. riesgo

rite n. rito

ritual n., adj. ritual

rivalry n. rivalidad

river n. río

roach n. cucaracha

road n. camino; rumbo; sendero

roar v. rugir; bramar (tempestad); reírse estripitosamente; correr con estrnendo (locomotora)

rob v. robar; túnica

robe n. bata

robust adj. robusto

rock n. roca; peñasco; peñón

roll n. rollo (papel, tejido); bamboleo; fajo (dinero) lista

romance n. amorío; romance; romanza

romantic adj. romántico

roof n. tejado; techo; azotea

room n. sitio; cuarto; habitación

rooster n. gallo

root n. raíz

rope n. cuerda; soga; cordel

rose n. rosa

rosy adj. rosado; optimista; prometedor; favorable

rotate v. girar; rotar

rough adj. tosco; áspero

roulette n. ruleta

round prep. alrededor de; adj. redondo; completo

route *n.* ruta
routine *n.* rutina
royalty *n.* realeza; *pl.* regalías; derechos de autor
rub *v.* rozar; fregar; friccionar; frotar
rubbish *n.* basura; disparate; tontería
ruby *n.* rubí
rudder *n.* timón; norma; guía
rude *adj.* tosco; rudo
rudiment *n.* rudimento
rug *n.* alfombra; tapiz
ruin *v.* arruinar; *n.* ruina
rule *v.* gobernar; dominar; fallar; *n.* regla; guía; costumbre; línea recta
rumor *n.* rumor; chisme
run *v.* correr; postular (política); competir
running *adj.* corriente; continuo (comentario, ritmo); corrido (lectura, escritura)
rural *adj.* rural
rust *n.* orín; moho
rustic *adj.* rústico
ruthless *adj.* despiadado; cruel
rye *n.* centeno

S

Sabbath *n.* Sabat; día de descanso
saber *n.* sable
sabotage *v.* sabotear; *n.* sabotaje
saccharin *n.* sacarina
sack *n.* saco
sacrament *n.* sacramento
sacred *adj.* sagrado
sacrifice *v.* sacrificar; *n.* sacrificio
sacrilege *n.* sacrilegio
sad *adj.* triste
sadden *v.* entristecer
saddle *v.* ensillar
sadism *n.* sadismo
safari *n.* safari
safe *adj.* seguro; ileso; digno de confianza; inocuo
safety *n.* seguridad
sag *v.* combar(se)

saga *n.* saga
sage *n.*, *adj.* sabio; cuerdo; juicioso; *n.* sabio; salvia
sail *v.* navegar, *n.* vela
sailor *n.* marinero
saint *n.*, *adj.* santo
sake *n.* consideración; motivo; causa
salad *n.* ensalada
salamander *n.* salamandra
salary *n.* salario; sueldo
sale *n.* venta; liquidación
saline *n.* salino
saliva *n.* saliva
sallow *n.* amarillento
sally *n.* salida; ímpetu; ocurrencia
salmon *n.* salmón
salon *n.* salón
salt *n.* sal
salutation *n.* saludo; salutación
salute *v.* saludar; dar la bienvenida
salvage *n.* salvamento
salvation *n.* salvación
salve *n.* ungüento; emplasto
salvo *n.* salva; excepción
same *adj.* mismo; igual; idéntico; monótono
sample *v.* probar
sanatorium *n.* sanatorio
sanctify *v.* santificar
sanction *n.* sanción
sanctity *n.* santidad
sanctuary *n.* santuario
sand *n.* arena
sandal *n.* sandalia; huarache; zapatilla
sandstone *n.* arenisca
sandwich *n.* bocadillo; emparedado
sandy *adj.* arenoso; color de arena (cabello)
sane *adj.* sensato; cuerdo
sanitarium *n.* sanatorio
sanitary *adj.* sanitario
sanitation *n.* instalación sanitaria; saneamiento
sanity *n.* cordura; sensatez; juicio
sap *n.* savia; vitalidad
sapphire *n.* zafiro
sarcasm *n.* sarcasmo

sarcastic *adj.* sarcástico
sarcophagus *n.* sarcófago
sardine *n.* sardina
sari, saree *n.* sari
sash *n.* faja; cinturón; marco de ventana
sate *v.* saciar; satisfacer
satellite *n.* satélite
satiate *v.* saciar
satin *n.* raso; satén; satín
satire *n.* sátira
satisfaction *n.* satisfacción
satisfy *v.* satisfacer
saturate *v.* saturar
Saturday *n.* sábado
satyr *n.* sátiro
sauce *n.* salsa
saucer *n.* platillo
sausage *n.* salchicha; chorizo; embutido
savage *n., adj.* salvaje
save *v.* ahorrar; salvar; reservar (asiento); cuidar (ojos, voz)
saving *n.* economía
savior *n.* salvador
savor *n.* sabor; sazón
saw *n.* sierra; serrucho
saxophone *n.* saxofón
say *v.* decir; expresar
saying *n.* dicho
scab *n.* costra
scaffold *n.* andamio; cadalso
scald *v.* escaldar
scale *n.* escala; escama; capa de óxido
scallop *n.* venera; festón
scalp *n.* pericráneo
scalpel *n.* escalpelo
scan *v.* escudriñar
scandal *n.* escándalo
scandalize *v.* escandalizar
scant *adj.* escaso; insuficiente
scanty *adj.* escaso; corto; reducido
scar *n.* cicatriz
scarce *adj.* escaso
scare *v.* asustar
scarf *n.* bufanda
scarlet *n.* escarlata
scatter *v.* esparcir
scavenger *n.* basurero; animal que come carroña

scene *n.* vista; escena
scenery *n.* paisaje; decoraciones
scent *n.* pista; olor; aroma; fragancia
schedule *n.* horario
scheme *v.* intrigar
schism *n.* cisma
schizophrenia *n.* esquizofrenia
scholar *n.* erudito; alumno; becario
scholarship *n.* erudición; beca
scholastic *adj.* escolar; académico
school *n.* escuela; cardumen (peces)
science *n.* ciencia
scientist *n.* científico
scissors *n.* tijeras
scoff *v.* mofarse; burlarse
scold *v.* regañar; amonestar
scoop *n.* paleta; cucharón
scooter *n.* patinete; patineta
scope *n.* alcance; propósito
scorch *v.* chamuscar
score *n.* cuenta; resultado; nota; partitura (música)
scorn *n.* desdén; desprecio
scorpion *n.* escorpión
scotch *v.* frustrar; suprimir
scour *v.* fregar; recorrer
scout *n.* explorador
scowl *v.* fruncir el entrecejo
scraggy *adj.* áspero; enjuto
scramble *v.* mezclar desordenada o confusa mente; bregar; reñir por
scrap *n.* fragmento; sobras
scrape *v.* raer; raspar
scratch *v.* rayar; ras guñar; rascar
scrawl *n.* garabatos
scream *n.* grito
screen *n.* biombo; pantalla
screw *v.* atornillar; *n.* tornillo
scribble *v.* garrapatear; garabatear
scrimmage *n.* escaramuza; riña; trifulca
script *n.* letra cursiva; guión o

libreto
scrub v. fregar
scruple n. escrúpulo
scrutinize v. escudriñar; escrutar
scrutiny n. escrutinio; inspección minuciosa
scuffle v. pelear; forcejear
sculptor n. escultor
sculpture v. esculpir, n. escultura
scurvy n. escorbuto
scuttle v. echar a pique; anular; arruinar
scythe n. guadaña
sea n. mar
seal n. foca; sello; timbre; v. cerrar
seam n. costura; juntura
seaman n. marinero
seamstress n. costurera
seamy adj. asqueroso; despreciable
seance n. sesión de espiritismo
seaport n. puerto de mar
sear v. marchitar; chamuscar
search v. buscar; inquirir
seashore n. orilla del mar; costa; ribera; litoral
seasickness n. mareo
season n. estación; temporada; sazón
seasoning n. condimento
seat v. sentar; n. asiento; escaño; curul; centro (cultura, comercio, erudición); sede (gobierno)
seaweed n. alga marina
seclude v. aislar; apartar; retraer
seclusion n. retiro; recogimiento
second n., adj. segundo
secondary adj. secundario
second-hand adj. de segunda mano
second-rate adj. inferior
secrecy n. secreto; encubrimiento
secret n., adj. secreto
secretary n. secretario
secrete v. secretar; ocultar
secretion n. secreción
sect n. secta
section n. sección
sector n. sector

secular adj. secular
secure adj. seguro
security n. seguridad
sedate adj. sosegado; serio
sedative n. sedativo; sedante; calmante
sedentary adj. sedentario
sediment n. sedimento
sedition n. sedición
seduce v. seducir
seduction n. seducción
see v. percibir; ver
seed n. semilla; simiente
seek v. buscar; solicitar
seem v. parecer
seemly adj. decoroso; correcto
seep v. rezumarse; filtrarse
seer n. profeta; adivino; vidente
segment n. segmento
segregate v. segregar
segregation n. segregación
seismograph n. sismógrafo
seize v. apoderarse de; asir
seizure n. confiscación; secuestro; ataque; acceso (enfermedad)
seldom adv. rara vez
select adj. selecto; v. elegir
selection n. selección
self n. see myself, yourself
self-command n. dominio de sí mismo; aplomo
self-confidence n. confianza en sí mismo
self conscious adj. tímido
self-control n. dominio de sí mismo
self-evident adj. patente; manifiesto
self-explanatory adj. evidente; obvio
self-government n. autonomía
selfish adj. egoísta; interesado
selfless adj. desinteresado
self-reliance n. confianza en sí mismo
sell v. vender
semantics n. semántica
semblance n. parecido; apariencia
semester n. semestre

semicircle *n.* semicírculo
semicolon *n.* punto y coma
semifinal *adj.* semifinal
seminar *n.* seminario
seminary *n.* seminario
semiofficial *adj.* semioficial
semiprecious *adj.* semiprecioso
semiweekly *adj.* bisemanal
senate *n.* senado
senator *n.* senador
send *v.* mandar; enviar
senile *adj.* senil
senior *adj.* superior; mayor; más antiguo; escolar del último año
seniority *n.* antigüedad; precedencia
sensation *n.* sensación
sense *v.* intuir; percibir; *n.* sentido sensación juicio
senseless *adj.* sin sentido; insensato
sensibility *n.* sensibilidad
sensible *adj.* razonable; sensato; apreciable; sensible
sensitive *adj.* delicado; sensitivo
sensitivity *n.* delicadeza; sensibilidad
sensory *adj.* sensorio
sensual *adj.* sensual; voluptuoso
sensuous *adj.* sensorio; sensorial
sentence *n.* frase; oración; sentencia; condena
sentiment *n.* sentimiento
sentinel *n.* centinela
sentry *n.* centinela
separate *v.* separar(se)
separation *n.* separación
September *n.* septiembre
septic *adj.* séptico
sepulchre *n.* sepulcro
sequel *n.* resultado; secuela; continuación
sequence *n.* sucesión; serie; secuencia
sequester *v.* separar; aislar
sequestered *adj.* aislado; secuestrado (jurado)
sequin *n.* lentejuela
seraph *n.* serafín

serenade *n.* serenata
serene *n.* sereno
serenity *n.* serenidad
serf *n.* siervo
sergeant *n.* sargento
serial *adj.* en serie
series *n.* serie
serious *adj.* serio; formal; grave (enfermedad)
sermon *n.* sermón
serpent *n.* serpiente
serum *n.* suero
servant *n.* sirviente; servidor
serve *v.* servir; entregar notificación
service *n.* servicio
serviceman *n.* militar
servile *adj.* servil
session *n.* sesión
set *v.* fijar; poner(se)
setback *v.* detener; frenar
setting *n.* engaste; (joyas); fondo (musical); puesta (sol)
settle *v.* arreglar; resolver
settlement *n.* colonización
settler *n.* colono
seven *adj., n.* siete
seventeen *adj.* diecisiete
seventh *n., adj.* séptimo
seventy *n., adj.* setenta
sever *v.* cortar
several *adj.* varios; diversos
severe *adj.* severo; riguroso; estricto; grave
sew *v.* coser
sewer *n.* albañal; alcantarilla
sextet *n.* sexteto
sexual *adj.* sexual
shabby *adj.* raído; en mal estado
shack *n.* choza
shackle *n.* grillete; argolla
shade *v.* oscurecer(se); sombrear, *n.* sombra
shading *n.* sombreado; matizado
shadow *n.* sombra
shadowy *adj.* umbroso; vago
shady *adj.* sombreado; dudoso
shaft *n.* eje; pozo; (de ascensor)
shake *v.* estrechar; temblar
shaky *adj.* tem

bloroso; movedizo; indigno deconfianza; poco sólido

sham v. fingir(se), adj. fingido;falso

shambles n. desorden; matadero

shame n. vergüenza

shampoo n. champú

shanty n. choza; casucha

shape v. formar, n. forma

shapely adj. bien formado

share n. parte; cuota; reja del arado; v. compartir

shark n. tiburón; estafador

sharp adj. vivo; cortante; afilado; definido; agudo; atento; sostenido (musica)

sharpen v. afilar; sacar punta

shatter v. hacer(se) pedazos

shave v. afeitar(se); desbastar; cortar en tajadas finas

shaver n. máquina de afeitar

shawl n. chal; pañolón

she pron. ella

shears n. tijeras grandes

shed v. quitarse; verter; mudar la piel (reptiles)

sheen n. lustre; brillo

sheep n. oveja

sheepish adj. tímido

sheer adj. escarpado; transparente; fino

sheet n. sábana; hoja; lámina

shelf n. estante; anaquel; plataforma submarina

shell n. cáscara; corteza; carapacho; caparazón; concha; cásula; casquill (armas)

shellfish n. marisco

shelter n. refugio; santuario; protección

shepherd n. pastor

sherbet n. sorbete; helado (generalmente sin leche)

sheriff n. sheriff; alguacil de policía

sherry n. jerez

shield n. escudo; placa de policía; caparazón (zoologia)

shift v. mover(se); cambiar

shimmer v. rielar; relucir

shin n. espinilla; canilla

shine v. pulir; brillar; destacarse

shingle n. ripia; tejamanil; letrero de consultorio

shiny adj. brillante

ship n. barco

shipment n. embarque; envío

shipwreck n. naufragio

shirk v. evitar; esquivar

shirt n. camisa

shiver v. temblar

shock n. susto; choque; postración nerviosa

shoddy adj. de pacotilla; mal hecho

shoe n. zapato

shoehorn n. calzador

shoelace n. cordón de zapato

shoot v. espigar; disparar; filmar (escena)

shop n. taller; tienda

shopkeeper n. tendero

shore n. playa; costa; orilla

short adj. breve; corto; pequeño; reducido

shortage n. deficienca; escasez

shortcut n. atajo

shorten v. acortar(se)

shorthand n. taquigrafía

shorttempered adj. de mal genio

shot n. tiro; tirador

should aux. v. past form of **shall**

shoulder n. hombro

shout v. gritar; n. grito

shovel n. pala

show v. mostrar(se); demostrar; n. spectáculo

shower v. ducharse; n. ducha

shred v. hacer tiras

shrew n. arpía

shrewd adj. sagaz; prudente

shrimp n. camarón; hombre pequeño

shrine n. relicario; lugar sagrado

shrink v. encoger(se); acobardarse

shrivel v. encoger(se); secar(se); consumirse

shroud *n.* mortaja; sudario
shrub *n.* arbusto
shrubbery *n.* arbustos; maleza
shudder *v.* estremecerse
shuffle *v.* arrastrar los pies;
  barajar (cartas, naipes)
shun *v.* evitar; apartarse de;
  huir de
shut *v.* cerrar(se); encerrar
shutter *n.* contraventana;
  postigo; obturador (fotografía)
shuttle *n.* lanzadera
shy *adj.* tímido
sic *v.* atacar; incitar a atacar
sick *adj.* enfermo; mórbido; harto
  de algo
sicken *v.* enfermar(se)
sickle *n.* hoz
sickness *n.* enfermedad
side *n.* partido; lado; costado; cara
  (monedas); falda (montaña)
sideburns *n.* patillas
sidewalk *n.* acera; vereda
sideways *adv.* oblicuamente; de
  soslayo
siege *n.* sitio; cerco
sieve *n.* coladera; tamiz; cedazo
sift *v.* tamizar; cernir
sigh *n.* suspiro, *v.* suspirar
sight *n.* visión; vista; mira
  (armas; instrumentos ópticos)
sightless *adj.* ciego
sightseeing *n.* visita a puntos de
  interés
sign *n.* signo; señal
signal *n.* señal
signature *n.* firma
significance *n.* significación;
  significado; importancia
signify *v.* significar; indicar
silence *n.* silencio
silent *adj.* silencioso
silhouette *n.* silueta
silica *n.* sílice
silicon *n.* silicio
silk *n.* seda; barba del maíz
silky *adj.* sedoso
silly *adj.* bobo; necio; ridículo
silo *n.* silo
silt *n.* sedimento
silver *n.* plata; monedas de plata;
  servicio o vajilla

silverware *n.* vajilla de plata
simian *a.* símio
similar *adj.* similar; parecido
simmer *v.* hervir a fuego lento
simper *v.* sonreírse afectada-
  mente
simple *adj.* simple; fácil; natural;
  sin afectación
simplify *v.* simplificar
simply *adv.* sencillamente
simulate *v.* simular
simultaneous *adj.* simultáneo
sin *n.* pecado; transgresión;
  vicio
since *conj.* puesto que, *prep.*
  después; desde
sincere *adj.* sincero
sincerity *n.* sinceridad
sinecure *n.* sinecura; prebenda
sinew *n.* tendón
sing *v.* cantar; silbar
  (proyectiles, oídos); zumbar
  (oídos); dar información
singer *n.* cantante
single *adj.* único; soltero; individual
singular *adj.* singular; extraño;
  extraordinario
sinister *adj.* siniestro
sink *v.* hundir(se)
sinner *n.* pecador
sinus *n.* seno
sip *n.* sorbo trago; *v.* sorber;
  beber a tragos
sir *n.* señor; don; caballero
sire *n.* padre; padrón; padrote;
  manera de dirigirse al rey
siren *n.* sirena
sirloin *n.* solomillo lomo
sister *n.* hermana
sister-in-law *n.* cuñada
sit *v.* sentar(se)
site *n.* sitio
situation *n.* situación
six *adj., n.* seis
sixteen *adj., n.* dieciséis
sixth *n., adj.* sexto
sixty *adj., n.* sesenta
size *n.* talla; tamao
sizzle *v.* chisporrotear; chirriar
skate *v.* patinar
skeleton *n.* esqueleto

skeptic *n.* escéptico
skeptical *adj.* escéptico
ski *v.* esquiar
skill *n.* destreza; habilidad
skin *n.* piel
skinny *adj.* flaco
skirt *n.* falda; saya; pollera
skull *n.* cráneo
skunk *n.* zorrillo; zorrino; mofeta
sky *n.* cielo
skyscraper *n.* rascacielos
slacken *v.* aflojar
slacks *n.* pantalones
slander *v.* calumniar, *n.* calumnia
slap *v.* pegar; abofetear
sled *n.* trineo
sleep *v.* dormir
sleeve *n.* manga
sleigh *n.* trineo
slender *adj.* delgado; esbelto
slice *v.* rebanar; tajar, *n.* tajada;
  lonja
slide *v.* deslizarse; tobogán
slim *adj.* delgado; débil
  (esperanza, oportunidad)
slipper *n.* zapatilla
slit *v.* cortar; rajar; *n.* fajo
slope *v.* inclinar(se), *n.* inclinación; estar en declive; cuesta
slow *adj.* torpe; lento; gradual
slowly *adv.* despacio
sly *adj.* astuto, taimado
smack *v.* besar; sonoramente;
  bofetada
small *adj.* pequeño
smart *adj.* listo; fresco
smell *v.* oler
smile *n.* sonrisa, *v.* sonreír(se)
smoke *v.* fumar, *n.*
  humo
smooth *adj.* suave;
  liso; pulido;
  sereno
snail *n.* caracol;
babosa
snake *n.* culebra
snapshot *n.* foto; informal
sneeze *n.* estornudo, *v.* estonudar
snore *n.* ronquido,
  v. roncar
snow *v.* nevar, *n.*
  nieve

so *conj.* por tanto, *adv.* así; tan
soak *v.* remojar; empaparse
soap *n.* jabón
sober *adj.* sobrio; solemne
soccer *n.* futbol
sociable *adj.* sociable
social *adj.* social
socialism *n.* socialismo
socialize *v.* socializar
society *n.* sociedad
sodium *n.* sodio
sofa *n.* sofá
soil *v.* ensuciar manchar, *n.*
  abono; suciedad; tierra
solar *adj.* solar
soldier *n.* soldado
solely *adv.* solamente
solemn *adj.* solemne
solicit *v.* solicitar
solid *n., adj.* sólido
solidarity *n.* solidaridad
solitary *adj.* solitario
soluble *adj.* soluble
solution *n.* solución
solve *v.* resolver; solvcionar
somber *adj.* sombrío
some *pron.* algunos, *adj.* alguno
somebody *pron.* alguien
someday *adv.* algun día
someone *pron.* alguien
something *n.* algo
sometimes *adv.* a veces
son *n.* hijo
song *n.* canción
soninlaw *n.* yerno
soon *adv.* pronto
soothe *v.* calmar
soprano *n.* soprano
sordid *adj.* vil; sórdido
sorry *adj.* triste; afligido; arrepen-
tido
soul *n.* alma; espíritu
sound *n.* ruido
soup *n.* sopa
sour *adj.* agrio; ácido
south *n.* sur
southeast *n.* sudeste; sureste
southwest *n.* sudoeste; suroeste
sovereign *n., adj.* soberano
space *v.* espaciar, *n.* espacio
spacious *adj.* espacioso
spaghetti *n.* espagueti

spasm *n.* espasmo; convulsión; arrebato
spastic *adj.* espástico
spatula *n.* espátula
speak *v.* decir; hablar
spear *n.* lanza; pica
special *adj.* especial
specialist *n.* especialista
specialize *v.* especializar(se)
specialty *n.* especialidad
species *n.* especie
specific *adj.* específico
specify *v.* especificar
spectacle *n.* espectáculo
spectacular *adj.* espectacular
speed *v.* apresurarse; acelerar
spell *v.* deletrear
spellbind *v.* encantar; embelesar
spelling *n.* ortografía; deletreo
spend *v.* gastar; pasar (tiempo)
spermwhale *n.* cachalote
sphere *n.* esfera
spherical *adj.* esférico
spice *n.* especia
spicy *adj.* picante; sazonado; atrevido
spider *n.* araña
spill *v.* verter(se); derramar
spinach *n.* espinaca
spinal *adj.* espinal
spine *n.* espinazo; espina dorsal
spiral *adj.*, *n.* espiral
spirit *n.* espíritu
spit *v.* escupir
spite *n.* rencor mala voluntad
splinter *n.* astilla
split *v.* dividir; separar (se); rajar
spoil *v.* echar(se) a perder; estropear(se); malcriar; consentir
spoken *adj.* hablado
sponge *n.* esponja
spontaneous *adj.* espontáneo
spoon *n.* cuchara
spoonful *n.* cucharada
sporadic *adj.* esporádico
spore *n.* espora
sport *n.* deporte
sportsman *n.* deportista
spot *n.* mancha; lugar; punto
spotty *adj.* manchado

spouse *n.* esposa; esposo
spread *v.* diseminar; regar; extender; propagar
spring *n.* primavera; fuente; resorte *v.* saltar; hacer surgir o brotar
springtime *n.* primavera
spruce *n.* picea; abeto
spurious *adj.* espúrio; falso
spy *v.* espiar; divisar
squadron *n.* escuadrón
squalid *adj.* desaliñado
square *adj.*, *n.* cuadrado
squeak *n.* chirrido, *v.* chillar; delatar
stability *n.* estabilidad
stable *adj.* estable; firme; uradero
stadium *n.* estadio
stage *n.* etapa; escenario
stain *n.* mancha
stair *n.* escalón; peldaño
stairway *n.* escalera
stamp *n.* sello; estampilla; molde; impresión
stampede *n.* estampida
stand *v.* colocar; estar de pie
standing *adj.* derecho; recto; vertical
staple *n.* grapa; producto o artículo principal; basico
stapler *n.* grapadora
star *n.* estrella; astro
starless *adj.* sin estrellas
starry *adj.* estrellado; brillante
start *v.* comenzar; empezar; asustarse
state *n.* estado
static *adj.* estático
station *n.* estación
statistic *n.* estadística
statue *n.* estatua
stay *v.* quedar(se); posponer
steal *v.* robar
steam *v.* empañar; encolerizarse *n.* vapor; vaho; energía
steamy *adj.* vaporoso; húmedo
stem *n.* tallo; tronco; vástago
step *n.* escalera; de mano; pisada; intervalo (musica); paso
stepbrother *n.* hermanastro
stepdaughter *n.* hijastra
stepfather *n.* padrastro

stepmother n. madrastra
stepsister n. hermanstra
stepson n. hijastro
sterility n. esterilidad
stick n. palo
sticky adj. viscoso; pegajoso
stiff adj. rígido; tieso; tirante
still adj. tranquilo; inmóvil
stimulant n. estimulante
stimulate v. estimular
stink v. hedor; malolor
stipulate v. estipular
stipulation n. estipulación
stocking n. media; calceta
stoical adj. estoico
stomach n. estómago
stone n. piedra
stop v. terminar; parar; suspender
stoplight n. semáforo
store n. almacén; tienda
stork n. cigüeña
storm n. tempestad
story n. piso; historia; cuento
stove n. estufa
straight adj. directo; recto;
    continuo; consecutivo; franco
strange adj. extraño; raro
strategic adj. estratégico
strategy n. estrategia
straw n. paja
strawberry n. fresa
stream n. arroyo; flujo
street n. calle
strength n. vigor; fuerza
strict adj. estricto
strike v. atacar; golpear
string n. cordel; hilo; cuerda;
    sucesión
stripe n. raya; franja
striped adj. rayado; listado
strong adj. robusto; fuerte
structural adj. estructural
student n. estudiante
studio n. estudio; taller
study v. estudiar; n.
    estudio
stupendous adj. estu-
    pendo
stupid adj. estúpido
style n. modo; estilo
subdivide v. subdividir
subject adj., n. sujeto

subjective adj. subjetivo
sublease v. subarrendar
sublimate v. sublimar
sublimation n. sublimación
submerge v. sumergir(se)
submission n. sumisión
subnormal adj. subnormal
subscribe v. suscribir(se)
subscription n. subscripción
substance n. esencia; sustancia
substantial adj. sustancial
substitute n. sustituto, v.
    sustituir
subtract v. sustraer
suburb n. suburbio
subway n. metro; tren
    subterráneo
succeed v. suceder; tener éxito
success n. éxito
succession n. sucesión; serie
successor n. sucesor
such adv. tan, pron., adj. tal
suction n. succión
suffer v. sufrir
sufficiency n. suficiencia
suffocation n. sofocación
sugar n. azúcar
suggest v. sugerir
suggestion n. sugestión; sug-
    erencia
suit n. traje; terno; demanda;
    galanteo
sum v. sumar, n. suma
summary adj. sumario; resúmen
summer n. verano
sun n. sol
Sunday n. domingo
sundown n. puesta del sol
sunflower n. girasol
sunglasses n. gafas de sol
sunlight n. luz del sol
sunrise n. salida del sol
superficial adj. superficial
superior n., adj. superior
supermarket n. supermercado
superstition n. superstición
supine adj. supino; indolente
supper n. cena
supplement n. suplemento
supplicate v. suplicar
suppose v. suponer
suppression n. supresión

supremacy n. supremacía
supreme adj. supremo
sure adj. seguro; firme; cierto; infalible
surely adv. seguramente
surface n. superficie
surgeon n. cirujano
surgery n. cirugía
surname n. apellido; apodo
surprise v. sorprender, n. sorpresa
survive v. sobrevivir
susceptible adj. susceptible
suspend v. suspender
suspension adj. suspensión
suspicious adj. sospechoso
sustain v. sustentar
swan n. cisne
swap v. cambiar; trocar
swat v. matar; (con golpe insectos); aporrear
swear v. jurar
sweat n. sudor, v. sudar
sweaty adj. sudoroso
sweet adj. dulce
swim n. natación, v. nadar
swimmer n. nadador
switch v. cambiar; fustigar; conectar; n. llavedeloz
sword n. espada
syllable n. sílaba
symbol n. símbolo
symbolic adj. simbólico
symbolism n. simbolismo
symbolize v. simbolizar
symmetry n. simetría
sympathy n. simpatía
syndicate v. sindicar; n. sindicato
synonym n. sinónimo
synonymous adj. sinónimo
synthetic adj. sintético
system n. sistema
systematize v. sistematizar

T

tab n. cuenta; lengüeta; indicador
tabernacle n. tabernáculo
table n. mesa

tablespoonful n. cucharada
tablet n. tableta
taboo, tabu adj. tabú
tabular adj. tabular
tabulate v. tabular
tacit adj. tácito
taciturn adj. taciturno
tack n. tachuela; virada
tackle n. equipo; carga
tact n. tacto
tactics n. táctica
tadpole n. renacuajo
taffeta n. tafetán
taffy n. caramelo; melcocha
tag n. etiqueta; marbete
tail n. cola; rabo
tailor n. sastre
taint v. hechar a peroler; corromper(se); contaminar(se)
take v. coger; tomar; sacar; sorprender; entender
takeoff n. despegue; parodia
tale n. cuento; rumor; chisme
talent n. talento
talented adj. talentoso
talisman n. talismán
talk v. decir; hablar; conversar
talkative adj. hablador
tall adj. alto
tallow n. sebo
tally n. cuenta; marca; muesca
talon n. garra
tambourine n. pandereta
tame adj. domesticado; sumiso; manso; soso
tamper v. estropear; falsificar
tan v. curtir; tostar (the skin)
tandem adv. en tándem
tang n. sabor fuerte
tangent n., adj. tangente
tangerine n. naranja mandarina o tangerina
tangible adj. tangible
tangle v. enredar(se)
tango n. tango
tank n. tanque;(mil) aljibe; depósito
tantalize v. atormentar; tentar; provocar
tantamount adj. equivalente

tap n. llave de agua; espita; intercepción (teléfono) grifo; golpecito
tape n. cinta; trencilla
taper v. afilar
tapestry n. tapiz
tapeworm n. tenia; solitaria
tapioca n. tapioca
tapir n. tapir; danta; macho de monte
tar v. alquitranar; embrear
tarantula n. tarántula
tardy adj. tardío; lento
target n. blanco; objetivo
tariff n. tarifa; arancel
tarnish v. deslustrar(se); em pañar
tarry v. tardar; detenerse
task n. tarea; labor
tassel n. borla; espiguilla (maíz)
taste n. sabor; gusto; preferencia
tasty adj. sabroso
tatter n. andrajo
tattered adj. harapiento; andrajoso
tattoo n. tatuaje
taunt n. mofa; sarcasmo; escarnio
taut adj. tieso; tirante; tenso; aseado
tavern n. taberna
tawny adj. leonado
tax n. impuesto; contribución; carga
taxi n. taxi
taxicab n. taxi
tea n. té
teabag n. sobre de té; (muñeca de te)
teach v. instruir; enseñar; educar
teacher n. maestro; profesora; profesor
teacup n. taza para té
team n. equipo
teammate n. compañero de equipo
teamster n. camionero; camionista
teamwork n. cooperación; trabajo colectivo

tear n. lágrima
tear v. rasgar(se); romper(se)
tease v. tomar el pelo; atormentar
teaspoon n. cucharilla
technical adj. técnico
technician n. técnico
technology n. tecnología
tedious adj. tedioso
telegram n. telegrama
telegraph n. telégrafo
telephone n. teléfono
telescope n. telescopio
television n. televisión
tell v. decir
temperamental adj. temperamental
temperature n. fiebre; temperatura
temple n. templo
tempo n. tempo; compás; ritmo
temporal adj. temporal
temptation n. tentación
ten adj., n. diez
tend v. tender a; inclinarse a
tendency n. tendencia
tenderly adv. tiernamente
tendon n. tendón
tennis n. tenis
tense v. tensar, adj. tenso
tension n. tensión
terminal adj., n. terminal
terminate v. terminar
terminology n. terminología
terrain n. terreno
terrestrial adj. terrestre
terrible adj. terrible
terrific adj. terrífico; espantoso; magnífico
terror n. terror; pavor
test v. examinar, n. examen
testify v. testificar; dar testimonio
text n. texto; tema
texture n. textura
than conj. de; que
thanks n. gracias
that adj. aquella; aquél; esa; ese
the def. art. la; el; las; los; lo
theater n. teatro

them *pron.* las; les; los; ellas; ellos

then *adv.* luego; entonces

theology *n.* teología

theorize *v.* teorizar

theory *n.* teoría

there *adv.* ahí; allí; allá

thermal *adj.* termal

thermometer *n.* termómetro

thesaurus *n.* diccionario

these *pron.* éstas; éstos; *adj.* estos; estas

they *pron.* ellas; ellos

thick *adj.* denso; grueso; espeso; torpe

thief *n.* ladrón

thigh *n.* muslo

thin *adj.* escaso; delgado; aguado

thing *n.* cosa

think *v.* creer; pensar

third *adj.* tercero

thirst *n.* sed

thirteen *n., adj.* trece

thirty *n., adj.* treinta

this *adj.* esta; este, *pron.* esto; ésta; éste

thorn *n.* espina; púa

thorny *adj.* espinoso; embrollado

thorough *adj.* completo; concienzudo

though *adv.* sin embargo, *conj.* aunque

thoughtful *adj.* pensativo; atento; considerado

thousand *n., adj.* mil

threaten *v.* amenazar

three *n., adj.* tres

throat *n.* garganta

throne *n.* trono

through *prep.* por; travésde

throw *v.* lanzar; echar; derribar

thumb *n.* pulgar

Thursday *n.* jueves

tibia *n.* tibia

tickle *v.* cosquillear

tide *n.* marea

tiger *n.* tigre

till *prep.* hasta

timber *n.* madero; madera de construcción

time *n.* hora; tiempo; vez

timid *adj.* tímido

timidity *n.* timidez

tip *n.* propina; punta; cabo; soplo (secreto); indicio

tire *v.* cansar(se)

tired *adj.* cansado

tiresome *adj.* molesto; tedioso; aburrido

tissue *n.* tisú; gasa; tejido

titanic *adj.* titánico

tithe *n.* diezmo

title *v.* titular, *n.* título

titter *v.* reír entre dientes

titular *adj.* titular

to *adv., prep.* hacia, *prep.* hasta; a

toad *n.* sapo

toast *v.* tostar; brindar

tobacco *n.* tabaco

toboggan *n.* tobogán

today *n., adv.* hoy

toe *n.* dedo del pie

toga *n.* toga

together *adv.* juntos

toil *v.* trabajar asiduamente; afanarse

toilet *n.* retrete; váter; tocador

toiletry *n.* artículo de tocador

token *n.* indicio; prenda; señal; ficha

tolerable *adj.* tolerable; regular

tolerance *n.* tolerancia

tolerant *adj.* tolerante

tolerate *v.* permitir; tolerar

toll *n.* peaje

tomato *n.* tomate; (jitomate)

tomorrow *adv., n.* mañana

ton *n.* tonelada

tone *n.* tono; tendencia

tongs *n.* tenazas; pinzas

tongue *n.* lengua; habla; lenguaje

tonic *n.* tónico

tonight *adv.* esta noche

tonnage *n.* tonelaje

tonsil *n.* amígdala; tonsila

too *adv.* además; también; demasiado

tool *n.* herramienta; instrumento

tooth *n.* diente; púa; mella

toothache *n.* dolor de muelas

toothbrush n. cepillo de dientes

top n. tapa; cima; copa (árbol); coronilla (cabeza); parte superior

topaz n. topacio

topcoat n. sobretodo

tophat n. chistera; sombrero de copa

topic n. tema; asunto; tópico

topical adj. (med.) tópico; deactvalidaol

topple v. venirse abajo

torch n. antorcha

torment v. atormentar

tornado n. tornado

torpedo n. torpedo

torrent n. torrente

torrid adj. tórrido; ardiente

torso n. torso

tortoise n. tortuga

tortuous adj. tortuoso

torture v. torturar

toss v. echar de un lado a otro; menear; tirar; lanzar

tot n. nene; nena

total n., adj. total

totalitarian adj. totalitario

totally adv. totalmente

tote v. inf. llevar; cargar

totem n. tótem

touch v. tocar(se)

touchy adj. irritable; delicado

tough adj. difícil; duro; tenaz

toughen v. endurecer(se); hacer(se) tenaz; templar

tour v. viaje; excursión; vuelta; circuito

tourism n. turismo

tourist n. turista

tournament n. torneo

tourniquet n. torniquete

tousle v. despeinar

tow v. llevar a remolque

toward prep. hacia

towel n. toalla

tower n. torre

town n. pueblo; ciudad

toxic adj. tóxico

toxin n. toxina

trace n. indicio; huella; rastro

trachea n. tráquea

track n. vía; pista; senda

tract n. extensión; tracto; región; zona

tractor n. tractor

trade v. comerciar; trocar; canjear

trademark n. marca de fábrica; marca registrada

tradition n. tradición

traditional adj. tradicional

traduce v. calumniar; difamar

traffic n. tráfico; tránsito

tragedy n. tragedia

tragic adj. trágico

trail v. arrastrar(se); rastrear; perseguir; quedarse detrás de

trailer n. remolque; casarremolque; avance publicitario (cine)

train n. tren; sucesión (ideas); cola (traje de novia)

trait n. característica; rasgo

traitor n. traidor

trajectory n. trayectoria

tramp v. andar con pasos pesados

trample v. pisotear

trance n. arrobamiento; estado hipnótico

tranquil adj. tranquilo

tranquillity n. tranquilidad

tranquillize v. tranquilizar

tranquilizer n. tranquilizante; calmante

transcend v. sobresalir; rebasar; trascender

transcribe v. transcribir

transcript n. transcripción; copia

transcription n. transcripción

transfer v. transferir; trasladar; transbordar

transference n. transferencia; traspaso

transform v. transformar

transformation n. transformación; conversión

transfusion n. transfusión

transgress v. traspasar; transgredir; excederse; extralimitarse

transient adj. transitorio; pasajero

transistor n. transistor

transit n. tránsito

transition n. tránsicón
transitive adj. transitivo
transitory adj. transitorio
translate v. traducir; descifrar
translation n. traducción
translucent adj. translúcido
transmission n. transmisión
transmit v. transmitir
transmitter n. transmisor
transom n. travesaño; dintel
transparent adj. transparente
transpire v. transpirar; suceder
transplant v. trasplantar
transport n. transporte, v. transportar
transportation n. transporte
transpose v. transponer
trap v. entrampar
trapeze n. trapecio
trash n. basura
trauma n. trauma
traumatic adj. traumático
travel v. viajar
treason n. traición
treasure n. tesoro
treasury n. tesorería; tesorero público
treat v. tratar; negociar; n. regalo delicia
treatise n. tratado
treatment n. tratamiento
treaty n. tratado; pacto
treble adj. triple; de soprano
tree n. árbol
trek v. caminar; hacer caminata fatigosa
trellis n. enrejado; espaldera
tremble v. temblar
tremendous adj. tremendo; formidable
tremor n. temblor
trial n. prueba; tanteo; juicio (derecho)
triangular adj. triangular
tribunal n. tribunal
tribute n. tributo
trick n. truco; trampa; engaño
trickle v. gotear; escurrir(se)
tricycle n. triciclo
tried adj. probado; confiable

trifle n. bagatela
trifling adj. sin importancia
trigger n. gatillo
trigonometry n. trigonometría
trillion n. billón
trim v. guarnecer; adornar; reducir; recortar
trinket n. dije
trio n. trío
trip n. viaje
triple v. triplicar(se)
triplet n. trillizo
tripod n. trípode
trite adj. gastado; trillado; trivial
triumph n. triunfo
triumphant adj. triunfante
trivial adj. trivial; frívolo
triviality n. trivialidad; frivolidaol
trolley n. tranvía
troop n. tropa; escuadrón; turba; caterva
trooper n. soldado de caballería; polica montado; policia esatal
trophy n. trofeo
tropic n. trópico
tropical adj. tropical
trot v. ir al trote; hacer trotar
troubadour n. trovador
trouble v. molestar(se); pre ocuparse
troublesome adj. molesto
trough n. abrevadero; comedero
troupe n. compañía (actores, circo)
trousseau n. ajuar
trout n. trucha
trowel n. paleta; desplantador
truant n. novillero; haragán; estudiante que se escapa de las clases
truce n. tregua
truck n. camión
true adj. verdadero; legitimo; exacto
truly adv. verdaderamente; realmente
trump n. triunfo (juegos); buena persona
trumpet n. trompeta
trunk n. tronco (de árbol, familia); baúl; trompa (elefante); tórax (insectos)

trust v. esperar; fiarse de; creer en n. fideicomiso; confianza

trustee n. fideicomisario

trustworthy adj. fidedigno; confiable

trusty adj. seguro; fiel; leal

truth n. verdad; realidad

truthful adj. veraz; verídico

try v. probar; intentar

tub n. bañera; tina

tuba n. tuba

tube n. tubo; caño; túnel subterráneo (trenes)

tuberculosis n. tuberculosis

tuck v. alforzar; plegar

Tuesday n. martes

tuft n. copete; mechón de pelo

tug v. tirar con fuerza; remolcar

tuition n. enseñanza; derechos de matrícula

tulip n. tulipán

tumble v. caer(se); dar volteretas; tambalearse

tumor n. tumor

tumult n. tumulto

tumultuous adj. tumultuoso

tuna n. atún

tundra n. tundra

tune n. aire; afinación

tunic n. túnica

tunnel n. túnel

turban n. turbante

turbid adj. turbio; confuso

turbine n. turbina

turbulent adj. turbulento

tureen n. sopera

turf n. césped; pista (carreras de caballos)

turkey n. pavo; fiasco; fracaso

turmoil n. tumulto; agitación; confusión

turn v. volver(se); girar; torcer (tobillo)

turnip n. nabo

turnout n. producción; concurrencia

turnpike n. autopista, especialmente con pago de peaje

turquoise n. turquesa

turret n. torrecilla; torreta

turtle n. tortuga

tusk n. colmillo; (de animales); diente grande y saliente

tussle n. agarrada; forcejeo; pelea

tutelage n. tutela

tutor n. tutor; preceptor; maestro particular

tuxedo n. smoking; traje de etiqueta masculino

TV n. televisión

twang n. tañido; timbre nasal

tweed n. tela de mezcla de lana

tweezers n. pinzas; tenacillas; bruselas

twelfth adj. duodécimo; doceavo

twelve adj., n. doce

twenty adj., n. veinte

twice adv. dos veces

twig n. ramita

twilight n. crepúsculo; decadencia; ocaso

twill n. tela cruzada

twin adj., n. gemelo; mellizo

twine n. guita; bramante; cordel

twinge n. dolor agudo; punzada

twinkle v. centellear; parpadear

twirl v. girar; piruetear

twist v. torcer(se); dislocar(se)

twitch v. crisparse

twitter v. gorjear

two adj., n. dos

tycoon n. magnate

type n. tipo

typhoid n. fiebre tifoidea

typhoon n. tifón

typical adj. típico

typify v. simbolizar; representar

typist n. mecanógrafo

typography n. tipografía

tyrannical adj. tiránico; despótico

tyrannize v. tiranizar

tyranny n. tiranía

U

ubiquitous adj. ubicuo

ubiquity n. ubicuidad

udder n. ubre

ugliness *n.* fealdad
ugly *adj.* feo
ukulele *n.* ukelele
ulcer *n.* úlcera
ulcerate *v.* ulcerar(se)
ulna *n.* cúbito; ulna
ulterior *adj.* ulterior
ultimate *adj.* último;
  fundamental; máximo
ultimatum *n.* ultimatum
ultra *adj.* excesivo
ultramodern *adj.* ultramoderno
ultrasonic *adj.* ultrasónico
ultrasound *n.* ultrasonido
ultraviolet *adj.* ultravioleta
umbrella *n.* paraguas; sombrilla
umpire *n.* árbitro
unabashed *adj.* desver
  gonzado; descarado
unable *adj.* incapaz;
  imposibilitado
unabridged *adj.* no abreviado;
  íntegro; completo
unaccented *adj.* sin acento;
  átono; inacentuado
unacceptable *adj.* inaceptable
unaccountable *adj.*
  inexplicable; irresponsable
unaccustomed *adj.* no acostum-
  brado; insólito
unacknowledged *adj.* no
  conocido; ignorado
unadorned *adj.* sin adorno
unaffected *adj.* sin afectación;
  natural; genuino
unafraid *adj.* sin temor
unaided *adj.* sin ayuda; solo
unambiguous *adj.* sin
  ambigüedad; inequívoco
unanimous *adj.* unánime
unanswerable *adj.*
  incontestable; irrebatible
unapproachable *adj.*
  inaccesible; inalcanzable
unarmed *adj.* desarmado
unassailable *adj.*
  inexpugnable; irreductible
unassisted *adj.* sin ayuda
unassuming *adj.* modesto;
  sencillo
unattended *adj.* desatendido
unattractive *adj.* sin atractivo

unauthorized *adj.* desauto
  rizado
unavoidable *adj.* inevitable
unaware *adj.* ignorante(de)
unawares *adv.* de improviso
unbeatable *adj.* invencible
unbeaten *adj.* invicto
unbecoming *adj.* que sienta
  mal; impropio; indecoroso
unbelief *n.* incredulidad
unbelievable *adj.* increíble
unbeliever *n.* incrédulo;
  escéptico
unbending *adj.* inflexible
unbiased *adj.* imparcial; neutral
unbind *v.* desatar; desamarrar
unblemished *adj.* puro;
  inmaculado
unborn *adj.* no nacido; nonato
unbounded *adj.* ilimitado
unbreakable *adj.* irrompible
unbridled *adj.* desenfrenado
unbroken *adj.* inviolado; sin
  romper
unbuckle *v.* deshebillar
unburden *v.* descargar; aliviar;
  desahogar
unbutton *v.* desabotonar(se)
uncaged *adj.* suelto de la jaula
uncanny *adj.* extraño; misterioso
unceasing *adj.* incesante
unceremonious *adj.* informal;
  abrupto; descortés
uncertain *adj.* indeciso; dudoso;
  perplejo; variable
uncertainty *n.* incertidumbre
unchangeable *adj.* inalterable
unchanged *adj.* inalterado
unchanging *adj.* invariable
uncharted *adj.* desconocido; inexplorado
uncivil *adj.* incivil; descortés
uncivilized *adj.* incivilizado;
  bárbaro; salvaje
unclasp *v.* separar; (manos
  estrechadas); desabrochar
uncle *n.* tío
unclean *adj.* sucio; impuro
unclear *adj.* confuso
unclog *v.* desatascar
uncomfortable *adj.* incómodo
uncommon *adj.* raro;

infrecuente; excepcional

uncommunicative *adj.* poco comunicativo reservado; taciturno

uncompromising *adj.* inflexible

unconnected *adj.* inconexo

unconscious *adj.* inconsciente

unconsidered *adj.* inconsiderado; insignificante

uncooked *adj.* crudo

uncounted *adj.* innumerable; no contado

uncross *v.* descruzar

undecided *adj.* indeciso

underestimate *v.* subestimar

underline *v.* subrayar; recalcar

underneath *adv.* debajo, *prep.* bajo

understand *v.* comprender; entender

undertake *v.* emprender

underwear *n.* ropa interior

undo *v.* desatar; deshacer (nudo); arruinar

uneasy *adj.* intranquilo

unfinished *adj.* incompleto; sin barnizar o pulir

unfold *v.* extender; abrir; desenrollar; dar a conocer

uniform *n.* uniforme

union *n.* unión

united *adj.* unido

universal *adj.* universal

unlucky *adj.* desdichado; infortunado; de mal agüero

unrest *n.* inquietud; disturbio

unseemly *adj.* indecoroso

unskilled *adj.* inexperto

unsophisticated *adj.* cándido; inexberto

unstable *adj.* inestable; fluctuante; irregular

unsteady *adj.* inseguro; tambaleante

until *prep.* hasta

untruthful *adj.* mentiroso

unusual *adj.* raro; inusitado; insólito

unwrap *v.* desenvolver

up *prep.* hacia arriba *adj.* ascendente, *adv.* arriba; para

arriba

upholstery *n.* tapicería

upon *prep.* sobre; encima de

upper *adj.* alto; superior; más elevado

uproar *n.* alboroto; conmoción

upset *n.* trastorno; *v.* volcar; derrotar

upstairs *adj.* arriba

uranium *n.* uranio

urban *adj.* urbano

urge *n.* impulso, *v.* incitar; estimular

urgent *adj.* urgente

um *n.* urna

us *pron.* nosotras; nosotros; nos

use *n.* uso, *v.* utilizar; usar

useless *adj.* inútil; inservible; inepto

usual *adj.* usual; habitual

utensil *n.* utensilio

utilitarian *n.* utilitario

utility *n.* utilidad; provecho; empresa de servicio público

utilize *v.t.* utilizar

utterance *n.* expresión; aserción

uterus *n.* útero

V

vacancy *n.* vacante

vacant *adj.* vacío

vacation *n.* vacación; vacaciones

vaccinate *v.* vacunar

vaccination *n.* vacunacion

vaccine *n.* vacuna

vacillate *v.* vacilar; titubear

vacillation *n.* vacilación; fluctuación

vacuity *n.* vacuidad

vacuum *n.* vacío

vagrant *n.* vagabundo; vago

vague *adj.* incierto; vago

vain *adj.* vano; inútil

vale *n.* valle

valedictory *n.* discurso de despedida

valentine *n.* novia o novio el día

de San Valentín; regalo; tarjeta;
del día de San Valentín
valid adj. válido
validate v. validar
validity n. validez; vigencia
valise n. maleta; valija
valley n. valle
valor n. valor; valentía
valuable adj. valioso; costoso;
precioso
valuation n. valuación; avalúo;
tasación
value v. valuar, n. valor; mérito;
aprecio
valve n. válvula
van n. vanguardi; camión de
mudanzas (militar)
vane n. veleta; aspa
de molino
vanguard n. vanguardia
vanilla n. vainilla
vanish v. desaparecer;
desvanecerse
vanity n. vanidad
vanquish v. vencer; conquistar;
dominar
vantage n. ventaja; provecho
vapid adj. insípido; soso
vapor n. vapor; vaho
vaporize v. vaporizar(se)
vaporous adj. vaporoso; etéreo;
nebuloso
variability n. variabilidad
variable n., adj. variable
variation n. variación
varicose adj. varicoso
varied adj. variado
variety n. variedad;
diversidad
various adj. variado; diverso;
numerosos; diferente
varnish n. barniz
varsity n. equipo principal de
una universidad
vary v. variar; desviarse;
cambiar; discrepar
vase n. jarrón; florero
vast adj. vasto; extenso
veal n. ternera
vegetable n. legumbre; verdura;
hortaliza; vegetal
vegetarian n. vegetariano

vegetation n. vegetación
vehicle n. vehículo
vein n. vena; humor; genio; veta
velocity n. velocidad
venality n. venalidad
vend v. vender; expender
venerable adj. venerable
veneration n. veneración
venial adj. venial
venom n. veneno; ponzoña
venomous adj. venenoso;
ponzoñoso; maligno
ventilate v. ventilar; airear
ventral adj. ventral;
abdominal
ventricle n. ventrículo
venturesome adj. aventurado;
arriesgado
veracious adj. veraz; verídico
verb n. verbo
verbal adj. verbal; oral
verbose adj. verboso; prolijo
verbosity n. verbosidad
verdict n. veredicto; fallo
verify v. verificar
vermouth n. vermut
vernal adj. vernal; primaveral;
juvenil
verse n. versículo; verso
version n. versión
vertebra n. vértebra
vertebrate adj. vertebrado
vertical adj. vertical
very adj. mismo; puro; adv. muy;
mucho
vessel n. vaso; (sanguíneo);
receptácul; embarcación
vest n. chaleco
veteran adj., n. veterano
vibrant adj. vibrante
vibrate v. oscilar
vibration n. vibración
vicar n. vicario
vice n. vicio; defecto; prefijo
significa suplente
vicepresident n. vicepresidente
vicinity n. vecindad
vicious adj. depravado; vicioso;
cruél
victim n. víctima
victimize v. hacer víctima;
engañar

victorious *adj.* victorioso
victory *n.* victoria
view *v.* contemplar; examinar
vigilance *n.* vigilancia
vigor *n.* vigor
vigorous *adj.* vigoroso
village *n.* aldea; caserío
vindicate *v.* vindicar; justificar
vine *n.* vid; parra;
  enredadera
vinegar *n.* vinagre
viola *n.* viola
violation *n.* violación
violent *adj.* violento
violet *adj.* violado; color
  violeta
violin *n.* violín
virtual *adj.* virtual; verdadero
virtually *adv.* virtualmente;
  casi
virulent *adj.* virulento
virus *n.* virus
vise *n.* prensa de tornillo
visibility *n.* visibilidad
visible *adj.* visible; evidente
vision *n.* visión
visionary *n.* visionario
visit *n.* visita, *v.* visitar
visitation *n.* visitación
visor *n.* visera
visual *adj.* visual
visualize *v.* representarse en la
  mente; concebir; planear
vital *adj.* vital
vitality *n.* vitalidad
vitamin *n.* vitamina
vitreous *adj.* vítreo
vivacious *adj.* vivaz; animado;
  vivaracho
vivacity *n.* vivacidad; animacion
vivid *adj.* intenso; vivo; gráfico
vocabulary *n.* vocabulario
vocal *adj.* vocal
vocalist *n.* cantante; vocalista
vocation *n.* vocación
vogue *n.* moda; boga
voice *n.* voz
void *adj.* nulo; vacío
volcanic *adj.* volcánico
volcano *n.* volcán
volition *n.* voluntad; volición
volley *n.* descarga; voleo; salva
  (cañonazos)
volt *n.* voltio
voltage *n.* voltaje
voluble *adj.* hablador; voluble;
  charlatán
volume *n.* cantidad; volumen
voluntary *adj.* voluntario
volunteer *n.* voluntario
voluptuous *adj.* voluptuoso
votary *n.* devoto; partidario
vote *v.* votar, *n.* voto; sufragio
voter *n.* votante
votive *adj.* votivo; exvoto
vouch *v.i.* comprobar; garantizar
  algo; atestiguar
vowel *n.* vocal
voyage *v.* viajar (por mar, aire),
  n. viaje
vulgar *adj.* vulgar
vulnerable *adj.* vulnerable
vulture *n.* buitre; homber rapaz

W

wacky *adj.* loco; chiflado
wad *n.* fajo; taco; rollo; bolita
waddle *v.* anadear;
  contonearse
wade *v.* vadear; pasar con
  dificultad; chapotear
wag *v.* menear(se); mover (cola,
  dedo)
wage *n.* salario; sueldo; paga
wager *v.* apostar
wagon *n.* carro; carretón;
  vagón
waif *n.* niño abandonado
wail *v.* lamentarse; sollozar
waist *n.* cintura
waistcoat *n.* chaleco; justillo
waistline *n.* talle; cintura;
  pretina
wait *n.* espera, *v.* esperar
waiter *n.* camarero; mesero
waitress *n.* camarera; mesera
waive *v.* renunciar a;
  abandonar
waiver *n.* renuncia; abandono
wake *v.* despertar(se); velar a un
  muerto
waken *v.* despertar(se); caer en
  la cuenta

walk n. caminata; v. caminar; andar

walkover n. triunfo o tarea fácil

wall n. pared; muro; tabique; tapia; barrera; paredón

wallet n. cartera; billetera

wallop v. zurrar; azotar

wallow v. revolcarse

wallpaper n. papel pintado para empapelar

walnut n. nogal (nuez)

walrus n. morsa

waltz n. vals

wand n. vara; varita mágica

wander v. desviarse; vagar

want v. querer; requerir; desear

wanting adj. deficiente; avsente

wanton adj. lascivo; libertino desenfrenado; injustificable; cruel; insensible; perverso

ward v. desviar; resguardar

warden n. guardián; alcaide

ware n. mercancía

warehouse n. almacén; depósito

wariness n. precaución; cautela

warm v. calentar(se); adj. caluroso; caliente

warmhearted adj. afectuoso; bondadoso; cariñoso

warmth n. calor; simpatía; cordialidad

warn v. advertir; avisar

warning n. advertencia; aviso

warp v. alabear; pervertir; torcer; falsear

warped adj. combado; adunco

warrant n. autorización; garantía; decreto; orden; justificación

warranty n. garantía

warren n. conejera; madriguera

warrior n. guerrero

wart n. verruga

wary adj. cauteloso; precavido

was pret. of **be; ser, estar**

wash v. lavar(se)

washcloth n. paño para lavarse

washing n. lavado

washroom n. lavabo; cuarto de aseo

washtub n. tina o cuba de lavar

wasp n. avispa

wastage n. desgaste; merma; despilfarro; desperdicio

waste n. pérdida; v. desperdiciar; desgastarse

watchdog n. perro guardián

wastrel n. derrochador

watch n. reloj, v. mirar; observar

watchful adj. vigilante; desvelado; alerta; atento

water n. agua

waterbottle n. cantimplora; garrafa

waterfall n. cascada; catarata; salto de agua

waterfowl n. ave acuática

waterway n. canal navegable; vía fluvial

watt n. vatio

wave v. ondular; n. onda; ola; oleada; ondulación (cabello)

waver v. oscilar; vacilar

wavering adj. irresoluto, vacilante

wavy adj. ondulado

wax n. cera

way n. camino; modo; dirección

waylay v. acechar; saltear asaltar

wayside n. borde del camino

wayward adj. voluntarioso

we pron. nosotras; nosotros

weak adj. débil; aguado (té café)

weaken v. debilitar(se); atenuar(se); aflojar(se)

weakness n. debilidad

wealth n. riqueza; abundancia

wealthy adj. rico; opulento

wean v. destetar; desmamar

weapon n. arma; proyectil

wear v. desgastar(se); llevar o traer puesto

wearisome adj. fastidioso;

penoso
weary *adj.* fatigado; aburrido; fastidioso
weasel *n.* comadreja
weather *n.* tiempo; clima
weatherman *n.* pronosticador de tiempo; meteorólogo
weave *v.* tejido; textura
weaver *n.* tejedor
weaving *n.* tejeduría; tejido
web *n.* tela; tejido; telaraña
webfooted *adj.* palmípedo; palmeado
wed *v.* casar(se) con
wedding *n.* boda; casamiento
wedge *n.* cuña
Wednesday *n.* miércoles
weed *v.* escardar; desherbar; desyerbar
week *n.* semana
weekday *n.* día laborable o de trabajo
weekend *n.* fin de semana
weekly *adj.* semanal
weep *v.* llorar; llorar a lágrima viva
weeping *a.* lloroso; plañidero
weigh *v.* pesar; sopesar
weight *n.* pesa; peso; influencia
weightless *adj.* ingrávido
weird *adj.* extraño; fantástico; raro
welcome *adj.* bienvenido; grato
weld *v.* soldar; unir
welfare *n.* bienestar; prosperidad
well *adv.* pues; bien; con razón *n.* fuente; manantial; poz
wellbeing *n.* bienestar
wellbred *adj.* bien criado; de maneras refinadas
welldisposed *adj.* bien dispuesto; receptivo
wellknown *adj.* muy conocido; familiar
welloff *adj.* adinerado; acomodado; próspero
wellread *adj.* leído; instruido; culto
welltimed *adj.* oportuno; preciso
welltodo *adj.* acaudalado;

próspero; acomodado
welt *n.* verdugón; ribete
welter *v.* revolcar(se); sumergirse (en vicios)
were *pret. pl. of* be; ser, estar
west *n.* oeste
western *adj.* occidental
wet *v.* mojar(se); remojar; empapar(se)
whack *v.* golpear; vapulear
whale *n.* ballena
whalebone *n.* ballena (barba)
wharf *n.* muelle; desembarcadero
what *pron.* qué; lo que; cuál
whatever *pron.* todo lo que
whatnot *n.* estante; rinconera
wheat *n.* trigo
wheedle *v.* engatusar; halagar
wheel *n.* rueda; volante; timón
wheelbarrow *n.* carretilla
wheelchair *n.* silla de ruedas
when *conj.* cuando
whence *adv.* de donde
whenever *adv.* siempre que
where *conj., adv.* donde; *adv.* adonde
whereas *conj.* visto que
whereupon *adv.* con lo cual
wherever *conj.* dondequiera que
whether *conj.* si
whey *n.* suero de la leche
which *pron.* lo que; cual
whichever *pron.* cualquiera
whiff *n.* olorcillo
while *conj.* mientras (que)
whim *n.* capricho; antojo
whimper *v.* lloriquear; gimotear
whimsical *adj.* caprichoso; extravagante
whine *v.* gimotear
whinny *n.* relincho
whip *v.* batir; azotar
whir *v.* zumbar
whirl *v.* girar rápidamente; remolinear
whirlpool *n.* remolino; vórtice; virgine
whirlwind *n.* torbellino
whiskers *n.* barbas; bigotes
whisper *n.* cuchicheo; *v.* cuchichear

whistle v. silbar
white n., adj. blanco
whitecollar adj. oficinesco;
(personal) de oficina
whiten v. blanquear
whither conj. adonde
whittle v. cortar poco a poco
whiz v. silbar; rehilar; zumbar
who pron. él; (la, los, las)
quién(es); que
whoever pron. quienquiera que
whole n., adj. todo; n. total;
entero; adj. coinpleto
wholehearted adj. sincero;
franco; cordial
wholesale n. venta al por
mayor
wholesome adj. saludable; sano;
salutífero
wholly adv. completamente
whom pron. a quién
whomever pron. a quien quiera
whoop n. alarido; chillido (buho)
whose pron. de quien(es); de
quién(es)
why adv. por qué
wick n. mecha; pabilo
wicked adj. malicioso; malvado;
perverso
wicker adj. de mimbre
wide adj. ancho; dilatado;
extenso
widen v. ensanchar(se)
widespread adj. extendido;
difuso; diseminado; propagado
widow n. viuda
widower n. viudo
width n. anchura; ancho
wield v. ejercer; mandar;
manejar
wife n. esposa
wig n. peluca
wiggle v. menear(se);
cimbrearse; culebrear
wild adj. descabellado; silvestre
wild boar n. jabalí; jabalina
wilderness n. yermo; desierto
wile n. ardid; astucia
will v. querer
willful adj. voluntarioso; terco;
premeditado
willing adj. dispuesto

willow n. sauce
wilt v. marchitar(se)
win n. victoria, v. lograr;
ganar
wince v. respingar; retroceder
wind n. viento; enrollar;
enroscar
wind n. viento; enrollar;
enroscar
windfall n. ganacia inesperada
windmill n. molino de viento
window n. ventana
windy adj. ventoso; verboso
wine n. vino
winery n. lagar; vinería
wing n. ala
wink v. guiñar
winner n. ganador
winnings n. ganancias
winter n. invierno; limpiar
wipe v. enjugar; secar; borrar
wire n. alambre
wisdom n. sabiduría
wise adj. acertado; sabio; sagaz;
wish n. deseo; v. desear
wishful adj. deseoso; ansioso
witch n. bruja
with prep. con
withdrawal n. retirada
withdrawn adj. ensimismado
withhold v. retener; negar
(permiso, autoridad)
within adv. dentro; adentro; por
dentro
without adv. por fuera
withstand v. resistir; aguantar
witness n. testigo
witty adj. salado; ingenioso
wobble v. bambolear; tambalear
woe n. aflicción; infortunio
wolf n. lobo
woman n. mujer
womb n. matriz; útero
wonder v. asombrarse; tener
curiosidad; preguntarse
wonderful adj. maravilloso
wood n. madera
wooden adj. de madera; sin
expresion; tieso; rígido
woodland n. monte; región
arbolada
wool n. lana

word n. palabra; promesa; noticia

work v. trabajar, n. obra; trabajo

worker n. trabajador

workshop n. taller

world n. mundo m. mundano

worldwide a. mundial

worm n. gusano; lombriz

worn adj. usado; raido; gastado

worry v. inquietar(se); preocupar(se); fastidiar; incomodar

worship v. venerar; adorar; idolatrar

worth n. valor; valia; mérito

worthless adj. despreciable; inservible; sin valor

wound v. herir

wrap v. envolver; finalizar; cubrir

wrath n. ira; furia

wreck v. naufragar, destrozar n. ruina

wrinkle v. arrugar(se), n. arruga; invento; novedad

wrist n. muñeca (de la mano)

write v. escribir

writer n. escritora; escritor

writing n. escrito

wrong adj. equivocado

wrongful adj. injusto; falso

wrongheaded adj. terco; obstinado

wrought adj. forjado; trabajado; fraguado; elaborado

wry adj. torcido; irónico; sesgado

X

xray v. radiografiar, n. radiografía

Y

yacht n. yate

yank v. dar un tirón

Yankee n. yanqui

yard n. yarda; patio; corral

yardgoods n. tejidos; telas

yardstick n. vara de medir; criterio; norma

yarn n. hilado;estambre; cuento (increíble)

yawn n. bostezo, v. bostezar

year n. año -**book** anuario m.

yearling n. primal; añojo

yearly adv. anualmente

yearn v. suspirar; anhelar

yearning n. anhelo; deseo vivo

yeast n. levadura

yell n. alarido grito; v. decir a gritos; aullido m.; aullar

yellow n., adj. amarillo

yeoman hacendado

yes adv. sí

yesterday n. ayer

yet adv. todavía; aún; pero

yew n. tejo

yield v. rendir(se); ceder; producto

yolk n. yema(de huevo)

yonder adv. allí

yore n. antaño

you pron. vosotras; vosotros; tú; usted; ustedes

young adj. joven; hijuelos

youngster n. jovencito; mozalbete

your adj. su/s; tu/s; vuestra/s; vuestro/s; de usted(es)

yours pron. tu; vos; vosotros; vosotras

yourself pron. usted mismo; tú mismo

youth n. los jóvenes; juventud; joven

youthful adj. juvenil; vigoroso; nuevo; fresco

yule n. Navidad

Z

zeal n. ardor; fervor; celo

zealous adj. celoso; entusiasta

zebra n. cebra

zenith n. cenit

zero n. cero

zero hour n. momento crítico

zest n. gusto; deleite; placer

zinc n. cinc

zone n. zona

zoo n. jardín zoológico

zoological adj. zoológico

zucchini n. cidra cayote de verano